CW01497127

The Woman Who Fought an Empire

The Woman Who Fought an Empire

Sarah Aaronsohn and Her Nili Spy Ring

GREGORY J. WALLANCE

POTOMAC BOOKS

An imprint of the University of Nebraska Press

Library of Congress Cataloging-in-Publication Data
Names: Wallance, Gregory, author.
Title: The woman who fought an empire: Sarah Aaron-
sohn and her Nili spy ring / Gregory J. Wallance.
Description: Lincoln: Potomac Books, An imprint of
the University of Nebraska Press, 2018. | Includes bibli-
ographical references and index.
Identifiers: LCCN 2017034902
ISBN 9781612349435 (cloth: alk. paper)
ISBN 9781640120044 (epub)
ISBN 9781640120051 (mobi)
ISBN 9781640120068 (pdf)
Subjects: LCSH: Aaronsohn, Sarah. | Spies—Palestine—
Biography. | Zionists—Palestine—Biography. | NILI
(Organization: Palestine) | World War, 1914–1918—Secret
service—Great Britain. | Espionage, British—Palestine.
Classification: LCC DS125.3.A864 W35 2018 | DDC
940.4/8641092 [B]—dc23
LC record available at https://lccn.loc.gov/2017034902

Set in Adobe Garamond Pro by Mikala R Kolander.

In memory of my father, Don Wallance

Englishmen often talk about "playing the game," but even during the war few Britishers played it to a finer finish than this Jewish girl.

CAPT. L. B. WELDON of British Naval Intelligence, *"Hard Lying": Eastern Mediterranean, 1914–1919*

CONTENTS

ACKNOWLEDGMENTS

I am deeply grateful to the Beit Aaronsohn Nili Museum Archive in Zichron Ya'akov, Israel. The Beit Aaronsohn staff provided me with copies of Sarah Aaronsohn's letters and other archival materials, and unfailingly answered my questions and those of my interpreters. Given the volume of letters and materials in Hebrew, Russian, and French, I required the assistance of multiple interpreters and researchers. They included, in Israel, Ivgi Oanemos (both Hebrew and Russian), Jonathan Friedler and Research Assistant Yael Diamond of Diamond Services; in the United States, Cecilia Kleiman; and in Paris, Lisanna Wallance. In Kew, England, Bob O'Hara and Phil Tomaselli at Public Record Searches performed invaluable research in the National Archives. The staff of the Israel Defense Forces Archives assisted in locating an oral history that was helpful in constructing a narrative of key events, and the First Aliyah Museum in Zichron Ya'akov provided helpful background and materials on the town and its early settlers. The National Library of Israel, the Khan Museum of Hadera, and the Central Zionist Archives in Jerusalem also provided assistance in locating archival materials. I am grateful to the persons with busy schedules who took time to answer questions or provide guidance, including Yuval Ben-Bassat, Uri Bar-Joseph, Ronald Florence, Kevin Morrow, and Yigal Sheffy. Michael Ben-Jacob helpfully provided guidance on the Midrash Rabba (a compilation of rabbinic homiletic literature). Yigal Sheffy's *British Military Intelligence in the Palestine Campaign, 1914–1918* and Ronald Florence's *Lawrence and Aaronsohn* were also invaluable resources. Any questions of interpretation or emphasis, of course, are my responsibility. Much credit goes to the team at the University of Nebraska Press/Potomac Books, including Tom Swanson and Natalie O'Neal, for their dedicated work in preparing the book for publication. I owe an enormous debt to my agents, Peter Bernstein and Amy Bernstein at the Bernstein Literary Agency. And the support and encouragement of my wife, Lies van Veen, as much as anything else, made this book possible.

A NOTE ON TERMINOLOGY

I have adopted the usage of Middle East historians such as Eugene Rogan and Scott Anderson and frequently use "Ottoman" and "Turkish" interchangeably and Western spellings for cities, such as Beirut or Damascus. Even in English works, Jewish, Arab, and Turkish names can be spelled a variety of ways. For example, Sarah's settlement in Palestine has been spelled Zikron Ya'aqov, Zichron Ya'akov, Zichron Yaakov, and Zichron Yaacov. In general, I have attempted to use the version most commonly found in English-language works on the Middle East in World War I, but even then there is sometimes a close split, as with the case for Sarah's settlement. My somewhat arbitrary choice is Zichron Ya'akov. In some instances, where a letter's or memoir's usage conflicts with contemporary usage, such as Istanbul, I have used the city's name in the letter or memoir—in this instance, Constantinople.

MAJOR CHARACTERS

The Aaronsohn Family
Ephraim (father)
Malka (mother)
Aaron
Zvi
Samuel
Alexander
Sarah
Rivka

The Feinberg Family
Israel (father)
Fanya (mother)
Avshalom
Tzila
Shoshana

British Intelligence Officers in Egypt (1915 Rank)
Maj. Wyndham Deedes
Capt. Stewart Newcombe
Lt. Leonard Woolley
2nd Lt. Thomas E. Lawrence

Other British Figures
Gen. Sir Archibald Murray
Gen. Sir Edmund Allenby
Prime Minister David Lloyd George

First Lord of the Admiralty
    Winston Churchill
Sir Mark Sykes

The Rulers of the Ottoman Empire
Djemal Pasha
Enver Pasha
Talaat Pasha

The Nili Spies (Partial List)
Eitan Belkind
Naaman Belkind
Liebl Bernstein
Menashe Brunstein
Tova Gelberg
Yitzhak Halperin
Yosef Lishansky
Dr. Moshe Neumann
Nissan Rotman
Liova Schneersohn
Reuven Schwartz

American Figures
Henry Morgenthau,
    U.S. ambassador to the
    Ottoman Empire

The Woman Who Fought an Empire

Introduction

World War I, one of the greatest disasters in human history, transformed the role of women in espionage. In prior conflicts, women spies had generally been amateurs who operated informally and on a small scale. By giving rise to the modern, centralized, and well-funded intelligence organization, the war created opportunities for women to spy as part of or even to run major spy networks.

Ironically enough, despite the many courageous women who skillfully spied in that war, the best known today is Mata Hari, the nude dancer and courtesan who had no significant espionage achievements but still found herself in front of a French firing squad in 1917. Mata Hari came to define the image of the female spy in the public imagination as an erotic espionage agent, or as a femme fatale, whose principal talent is seduction. That false and unfair image persists today in popular culture and, having endured for a century, must be discarded.[1]

Sarah Aaronsohn is the curative for the damaging Mata Hari stereotype of women spies. She was the intelligent, beautiful, brave, willful sister of an equally willful, world-famous scientist, and the skilled leader of a mostly male spy ring at a time when women held an inferior status in society. Her cloak-and-dagger exploits played an important role in the collapse of the Ottoman Empire and the outcome of World War I.

Sarah was born in 1890 in Palestine, then part of the Ottoman Empire, to Jewish emigrants from Romania. When World War I began in 1914, Sarah was married to a Jewish businessman in Constantinople (now Istanbul), the capital of the Ottoman Empire. Wartime postal restrictions and censorship limited Sarah's ability to get news from her family in the Zichron Ya'akov settlement in Palestine, and she grew increasingly homesick. In late 1915 Sarah decided to return to Zichron for an extended visit. By a coincidence of timing and geography, Sarah's three-week trip took her through the heart of the genocide the Turks conducted against the Armenians.

The nightmarish journey convinced the deeply shaken Sarah that unless the British defeated the Ottoman Empire, and a homeland for Jews was created in Palestine under British rule, the same fate would befall the Jews of Palestine. Little more than a year later and at age twenty-seven, Sarah became the leader of a pro-British spy network code-named Nili in the Ottoman Empire. The spy ring had originally been formed by her brother Aaron, a world-famous agronomist, and Avshalom Feinberg, a fearless young man from another settlement. But it was under Sarah's leadership that Nili provided the British crucial intelligence in their war against the Ottoman Empire for control of the Middle East. Sarah's loyalty, however, was decidedly not to Britain. "My only concern is with saving my Jewish brothers and sisters," Sarah told a British officer. "Had it not been for them, do you think I would be working for you?"[2]

Operating from behind enemy lines, Sarah recruited spies; conducted her own espionage in places like Jerusalem, Nazareth, and along the Mediterranean coast; managed the unruly Nili men, several of whom were in love with her; and delivered her intelligence reports to a British spy ship that made clandestine visits to Palestine from British-controlled Egypt. A British intelligence officer in Egypt later said that Nili was "the most valuable nucleus of our intelligence service in Palestine during the war."[3]

Sarah's inspiring story has led some of Nili's chroniclers to make Sarah seem as if she had stepped out of a painting of an Old Testament scene, as more of a brave and self-sacrificing saint than a flesh-and-blood woman. One purpose of *The Woman Who Fought an Empire* indeed is to celebrate Sarah's singular bravery and commitment, but another is to show that her dedication occasionally went beyond the pale and that she was not without emotional conflict, fear, self-doubt, dark moods, and her own needs.

Ultimately, Sarah's vision was realized when the British, with the assistance of her espionage, defeated the Ottomans. Palestine came under

British rule in what is called the British Mandate, the springboard to an independent Jewish state. Sarah's story and the events swirling around her are the story of the creation of Israel and the modern Middle East.

For years after World War I, Jews living under the British Mandate scorned Sarah and her spies as irresponsible and reckless. Even after the state of Israel was created in 1948, Israeli governments did not officially recognize the achievements of Sarah and her spies. That ended in 1967 as the result of a dramatic discovery in the desert.

As I learned during my research, there is more to Sarah's story than espionage. Her letters as well as the letters written by family members and fellow spies reveal daring and committed young people tied to one another by enviably deep bonds of devotion and loyalty; indeed, their commitment to establish a Jewish homeland in Palestine appears inseparable from their commitment to one another. The dashing Avshalom Feinberg, who was also a poet, conceived the idea of young Palestinian Jews spying for the British. He once wrote to Sarah of those bonds.

"What connects us more than blood and fellowship is our love, is the habit of being together and the suffering we have shared. These are things that will not die."[4]

1

I Will Be Really Happy When I Am Home

In 1882 Ephraim and Malka Aaronsohn, and their young sons—Aaron, age six, and Zvi, age four—sailed from Romania on the steamer *Thetis*. They were among several hundred Jews on the *Thetis* escaping Romania's intensifying pogroms and vice-like restrictions on Jewish economic activity. Many Romanian Jews gambled their futures on America, but the Jews on the *Thetis* took a bigger gamble. Their destination was Palestine, a backwater region of the province of Syria in the Ottoman Empire, which included what is now Israel. Among Palestine's population were 450,000 Arabs and 25,000 mostly ultraorthodox Jews in Jerusalem and a few other towns. These side-locked Jews lived in Palestine, not in the spirit of Zionism but to study ancient Hebrew texts and die on holy soil.

The Jews on the *Thetis*, by contrast, dreamed of a "return" to Zion. The Lovers of Zion society in Romania sponsored the families on the *Thetis* in the belief that Jewish settlements in Palestine would foster in diaspora Jews "holy feelings which the sheer weight of pain, want, and poverty had put to sleep for thousands of years" and lead to a Jewish revival in Palestine. The *Thetis* Jews were in the vanguard that would pave the way.[1]

The *Thetis* sailed across the Black Sea, through the Bosporus and Dardanelles, into the Mediterranean, and down to the coast of Palestine. The authorities in Palestine initially would not let the *Thetis* dock because the Ottoman government in Constantinople, suspicious that Jews were agents for British imperialists with designs on the Levant, had issued an edict against Jewish immigration. The *Thetis* steamed up and down the Palestinian coast, looking for a hospitable port, while on board the sanitary conditions for the Jews went from merely distasteful to perilously unhealthy. Port officials in Jaffa finally allowed the Jews to disembark.[2]

The Jaffa port officials had an ulterior motive for letting in the Jews. All of them were confined to Jaffa until they paid baksheesh, which was valued more highly by the local Ottoman bureaucrats with their red tarbushes than any pronouncements from Constantinople. The Ottoman bureaucratic bay for baksheesh was heard throughout the empire from minor bureaucracies in remote provinces to its very heart, the civil administrative offices in Constantinople in the block of government buildings called the Sublime Porte.[3]

The Jews, with the assistance of their local contacts, managed to come up with baksheesh, paid off the authorities, and were released after a week. Some sixty families went to Haifa in northern Palestine, where they stayed in a khan—a caravansary or rest stop—which in this case was a large courtyard with stone walls next to a stone house. They had no desire to remain any longer than necessary in Haifa with its many mosques and a few churches and where Jews lived within the Muslim district.[4]

A contingent of Romanian Jews headed south from Haifa, riding mules or sitting on ox-drawn wagons. They reached a narrow mountain path by nightfall, but the weary oxen declined to pull the wagons further. The men disassembled the wagons. Some hoisted the pieces and their belongings onto their shoulders and began to climb the mountain, while others lashed the liberated oxen up the steep path. Behind them came the women, carrying infants or holding the hands of the young children. The band of Jews and their animals climbed in the dark for several hours in a silence broken by the grunting of the oxen and the high-pitched howls and whines of jackals.[5]

Their destination was a hilltop perch on Mount Carmel near the coast of what is now northern Israel. The name "Mount Carmel" is a misnomer because there is no specific peak but rather a row of hills that once were the outcroppings of an ancient carbonate barrier reef. At the top of one hill, the Jewish settlers found Arab farm workers, or fellahin, living in decrepit mud-and-wattle huts. With their arrival, the desolate place, known as Zammarin to the Arabs, became one of the first Jewish settlements in the initial modern wave of Jewish immigration to Palestine called the First Aliyah (1882–1903). The new settlers began building huts and clearing fields.[6]

Wealthy Jewish patrons in Romania had purchased the land for the immigrants from Haifa speculators, who plainly got the better end of the deal. The sweeping view of Arab olive groves and the tranquil, blue Mediterranean was splendid, but otherwise Zammarin proved to be an inhospitable home. The Romanian tradesmen, shopkeepers, and peddlers had planned to survive by farming even though few had any agricultural experience. Promised funds did not arrive; it might have seemed to the settlers that rocks flourished better in the fields than their wheat and barley did; and the settlers were beset with malaria, yellow fever, mosquitoes, black flies, snakes, scorpions, and acute homesickness. ("My heart grieves mightily when I remember how we wandered so far away from our family nest," one resident wrote to her sister-in-law in Russia.)[7] The oppressive summer heat and the khamsin—the suffocating, dust-laden desert wind—were especially hard on the settlers.

The sensible ones returned to Romania, and the remaining Jews pawned their Torah scrolls. They survived mainly because of the seemingly divine intervention of Baron Edmond de Rothschild, scion of the French branch of the powerful Rothschild banking family. The baron, who believed that Palestine was the future of the Jewish people and not just their past, gave the settlers desperately needed funds but with the biblical-like condition that "he alone shall be the colony's sole Lord and that all things in its domain be under his rule."[8]

Not having much choice, the settlers agreed to the baron's terms. They even renamed their settlement Zichron Ya'akov (in Jacob's Memory) after the baron's father. Every aspect of their lives was dictated by the baron and his agents, from what crops could be grown to the construction details of their residences. On his inspection visits to Zichron Ya'akov (he sailed to Palestine on his private yacht), the baron scolded a housewife for reading Shakespeare instead of the Bible, questioned the children in the schoolhouse on their grasp of arithmetic, and rebuked a mother for failing to cover a crib with mosquito netting. As he walked to the synagogue, villagers handed the baron petitions "as though he were Caesar approaching the Forum." Any utterance of the baron's name was invariably followed by the phrase, "May God be merciful on him." When the baron departed after one visit, Bedouin horsemen, who had come to see "the Sultan of the Jews," saluted him by firing their rifles into the air.[9]

The modern-day Moses and his flock realized their dream. By 1914 the primitive hamlet had become a prosperous village of nearly a thousand inhabitants and almost a hundred buildings, including a hospital and a bank; it had running water; and it offered horse-drawn coach service to Haifa and Jaffa. The baron recruited the eminent physician Dr. Hillel Yaffe to run a clinic for treating malaria patients. Zichron even boasted vineyards and a winery with huge underground wine cellars, although the wine could not be sold in the predominantly Muslim Ottoman Empire and had to be exported. Eucalyptus trees imported from Australia provided shade where no trees had ever grown, and the dusty trails had been replaced by passable dirt roads bordered with thorny acacia that, in season, were laced with sweet-smelling yellow blossoms. One American visitor in that period, however, viewing Zichron through the prism of American prosperity, thought it had the look of a squat Russian village.[10]

Even so the settlers could be justly pleased with what they had accomplished, but any candid assessment of Zichron's progress had to acknowledge the baron's indispensable bounty and the economic advantage of an endless source of low-cost labor from the Arab village farther down the slopes of Mount Carmel. As Zichron grew, fewer and fewer Jews worked in the settlement's fields, which more resembled those of plantations whose workers were Arabs.

The baron's other settlements took root as well, such as Petah Tikva, Rishon LeZion, Rosh Pinah, Hadera, and others; they were all part of an archipelago of tiny Jewish islands gamely struggling in the Ottoman Empire. By 1914 the Jewish population of Palestine was approximately eighty thousand people, including a new Jewish settlement next to the port of Jaffa called Tel Aviv. The Jews of Zichron and the other settlements, collectively referred to as the *yishuv*, went about their lives as Ottoman subjects.

Aaron and Zvi Aaronsohn had been born in Romania. The rest of the Aaronsohn children were born in Palestine. Two more boys, Samuel and Alexander, were followed by the first girl, Sarah, in 1890. The last Aaronsohn child, Rivka, was born two years later.

The family's affectionate name for Sarah was Sarati, "my Sarah." Much of Sarah's youth was devoted to household chores, from washing the stone floors, to scrubbing the wooden dining table with sand and water, to endless sewing and mending of the family's clothes, such as her brother Zvi's shirts for his pending wedding. In *Mandrakes from the Holy Land*, novelist Aharon Megged imagines Sarah as a teenager, helping to prepare and serve a family dinner while wearing "a festive white dress and a large bow tie on her breast, her light hair gathered on her nape by a black ribbon."[11]

Sarah was educated at the village school, where she learned French, Hebrew, and Arabic, plus some history, religion, and agronomy. Paris was then the world center of literature, science, art, music, and fashion, and French culture radiated like bright sunlight even into remote Palestine. The franc was common currency in the Jewish settlements, even though the official currency of the Ottoman Empire was the lira, and Zichron Ya'akov, much to the pride of its inhabitants, became known as "Little Paris." The curriculum at Sarah's school was modeled on the programs of the Alliance Israélite Universelle, founded by a French statesman in 1860 to, among other purposes, promote the education of Jews in the Middle East. But formal schooling for girls ended at age twelve, and thereafter Sarah was self-taught, reading books in several languages. Sarah, who lacked any trace of the Romanian shtetls, saw herself not as a child of struggling settlers in a malarial backwater town but as a pioneering Jew and audacious redeemer of a long-lost dream. While Yiddish was the primary language of the Aaronsohn home, the family talked enthusiastically of the reintroduction of Hebrew as a spoken, everyday language in Palestine.[12]

When the first modern Hebrew dictionary appeared, Sarah and Rivka, then ages fourteen and twelve, wrote its author, Eliezer Ben-Yehuda, to express their gratitude for the "first five books of your great dictionary, and to tell you that we cannot wait for you to publish the next ones." In their letter, the sisters pointed out that currently Hebrew is limited to "very general terms" and that "we do not have a name for each flower and plant, for each bird, for all the little insects that buzz in our ears when we walk in the fields." The sisters blamed the schools of the pioneer Jewish settlements, where children were not "educated to look and observe." If children were encouraged to collect plants, insects, and stones and to bring them to school, "then a name would be found for each one of these." Once they too had failed to pay attention to the objects around them, but their big brother Aaron had changed that. "Our brother never returns home from his journeys without bringing many plants, stones, pieces of metal, etc. He looks after them as though they were pearls, writes down on a little note the origin of each object and gives it a strange name. We can almost say that he hugs and kisses them. He really loves spending time with them. Little by little we are being infected with his 'craziness.'"

The sisters expressed their gratitude to Ben-Yehuda "for making our love for the language even stronger." Then, politely, almost apologetically, the sisters inquired, "Might we also dare draw your attention to some doubts and questions?" Sarah and Rivka proceeded to identify certain definitions they didn't understand or, implicitly, didn't agree with. Helpfully, they provided a list of questions for the great author to answer. Ben-Yehuda was so impressed that he published the sisters' letter in his newspaper, *Hashkafa*.[13]

Sarah matured into a striking young woman. Her blue eyes, oval face, erect posture, and full, sensuous figure would have found approval in the Belle Époque of Paris but not so in straitlaced Zichron Ya'akov. The slightly upward tilt of Sarah's head signaled her independent-mindedness, which was not an attitude Jewish women in the settlements typically displayed. The Jewish pioneer spirit in Palestine was not so bold as to grant women political and social equality with men. In 1886 when young women in the settlement of Petah Tikva demanded the right to vote at settlement meetings, even their own mothers opposed them.

Characters in the novels of Nehamah Pukhachewsky, a woman who came to Palestine in 1889 from Russia, reflect the bitterness of pioneer women at their inferior status. The character Zipporah Dori, a farmer's wife, attended a settlement assembly convened to address a vital issue.

But "they would not allow me to speak. Their reason was that I was only a guest at the meeting and not an official participant. Grievously offended, I wondered . . . cannot a poor wretched soul like me contribute anything?" She answered her own question: "A woman has no rights whatsoever. . . . A woman's place is in the kitchen, behind the stove and not among the chosen delegates of the people!"[14]

Jewish gender role expectations were lost on Sarah. She reportedly was among the first women in Palestine to decline to wear corsets, was an excellent shot and horsewoman, hunted with men from the village, and argued about politics and the future of Palestine with her brothers. Sarah often rode her fast mare into the countryside by herself, taking only a pistol for protection. "My mare was so swift, it was like flying," Sarah recalled years later for a visitor to the Aaronsohn home, with evident delight at the memory. "With my feet in the [stirrups] I'd stand erect and throw away my wide straw hat and then catch it sailing through the air." Sarah sewed her own dresses, which many Zichron women secretly admired, but she also occasionally wore men's agricultural clothes without concern for what anyone might think. Young men tended to fall in love with her.[15]

For all her independent-mindedness, Sarah's identity was knitted into that of her family. In small towns there is often a family that stands apart, perhaps because the children are striking in appearance, a member has a claim to distinction, the clan acts like royalty, or the family has a grand house. In the case of the Aaronsohn family, it may have been all of the above. The Aaronsohn children were unusually good-looking. At a young age Sarah's older brother Aaron gained worldwide recognition as an agronomist and became an influential figure in the Ottoman Empire. Sarah's mother, Malka—an otherwise practical, no-nonsense woman—raised her children to think of themselves as royalty. Malka's own mother had insisted that the family had descended from King David.[16]

By the early 1900s Ephraim and Malka had freed themselves from dependence on the baron and had become independent farmers. The family lived in Zichron's equivalent of a château, a rose-colored stucco house with a tile roof on an avenue lined with tall cypresses. The well-furnished interior included a living room with comfortable sofas and armchairs and a Persian rug; a dining room with a table covered by an embroidered tablecloth and a tall dark wood cabinet filled with crystal wine glasses, decanters, and such; and a snug kitchen with a large pantry containing porcelain plates and serving dishes decorated with bright red and purple flowers or elegant gold trim.

Aaron Aaronsohn was the dominant figure in that family. In 1893 agents of Baron de Rothschild, in the manner of talent scouts, spotted Aaron's promise and sent the brilliant but often combative fifteen-year-old—"how are you ever going to do anything if you quarrel with everybody?" his father once asked him—to France to study agronomy. Two years later Aaron returned to Palestine as a trained young scientist known for hard work (he rarely slept more than four or five hours a night, rising before dawn to read scientific periodicals or do research). For a time Aaron worked as an agricultural instructor at Metula, one of the baron's settlements, and later went into business as an importer of agricultural equipment.[17]

But throughout Aaron pursued botanical research on horseback and on foot, carrying with him an 1870s-era map of Palestine, a compass, a magnifying glass, and a .577/.450 Martini-Henry rifle. He became known as the Jew who gathered "wild grasses of no value." In 1906 on one of his explorations, Aaron discovered in the crevice of a rock on Mount Hermon patches of hardy wild wheat that had been thought extinct since ancient times. It was a long-sought, untainted strain that might rejuvenate existing wheat stocks, weakened by centuries of crossbreeding, to produce greater resistance to rust and drought. In a largely agrarian world, Aaron's discovery earned him an international reputation at age thirty, although ultimately the wild wheat did not dramatically improve existing stocks.[18]

In 1909 David Fairchild, a research botanist at the U.S. Department of Agriculture, invited Aaron to the United States to confer with American researchers on whether his discovery could improve wheat cultivation in the dry soils of the western plains. During his visit, Aaron asked Fairchild to introduce him "to some of the wealthy Jews in this country." Aaron met with, among others, Oscar Straus, the first Jewish cabinet member, whose brothers co-owned Macy's department store; Julian Mack, a well-connected judge in Illinois who became a close friend; Julius Rosenwald, the president of Sears, Roebuck & Company; Rabbi Judah L. Magnes of Temple Emanu-El in New York City; bankers Jacob Schiff and Paul M. Warburg; and Henrietta Szold, who later founded Hadassah, the Women's Zionist Organization of America.

Blue-eyed like Sarah, physically robust (reportedly, he could lift a horse off the ground and flip it on its side), deeply tanned, and filled with an inexhaustible warehouse of information to the point that he outtalked even the voluble Theodore Roosevelt during a subsequent trip to the United States, Aaron was a sensation among these American Jews. Legal scholar Felix Frankfurter, later a Supreme Court justice, once said of Aaron Aaronsohn, "I do not need the fingers of my two hands to include him among the most memorable persona I have encountered in my life." Frankfurter even began writing a biography of Aaron.[19]

Aaron explained to these distinguished Jews how agrarian technology could be used in Palestine to support a much larger Jewish population. His contention was not merely botanical but *political*, because it refuted the claims of both Jewish and non-Jewish anti-Zionists that Palestine was too arid to support a significant Jewish population. Impressed with Aaron's blend of science and Zionism, the American Jews donated $20,000 for Aaron to build an agricultural research station on a bluff overlooking the Mediterranean near Atlit, a tiny settlement about twelve miles north of Zichron. The research station's board of trustees was a roster of prominent American Jewry.[20]

The entrance road to the station could be accessed from the coastal road that ran between Haifa and Jaffa. A sign in English and Hebrew announced that the visitor was approaching the "Jewish Agricultural Experiment Station." The visitor turned off the coastal road and traveled down a road lined with stately Washingtonia palm trees planted by Aaron. The main building, about a mile from the Mediterranean, was a two-story cinder block structure with a laboratory and a research library; adjacent were storage buildings and an American midwestern-style windmill. Aaron's sisters, Sarah and Rivka, and their friends worked at the research station. Aaron succeeded in producing more wheat, barley, and oats per acre than many flourishing farms in Palestine did even though he had deliberately chosen an arid site.[21]

Agronomy would appear an unlikely basis for espionage. But Aaron's passion for disciplined observation, one that he passed on to Sarah and the other workers, would prove an invaluable asset for intelligence gathering, and the Atlit research station would turn out to be a suitable headquarters for a spy ring, whose recruits would include many of the young Jews who had worked there for Aaron. But that lay in the future.

Aaron Aaronsohn's success enabled him to build his own home next to his parents' house, creating a graceful compound for the intellectual and landed aristocrats of the Aaronsohn family. The interior motif of Aaron's home was heavy dark wood paneling, furniture inlaid with mother of pearl, and books—shelves and shelves of books. The grand feature of Aaron's home was a rotunda-shaped library filled with scientific works in German, French, and English. In the bedroom was a double-poster bed with a bas relief of wild wheat carved into the footboard. The bathroom had its own boiler, which provided hot water through a thin pipe to a showerhead above the bathtub; a wardrobe cabinet with glass doors; and a wooden scale that allowed the heavyset Aaron to keep track of his weight.[22]

In early 1912 Sarah's mother, Malka, died. One account suggests that some form of euthanasia may have been involved and speculates that such a drastic measure might have been necessary because Malka suffered from depression after her father was tortured to death during a Romanian pogrom. Essentially, though, the circumstances of Malka's death, and its impact on her husband and children, are a mystery.[23]

Later that year Aaron provided funds for the twenty-two-year-old Sarah to travel to Europe and arranged for her to stay with his European friends. Sarah apparently had never been to a foreign country. After visiting Paris, she went to Hamburg, Germany, arriving on October 18. Like many young travelers, she fretted about spending and eating too much but seemed especially concerned about not hearing any news from her brother, whom Sarah had expected would send her letters in care of her hosts and in advance of her arrival.

Sarah wrote Aaron the day after she arrived in Hamburg.

My dear Aaron,
As you can see, I am already here in Hamburg. I arrived yesterday morning. Mrs. Suskin came to pick me up at the railway station. The beautiful Hamburg welcomed me with a great weeping, darkness and pouring rain in the streets. I was hoping to find a letter from you here, but there wasn't one.

It's been more than two weeks since you've written to me. Why? I suppose that you are very busy these days. You must have been at the trustees' yearly meeting. Let me know what was decided and if the Americans were happy with you.

. . . My dear, I spent so much money in Paris, which is awful. I don't really know where it all went. At least I saw a lot; I bought what I needed, but not more than that.[24]

From Hamburg Sarah went to Berlin, arriving on November 7. Sarah wrote Aaron, wryly comparing Berlin to Zichron and again expressing concern over her spending.

It's already my third day here. On the first day I was greeted by beautiful snow, though it wasn't cold. They say it wasn't much snow this time and indeed, after a few hours, it melted and the streets were full of sludge and mud like our own streets. I haven't had a chance to see anything since it has been raining and gray all the time. I have only gone shopping with Ms. Berman and spent only a little money for food and the most necessary domestic supplies. There are so many beautiful and useful things here if only there was enough money! My dear, I have already taken 800 marks from the Suskins. It's awful how much money my journey is costing.

Sarah appeared not to have been impressed by European worldliness and culture—or with the bourgeois Jews she had met in Berlin.

To tell you the truth, I will be really happy when I am home. Here I am at a Jewish pension with Ms. Berman and her family, there are many Russians, everywhere Russians, wherever you move, you find them. Ms. Berman's sisters are modern girls and, of course, look askance at people like us. They study in the [music] conservatoire, play music, are very much concerned with their appearances, but I find them rather ignorant. I am, of course, ignorant, too and yet, even to my surprise, my aspirations are different than those of other people. When I am surrounded by people who are inferior to me, I cannot stand it. I like to be among people who are superior, so that I can draw from their knowledge and hear interesting things.

Sarah offered an especially acerbic opinion of the Jewish women she had encountered during her recent stay in Hamburg.

My dear, I have to confess that the people I met in Hamburg were not exactly to my liking either, particularly the women, who are not very cultured and usually have a sweet tooth and thus are fat like cows.

She complained again about not receiving any letters from Aaron—or his assistant at the agricultural research station, Avshalom Feinberg—and about the fact that, while her health was fine, she was putting on weight.

It has been several weeks and I haven't heard any news from you, or your secretary; indeed, he can write to me, or is he already such a *groisser macher* [big shot]? Still, you should let us know in some way, about yourself. Rivka also writes that she does not have any news from you.

. . . I don't have any other news. I am healthy but it seems that I have gained too much weight. I am not happy about this. I will try to lose some weight at home.[25]

Sarah returned in late 1912 to Zichron, where she and her sister, Rivka, could dress up in the afternoons after they had finished their chores and go for a walk, nodding pleasantly at their neighbors; and where Sarah could pay a visit to the home of a sheik in a nearby Druze village. On such a visit, seated at a low table piled with fruits and sweets, Sarah chatted in fluent Arabic with the sheik's young daughter, who dressed in black and wore a white scarf over the lower part of her face that revealed only her enchanting gray eyes. Unobtrusively placed near the entrance to the small house was a small door for the women of the household to escape through if a male stranger unexpectedly entered the home.[26]

2

Two Cannot Take Three Places— What Is Missing Is Missing

Her mother's death in 1912 meant that Sarah had to look after her widower father and younger sister, Rivka. Not long after Sarah became head of the Aaronsohn household, Avshalom Feinberg proposed marriage to Rivka, after he had seemingly courted both sisters.

Had his parents, Israel and Fanya, stayed in Russia, Avshalom Feinberg, with a lock of brown hair romantically falling across his forehead, likely would have become a daring revolutionary, endlessly quoting Marx (albeit with the faintest hint of mockery) and plotting against the czar with suicidal recklessness. Instead, the Feinbergs, Russian intellectuals, immigrated to Palestine and helped found Rishon LeZion a few miles south of Jaffa. There, the settlers established the first school whose curriculum was taught entirely in Hebrew.

Israel and Fanya left Rishon LeZion for Hadera, a settlement on the sandy Mediterranean coast, where Avshalom grew up. Hadera was adjacent to swamps, which meant that malaria was rife among its early settlers. The Arabs thought of the area as Bab-Il-Sahouneh (the gate to malaria), and the existing residents were astonished to see strangers in European dress on a visit to inspect the disease-ridden land. Many Jews died from malaria in the first few years of the settlement's existence, and thereafter residents of Hadera and their descendants maintained a perverse pride in the especially virulent nature of their malaria as compared, say, to the second-rate malaria in Atlit. "Those Atlit people should stop glorifying in the malaria that bred in their colony," an Hadera resident insisted. "Anyway, what do they know of malaria? They only had regular malaria!" In the end, Hadera managed to survive because Baron de Rothschild provided support, as he had with Zichron. With his money the settlers dried out the swamps by planting eucalyptus trees.[1]

When Avshalom was a small child, his father put him in the custody of an Arab scholar who had a small school. "He is your son," Avshalom's father said to the scholar. "Teach him." Avshalom learned to read and write Arabic and mastered the Koran; the Arab scholar regarded Avshalom as his best student. Avshalom became an experienced desert traveler, expert horseman and camel rider, and crack shot. At fifteen Avshalom went to Paris (as the settlements prospered, families began sending their offspring to study in Europe), where he spent four years in French schools. He made friends with notable French intellectuals, including Jacques Maritain, a Catholic philosopher, and Charles Péguy, a noted poet and essayist. As Aaron Aaronsohn's biographer Ronald Florence observed, while in Paris Avshalom was heavily influenced by "nationalist literature from newly emancipated countries." He wrote his family from Paris: "The time has come in which the small, oppressed peoples can take their place at the table, in the dining rooms of the nations, to nourish their physical body, and perhaps even enter the hall where all of the satiated may consider matters of faith, intellect and spirit!"[2]

After returning from Paris, Avshalom went to work for Aaron Aaronsohn at the Atlit research station, where he was both a protégé and a younger brother to the agronomist, who was thirteen years older. Avshalom met Sarah and Rivka through Aaron. He frequently rode his horse over to Zichron, where he and the sisters danced and sang with the villagers on warm nights after the harvest, went picnicking and swimming in the ancient harbor of Caesarea, and rode with other young people to parties at nearby settlements. Tall and muscular, Avshalom was a compelling, charismatic young man with restless, intense eyes who wrote poetry in several languages. Even standing still or sitting, Avshalom left an impression of impatient activity, as though time was running out on him. "We are passing like a cloud, like steam which disperses, and our song dies away without even an echo," he once wrote.[3]

Avshalom, Sarah, and Rivka—sometimes with their friends, sometimes just the three of them—spent days and nights in the hills, roaming on foot or horseback, lying on the rocks, listening to the jackals, or watching hungry foxes on a hunt. Whatever they did, Avshalom was always the center of their group, leading them in one direction or another on their aimless outings. Real and imagined dangers failed to trouble Avshalom in any visible way. His courage was infectious; no one worried about Arabs or getting lost or staying out so late that they had to make their way back in the dark. For those who knew him, Avshalom's passion, nerve, and imagination became precious.[4]

If Avshalom had any fear, it was of being trapped by life's stifling customs and conventions. Avshalom once wrote Sarah about his frustration that she had to be in Zichron for Passover and could not visit him in Hadera. "And as if it is not enough that the bloody Passover took us from slavery to freedom and then enslaved us again to its stupid rituals, it also keeps you from coming here." He disliked not knowing what Rivka was doing in Zichron when he was just miles away in Hadera. Soon, he predicted in a letter to Rivka, "someone will invent a machine by the means of which, according to the simple rules of physics, two people will be able to speak, and to see each other, when they are thousands of kilometers apart."[5]

Avshalom's imagination, though, had a darker side. His letters to Sarah and Rivka sometimes dwelt on death—specifically, his own. Perhaps Avshalom saw death as a sanctuary of last resort from banality, and there was an element of the poet intrigued with themes of mortality. At a time of strain in Avshalom's relationship with his father, an illness that befell his mother, and his own excruciating headaches, Avshalom mused in a letter how quickly he could "put a bullet through my temple" yet how long it would take for others to hear of his death and grieve. At the moment of his own death, Rivka would be reading a book about the "hero of some romance," and Sarah would be walking around Haifa, "light hearted and carefree." Moreover, despite the bonds among them neither sister would feel any emotion, not even a tremor in their hearts, until after he had been buried, "and then the sorrow would come."[6]

Avshalom could share with Sarah a love of French literature, recall for Rivka a rapturous night in Paris when he had listened to Beethoven's Ninth Symphony conducted by the famous Édouard Juda Colonne, and quote at length from the French poet and essayist Sully Prudhomme. But he could also pick fights—the Palestinian Jewish equivalent of a barroom brawl—perhaps for the excitement and, in some instances, because the fights were with Arabs. "I have lived among them all my life . . . there is no more cowardly, hypocritical, and false race than this one," Avshalom once said of Arabs.[7]

Baruch Ben-Azar, a friend since childhood ("I loved him like a brother . . . he was a fantasizer, imaginative, enthusiastic and temperamental"), was present in Jaffa when Avshalom got in a fight in a beachside Arab café. "It is likely that he was at fault," recalled Ben-Azar of the fight, "and the one to start the fight, but I stood with him and threw chairs." Once at a play in Jaffa, Avshalom bounded onto the stage after actors dressed as Russian thugs had just "hit" actors playing Jews who refused to fight back. He broke up the performance because he could not bear watching Jews meekly turn the other cheek, even if they were only acting.[8]

Sarah and Avshalom raced each other in swimming and on horses, and they sparred over ideas and principles. For a time Avshalom appeared to court both Sarah and Rivka, and he wrote them letters from Hadera. In one letter to Sarah in 1911, the year before her European tour, Avshalom promised to send her and Rivka "three parts of 'L'Homme qui rit' [The man who laughs] by Victor Hugo, enjoy reading it. I am also sending you (don't give it to anyone else) the book 'Versets' by Mr. André Spire." Avshalom wrote with a flourish: "I would send you [both] half of my heart as well, but what would you do with it? You don't even have dogs in your yard. Do you think it would be enough? Wouldn't it? Be well, my good Sarah. Truly yours in heart and soul."[9]

In June 1911 Sarah visited Avshalom in Hadera. It was a difficult time for Avshalom because his father had recently died, and his mother was gravely ill. Eventually she recovered, but at the time of Sarah's visit, Avshalom thought his mother might die. After Sarah left, he spent much of the night by his mother's bedside. The next day Avshalom wrote Sarah that his heart had ached from the "smells of sickness and sweat" and from gazing at the "poor body that each day of sickness took a bit of life away from." Then, in his mind, Sarah appeared. "Your image rose in front of my eyes, young and beautiful, smelling so nice, and healthy and cheerful, smiling your shiny smile and your eyes—your eyes that yesterday were so deep, so wet, so good, like a cold, clear spring on a hot summer's day, and little by little the quiet comfort returned to my heart."

He had the power to forgive his mother "for getting old and sick. I could even forgive myself for getting old." He asked Sarah to forgive "me all past and future rudeness, in deeds, word and thoughts. Forgive me because I am nothing more than just a man." Avshalom ended with an elegy to tears and kisses as expressions of sorrow and joy.

Tears and kisses are the two wonderful presents given to us by God. A tear is a drop of hell that is washed away from the heart, and takes the sadness away, a tear is a drop of happiness, too. And a kiss is a theft from the lost garden of Eden that everyone can permit himself. A kiss is a moment of unity—unity of the sun and the sea, the flowers and the butterflies, of all holy harmony of nature. And we, although we are heavy, ugly, and sinful, permit ourselves this beautiful gesture, because we still strive for heaven from time to time.[10]

When her mother died and Sarah took over responsibility for the Aaronsohn family, Avshalom fretted over her well-being. It became a frequent theme of his letters to her.

My heart worries a lot for you Sarahle. You should take better care of "my Sarah," as you are a "little mother" now; with a son [Aaron] (and what a son!), with a daughter [Rivka], with the house duties on your shoulders, and if not you, then who? But if you sleep too little, cry too much, eat too little and work too hard, you won't get far, the human machine has its limits. And in addition to all my troubles, I have to think of you and worry so much.[11]

Avshalom frequently wrote to Sarah, and he found it annoying that she did not write to him as often. "It is shameful how little you write to me, and still, thank you very much, my good girl, for your warm greetings. The Russians say: 'of the good, have a little.' I would actually take a lot, if it was my choice." Few of the letters that Sarah did write to Avshalom have survived and then apparently only a handful that she wrote in 1916. Any judgment about their relationship depends heavily on Avshalom's letters and the recollections of those around them, and they obviously omit Sarah's perspective. That Avshalom was deeply attached and affectionate to Sarah is certain. Whether he sought her out as a wife is not as clear. If he did, in the end, Sarah, proud and self-possessed, proved too much even for Avshalom. By nature, Sarah was not inclined to listen with silent admiration to a man, and she could not patiently indulge Avshalom's moods.[12]

And Sarah had moods of her own. Avshalom and Sarah evidently quarreled often. In June 1912 after one clash, Avshalom wrote Sarah a poem-like letter in which he declared that his happiness lay with Rivka.

Sarati
After all, we are two friends and I love you with all the efforts of my heart, although you make me furiously mad and you are a bad girl Sarahle, my dear!

This Saturday [Shabat] was sad, my heart was empty and the room was empty, still full with your presence.

I went to celebrate, to hide my shame away. But in the midst of celebration, I whispered to Avshalom: "Go! Go away from here!"

And yet I hope to find my happiness soon. And may this happiness be quieter and full of tenderness. And I ask you to send to me, without delay, your little sister in a "registered parcel."

We shall talk about you here, I promise, and think about you when the sun goes down. And in the moonbeams, we shall see something of your dreamlike eyes, and in the setting sun something of your ardent soul.

Avshalom[13]

Pale and petite Rivka, two years younger than Sarah, was quiet, if not withdrawn. She often wore her hair pulled into a bun and carefully parted down the middle. Her favorite pastime appeared to be reading. With less enjoyment, she organized her brother Aaron's botanical collections. Once she wrote Avshalom that she was "busy with my unending work. Just imagine, almost a million examples of herbs, all mixed up. For me it is a huge amount of work that takes up all my time and besides the fact that I get to know how to recognize and name every herb, I gain absolutely nothing from it." Rivka was overwhelmingly insecure in a family of robust, extroverted personalities. "I was always the little sister," Rivka recalled decades later, adding that Sarah was "so much braver and more beautiful." Some chroniclers of the Aaronsohn family tend to assume that an introvert like the self-effacing Rivka would never seriously interest or hold Avshalom and that Avshalom and Sarah were romantically involved.[14]

Avshalom's letters and poems to Rivka, in fact, are far more romantic and passionate than his letters to Sarah are. Avshalom uses terms of endearment such as "my Goddess," "my peppery fledgling," and "Rivka, my love." He wrote, "In my mind I hug your tiny body and embrace your huge soul and your precious heart," and "I will say only one thing and nothing will be left to say after it: I Love you! Love you! Love you!"[15]

Rivka's calm, retiring personality may have been a much-needed analgesic for Avshalom's turbulence. In one letter to Rivka, Avshalom imagined that she was sitting in a dining room, reading, the light giving a "golden hue to your hair. The two little 'snakes' [locks of her hair] that wriggle from your temples are hanging quiet and serene." Or "you are alone, sitting on the swing and thinking, your little foot is stepping to the rhythm of your thoughts, what they call in music: *battre la mesure*. At one moment you are quiet and calm and at the next there is a sudden little tempest rising in your mind, your little foot keeps tapping, one two, one two, the swing is rocking back and forth, and the little snakes are wriggling and dancing. Then your gaze drops down and it is quiet again."[16]

But Sarah is a constant presence in those letters to Rivka. In one Avshalom imagined that he, Rivka, and Sarah, along with their brother Alexander and Avshalom's sister Tzila, would live on an island with streams of clear water running through gardens, with nightingales singing "spring songs," and with a moon moving across the "blue screen" of the sky.

We won't need to die either and when the day comes, the boys will turn into green crowned date palms and next to them their girls will petrify into statues of white marble. A palm tree and a statue, a lover and his beloved one. Can't you see the blinding light of the gardens, can't you hear the whisper of the waves? Can't you smell the fragrance of the flowers?

Oh bluebird! How can I catch you?

Avshalom half-seriously suggested that Rivka act as his amatory emissary to Sarah. "Yes! Take Sarah and kiss her like you know how, leave the marks of your kisses on her neck and nape, and hug and squeeze her as hard as you can. Inshallah, when we add up the score, I will pay you back in kind."[17]

Avshalom and Rivka, though, were not easy on one another. Rivka wanted to remain a virgin until she married, a source of recurring tension because Avshalom's frustration only made Rivka feel more insecure. Once Avshalom and Rivka were apart for three weeks, hardly a long separation. When they saw each other again, Rivka was wounded by what she perceived as Avshalom's cool and reproachful attitude. She wrote Avshalom afterward:

I have suffered, waited, wished, striven, achieved and came to you. I heard nothing from you, you told me nothing, and just gave me your judging look, and reproached me sharply. . . . Avshalom, if you knew how painful your words were to me, how they burned from the inside, you would choose other words. For a moment I wanted to respond but I stopped myself and said nothing, as if some kind of self-pride washed over me to stop me from showing you that my love for you is stronger than your love for me. . . . I said to myself that after such a long time that we hadn't seen each other, you must have grown colder and have no use for me anymore, and what a strange thing I have become in your eyes, but I said nothing.

Avshalom's defense was that *she* had been cold to him. He wrote Rivka back that "no one would notice that I am indeed hungry and thirsty, that I have come to the spring to quench my thirst, but the spring is not there." He reminded her that "one night I asked and I met a wall of iron, of total refusal. When I saw how little you cared for my begging, and how you responded to my pain with cold decisiveness, I indeed thought and said, 'to beg you?' It is beneath my dignity! For I was not begging a stranger for a handout, but asking for the attention of my love."

But, Avshalom insisted, he nonetheless deeply loved her and that, in just three weeks, he had not grown "colder." "What are you talking about? When could I have grown colder? . . . Rivka, you sarcastic, needling girl, why? . . . My heart is all yours and you can do with it whatever you wish. Please have mercy on your property—my heart—and don't break it completely."[18]

Sarah—perhaps out of pride, perhaps from devotion to Rivka, perhaps because she was too levelheaded to marry someone like Avshalom—appears not to have vied with her sister for Avshalom's affection. Avshalom and Rivka announced their engagement.

In early 1913 Haim Abraham, a black-bearded Jewish businessman from Constantinople then on a business trip to Palestine, was introduced to Sarah's father as a potential husband for his elder daughter. Haim had been born in Bulgaria and moved to Constantinople when he was in his thirties. There he and his brother started an import/export company called Abraham Frères; the business required Haim to make frequent trips abroad. He was active in Jewish and Zionist groups in Constantinople, including Jewish sports organizations.

Sarah's father reported to her on Haim's business success, European manners, and well-regarded family in Constantinople. Sarah decided to marry Haim, then in his early forties, possibly without meeting him. In one respect Sarah's marriage reflects long-standing Jewish tradition: sisters must wed in age order, meaning Avshalom and Rivka could not marry until Sarah did. But Sarah, not one to abide by convention, may have made her own judgment that Haim was the right choice and would have married him even if Rivka had not become engaged to Avshalom.[19]

In late April Sarah visited Avshalom. They discussed her engagement to Haim. "Do what I advised you to do," he wrote Sarah afterward, "and when you have a moment to yourself, do some honest introspection and then, at the right time, your old friend will re-appear to make the final connection. You'll see that you are still not done with me, when the first dizziness passes—we shall meet again. After all, until the 'new times,' I am one of the four souls that love you. And as we know I always win first place." If Avshalom's advice was that Sarah should not marry Haim (the letter is not explicit), she did not take it.[20]

Aaron Aaronsohn was in Hamburg when news reached him in late May of Sarah's engagement to Haim Abraham. Aaron sent Sarah a congratulatory telegram, and she responded by letter on June 6.

My dear Aaron,
Thank you for the telegram with your blessing. I am now happy and relieved to know that you, too, have heard the news. To tell you the truth, I wanted to send you a telegram about my engagement, but then I thought that if you suddenly received such a telegram you would not understand who, with whom, etc., . . . so I decided that it would be better to write to you about it. The groom says that he knows who you are, but I doubt that you know him. That's why the very proper thing for you to do would be to pass through Constantinople on your way back, if that is not too much trouble, to meet him and to take a glance at his business as well.

Sarah mentioned in the same letter the imminent return of their brother Alexander, who had been living in the United States for the past several years. Sarah referred to him as the "little one" and expressed regret that their mother would not be there for the reunion with Alexander. "And the little one won't be arriving in time for Shavuot [religious holiday]. What a pity. You know how it will be both joyful and sad to have him among us, knowing that Mother did not live to see this day. When he went away, Mother cried, 'Who knows if I will be here when Alex returns.' May Allah make us happy and may our happiness shine bright together with our fortune, that was always Mother's wish. Alexander will be surprised when I tell him that I am a bride."

In her letters Sarah tended to first digress, such as writing about her brother Alexander's return and then, only after she had gotten well into writing the letter, would she bring up her really pressing concern. In this case it was Aaron's opinion of her plan to marry, as though his blessing, more than anyone else's, would be decisive in confirming the wisdom of her choice. "And you tell me the truth. Were you happy with this news or not? It would have been interesting to see your face. I am hopeful that the person I selected will be to your liking, inshallah, because I will then be even happier.

"What else can I tell you?" The days were mild, but the evenings were cold. She had spent a day at Atlit during the harvest, but "unfortunately, when you arrive, much will have been cut, such as the wheat, but you will see a great difference in the trees." The Washingtonia palms that Aaron had planted, she wrote, were "especially stunning, they grew very nicely." She ended the letter, "Thousand kisses and Shalom to you. Your Sarah."[21]

Sarah offered Rivka a double wedding, which Rivka declined. In March 1914 Sarah and Haim were married. At the wedding the Aaronsohn family appeared devastated by Sarah's imminent departure to Constantinople. A wedding photograph captures Sarah, resplendent in a white wedding dress and white veil.[22]

Sarah was destined to be unhappy in Constantinople, which the Turkish poet Tevfik Fikret called the "widowed virgin of a thousand men" because—despite having been ravished by conquerors, corruption, and intercommunal violence over twenty-six centuries—Constantinople retained an allure. It was a metropolis of mosques and minarets, four different religious calendars, and about a million inhabitants (there was no exact census), of whom approximately half were Turks. The rest were all manner of races and tribes; it was said that they dwelled beside, but not among, one another. The sign over a cobbler's shop, for example, might be painted in six different languages. The streets bustled with Greek butchers balancing long poles on their shoulders, the carcass of a pig hanging from each end; Christian and Mohammedan ice cream sellers setting up their stands; Albanians laying pavement; and Turks lighting fires under the hot water boilers and laying out thin cotton towels in the hammams.[23]

When Sarah arrived in 1914, Constantinople was struggling to overcome a primitive past. Until recently dogs had slept in the middle of the streets, undisturbed by pedestrians, horses, camels, donkeys, and vehicles, which carefully walked or drove around them. They had finally been removed, exiled to an island, and put to death. Fires had periodically consumed whole neighborhoods because the main residential building material was wood, and the firemen worked on a pay-as-you-go basis. They would not begin fighting a fire until they knew how much the owner of the building was willing to pay them, often resulting in time-consuming negotiations.[24]

Sarah had been accustomed to running a household in Zichron, but according to one account, her mother-in-law forbade her from going outside the home by herself, telling Sarah that it was unsafe for a young woman to venture into the streets alone. Henceforth, the mother-in-law explained, Sarah would spend her days with the women of the Abraham house, a free-born lioness in a cage.[25]

The mother-in-law's concerns might have been more justified a few years earlier, although even then the risks of walking alone in the Constantinople streets could hardly have exceeded the risks Sarah took in riding her horse alone into the Palestinian countryside. Until 1912 women were openly harassed on the streets of Constantinople. Muslim women in veils were routinely pinched, or worse, by men to determine whether the woman was old or young, fat or thin under the black veils. Unaccompanied women were often followed by elegantly dressed Turkish men in four-wheeled horse-drawn carriages. The men had their hair dyed black under a red fez, their eyebrows brushed upward, their cheeks shaved so smoothly that a fly could not get a grip and that were then softened with a pink powder, and their double chins bulging over stiff, straight collars. In 1912 a reform-minded city government announced that the harassment of women would be punished by exile. That sentence was meted out to several violators, and the incidents ceased.[26]

Sarah wrote Avshalom from Constantinople about her growing unhappiness concerning her isolation from family and friends in Zichron. Those letters did not survive (although, curiously, letters to other family members and friends from Constantinople did). Avshalom wrote Sarah on June 17, 1914.

> Your letters don't make me very cheerful but to be honest I expected it to be so and I am not at all surprised. I knew that going away, even under such circumstances as yours, is a wound that cannot heal so soon and it is obvious that it bleeds again with each letter. Maybe after many years the pain can ease a bit, but you cannot expect it to happen in the first weeks. And besides, still there is hope that it is just a temporary break, that even before you left, the longing to return had already sprouted in your heart and we were already waiting for you to come back.

For both himself and Rivka, "we couldn't know, my girl, just like you couldn't know it, what a 'big piece' of our heart you would take with you. Often, at home, I completely forget that my Sarah has gone."

Avshalom had recently been at the Aaronsohn family home in Zichron. "The garden doesn't have its old colors anymore and maybe even its fragrances have grown weaker." He had wandered into her old room.

> Your empty bed chases and disturbs the mind and gives it no rest, every piece of it, every thread of the blankets, everything in it speaks of you. And we, the two that have remained, sit closer to one another and try to forget. But it's the law of nature, two cannot take three places—and what is missing is missing. . . .
>
> How selfish these thoughts are. If we who stayed at home in "peace" are complaining so much, then how great your suffering must be. Because you, Sarah, are alone now, day and night, lonely and sad. Our heart is with you, the whole of our heart and all our love.

Avshalom ended the letter with some marital advice to the newlywed Sarah, although he might have been addressing his own relationship with Rivka. Effort and time, he assured Sarah, would eventually ensure the success of her marriage. "I adore love and know what it is worth. But even the biggest flame of love cannot do the slow and persistent work that is done by day-to-day life, that carves, shapes, refines and brings to perfection the characters and pathways of two people who are meant to be together."

Avshalom suggested that Sarah's marriage might lack sufficient erotic content. "You can say what you want, but two people, even if they are in love, as long as they aren't really familiar with each other, or—using the realistic language of our Bible—'don't know each other enough'—remain like two rivals that stand in front of one another, trying to catch every hint, every look, every sound that would help them to learn how to act." Her husband, Avshalom warned Sarah, had to dedicate more time to her and less to his business affairs. "It would be better, maybe, if he did less 'business' and inshallah you completely stopped missing us. If not, you will have to return earlier than we thought."[27]

We do not know what Sarah thought of this advice. But whatever the accuracy of Avshalom's analysis of Sarah's marriage, unquestionably she was increasingly homesick in Constantinople. Then a war started, further isolating Sarah from Avshalom, Rivka, and the rest of her family in Zichron.

3

Don't You Feel That a New Generation Is Born?

On June 28, 1914, a few months after Sarah had arrived in Constantinople, a Serbian nationalist assassinated Archduke Franz Ferdinand, heir to the Austro-Hungarian Empire, in Sarajevo. Europe's diplomats believed that the consequences would be confined to the Balkans, but they had miscalculated the impact of treaty and alliance obligations, troop mobilization timetables, and national pride, fear, and stupidity. After Serbia failed to meet the terms of an ultimatum from Austria-Hungary that effectively demanded the surrender of Serbia's sovereignty, Austria-Hungary declared war on Serbia with, in historian Barbara Tuchman's words, "the bellicose frivolity of senile empires." Russia mobilized to aid Serbia for reasons of historic allegiance and a Russian perception of geopolitical necessity. Germany, in rigid Teutonic fashion, considered itself lacking any alternative but to declare war on Russia to prevent the defeat of its ally Austria-Hungary. Inflexible German military doctrine, however, required an immediate all-out attack on Russia's ally France, which hadn't yet declared war on anyone. German armies marched into neutral Belgium as the first step toward an envelopment of Paris.

Germany's invasion of Belgium, a country on the English Channel, was unacceptable to England, which joined France and Russia (their alliance against Germany was called the Entente). Ironically, Czar Nicholas II of Russia, King George V of England, and Kaiser Wilhelm II of Germany were cousins. As children they had played together, and the late Queen Victoria of Great Britain was the grandmother of both King George and Kaiser Wilhelm. While signing a mobilization order, the kaiser complained about his cousins to his generals: "To think that George and Nicky should have played me false. If my grandmother had been alive, she would never have allowed it." Champagne was brought out to celebrate the mobilization of the German military for war. Today it seems like madness, but in the streets of the European capitals it made perfect sense to the exultant, cheering crowds of people, who apparently lacked any concept of what modern weapons could do to the human body.[1]

After a century of relative peace, within the space of a few weeks, most of the major European powers were at war with one another even though they had no significant political disagreements among them. Certainly no one, with the benefit of hindsight, would ever argue any of their disagreements was worth the deaths of nearly twenty million soldiers and civilians and an outcome that made inevitable a second world war that would kill several times that number. Without exception each belligerent country sincerely believed it was going to war in self-defense, and most people assumed the war would be over in a few months. It all started so quickly that the day after Great Britain's declaration of war on Germany, the *Daily Telegraph* in England displayed a front-page advertisement calling the attention of English tourists to "The Shortest & Most Comfortable Route to North Germany."[2]

The war began without the involvement of the Ottoman Empire, which in the previous six years had endured "a revolution, three major wars against foreign powers, and a number of internal disorders ranging from sectarian massacres to separatist revolts." The revolution in 1908 was led by Committee of Union and Progress, a group of reform-minded civilians and military officers that later became a political party (its members were sometimes called the Young Turks). The revolt ended what was essentially the theocratic absolute rule of the sultans, who had created the illusion of a cohesive empire, although the reality was that this multiethnic, multilingual, multireligious land was anything but cohesive. The Ottoman Empire was never a nation but only a jumble of separate and often hostile peoples under the military mastery of the Turks. As the English writer and explorer Gertrude Bell observed, "No country which turned to the eye of the world an appearance of established rule and centralized Government was, to a greater extent than the Ottoman Empire, a land of make-believe."

As the sons of harem concubines, the sultans were technically half-slave by birth. They were backward, uneducated, and, in some instances, brutal men. Murad III, sultan from 1574 to 1595, had his five brothers strangled to resolve any lingering questions about his succession. His son and successor, Mehmed III, strangled all nineteen of his brothers. Sultan Murad IV, who ruled from 1623 to 1640, liked to make incognito visits to taverns in Constantinople, where he personally beheaded anyone found smoking.[3]

At the time of the 1908 revolt, Sultan Abdul Hamid II had banned electric lights, trolleys, and telephones in Constantinople because he believed that a dynamo had something to do with dynamite, which could be used to assassinate him. In 1909 the Young Turks replaced him with Sultan Mehmed V, who had spent the first few decades of his life confined to Topkapi Palace in Constantinople. The Young Turks selected Mehmed V based in part on his boast that he had not read a newspaper in many years. Once Mehmed became sultan, no one even bothered to pretend to take him seriously.

By the outbreak of the war, three of the Young Turks had emerged as the ruling triumvirate of the Ottoman Empire and were promoted to pasha, the highest grade in both civil and military service. They were Talaat Pasha, minister of the interior; Enver Pasha, minister of war; and Djemal Pasha, the governor of Constantinople. During their rule in peacetime, the Ottoman government initiated public works projects, including electrification, public lighting, intercity railroads, paved roads, modern port facilities, and more efficient firefighting. Under wartime pressure, however, Talaat, Enver, and Djemal would match, if not exceed, the brutality of the dozens of sultans who had ruled the Ottoman Empire over six centuries.[4]

The three pashas governed an empire in a state of decline. For decades European imperialist powers, like hungry wolves, had been tearing out chunks of its outer provinces. In 1878 the Ottomans surrendered territory in the Balkans and eastern Anatolia after losing a war to Russia. That same year the British took the island of Cyprus in the Mediterranean, in 1881 the French occupied Tunisia, and in 1882 to safeguard the Suez Canal, the British established colonial rule over Egypt. Ottoman instability in the immediate prewar years only encouraged the European powers to bite off more of the empire. Despite the efforts of the Young Turks to bring the modern world to the empire, the modern world continued swallowing pieces of it. Between 1908 and 1912 the Ottoman Empire lost 40 percent of its landmass and a sixth of its population. Germany, for its part, concentrated on building relations with the Ottoman rulers, who were then searching for a strong ally and protector.[5]

Despite the loss of so much land and population, the Ottoman Empire was still a vast, potentially formidable realm at the outbreak of the war and a promising military ally for Germany in its war with the Entente. With 7,500 miles of borders and coastlines on the Black Sea, the Persian Gulf, the Red Sea, and the Mediterranean Sea, as one historian noted, the "sprawling Ottoman Empire was difficult to defend—but harder still to conquer." The population under direct control of the Ottoman government was somewhere in the range of twenty million to twenty-five million people, the majority of whom were Muslim.[6]

Upon observing that the European combatants had suffered a million casualties in less than six weeks of fighting, however, Talaat, Enver, and Djemal should have known better than to join the fray. But they feared an attack by Russia, to which the Ottomans had lost seven straight wars since the early 1700s. Ultimately the three pashas succumbed to seductive German promises of military and financial support and recovery of lost territory, especially Egypt and eastern Anatolia—in a sense, baksheesh. In October 1914 the Germans sent two million Turkish pounds in gold to Constantinople, to be released at the outbreak of hostilities with Russia; another three million pounds would be disbursed after the Ottoman Empire formally entered the war. In November the Ottoman Empire entered the war as an ally of Germany's.[7]

The German gold hardly offset the economic blow the war inflicted on the empire. After war broke out, blockades imposed by both sides curtailed trade with the outside world. The Ottoman navy mined the Dardanelles Strait to protect Constantinople from naval attack, and the British and French navies imposed blockades along the empire's coastlines.

Another shock to economic activity was the conscription of men for the army. In the summer of 1914, Enver Pasha had ordered all men between the ages of twenty-one and forty-five—including farmers, even though agriculture was a principal economic activity—to report for induction. In Constantinople the men, after their induction and assignment to a unit, were allowed to return home briefly to collect their belongings and bid their families farewell. A deafening band went from house to house, calling the conscripts away from their families.[8]

In August 1914 Sarah encountered two Jews from Haifa who gave her the startling news that her brother Alexander, Avshalom Feinberg, and other Zichron men had been inducted into the Ottoman army. Sarah sent a postcard to Rivka in Zichron: "Please write me everything and with details, otherwise I will be very upset. I am not at all calm and when you don't write, it just makes it worse."

She followed that with a long letter to "my lovely, little Rivka!" in which she reproached Rivka for not having written her for several weeks. "Why? Are there good reasons for this? . . . Not a moment passes when I don't think of you with worry and fear."

> It's needless to tell you how many tears I shed, all night, and the next day. I almost went out of my mind from looking at the pictures of you, Alex and Avshalom on the stand on my dressing table. I could not stop myself from crying. But, one gets used to everything, tears dry up and don't return so easily, and I calmed down. But you should know, my girl, that you do no good when you don't inform me about anything. Why are you silent? I have stopped writing in the last few days because of your silence and will write home each and every day. It might be that the post is irregular.

Constantinople newspapers had reported the German army's seemingly unstoppable drive through Belgium and France.

> From the news in the papers, Germany is winning for the time being. I hope our Turks will not join them. I am very afraid of war because our young men will be sent to the front. Write to me abso-

lutely everything, and in detail. . . . Is it at least peaceful there? We are concerned that the Arabs are starving and there will be theft and killing. Do you have sufficient provisions?

In her letter Sarah described the impact of the war in Europe on Constantinople, but at the time of this letter, the empire had not yet entered the war. "Here there isn't really any business activity. The shops open only out of habit because most of the workers are in the army. The wealthy have dismissed their servants and maids because they are afraid a war will start and it will be hard to find food, and so why do they need servants at their table, as well."

Sarah and her husband "have stopped buying anything new for the house because we are afraid to spend money now." Sarah wrote that "I haven't got a lot of work," suggesting that she might have been doing odd jobs, such as sewing. Rather, she was "staying at home all the time and not going out because nothing interests me." She and Haim had dreams, "castles in the air," to buy land in Palestine. "We decided that I shall go first and arrange everything. Father will help me, and a half year later Haim would come, and so on." The war had made that impossible. "So many dreams we had and then suddenly—this awful situation, is there anybody not affected by it?"

Sarah finally got to the real point: she was in the grip of an astonishingly painful homesickness.

How I long to see you. I swear, I would give everything to be among all of you just for a brief moment. . . . My longing for all of you is terrible and is growing every day.

I am looking at the garden and imagining that I am back home. I hear the carriages pass by and the noise is just like that of the carriages back home, bringing the young men from the fields, everything turns blurry, I close my eyes and feel like I am in Zichron. . . . I am in Constantinople but my mind and heart are in Zichron, believe me. I never thought I would go so crazy with homesickness when I have a fine house and everything I need.

People in Constantinople constantly reminded her of family, friends, and neighbors in Zichron, even the neighbors she had no interest in:

> I wish you could see how I find here every person from Zichron, people I never even looked at (Suzi). . . . When you come here, inshallah, I will show them all to you, from Bandarofsky to Rivka Goldstein, for example. . . . When, from a distance, I see two old women talking to each other, they appear to me like Basa and Hama and I see Mother with them, too. . . .
>
> What can I say? If I told you all that passes through my mind, a thousand pages would not be enough, so I'd better stop. I just gave you some examples so that you can imagine just how "crazy" I have become. I think that it is just you and me who go so mad in these situations, otherwise how can other people live abroad?

Sarah mentioned that "Autumn is already here with its new fashions, new hats, again the big hats are in fashion, just like the one I wore in Paris, with black below and white above. Do you remember? But I don't keep up with all the fashions these days." She ended the letter,

> I kiss you, write to me as soon as you can, the good things, if there are any, and the bad things, too. Kiss Father and everybody. Haim says hello to you all, he says that he is lucky to have met me. Say hello and greetings to Avshalom and his mother. Forgive me for this letter. If you only knew how many tears this one letter has cost me.
>
> One more kiss from your Sarah, love you very, very much.[9]

Two weeks later, in early September, the French and British halted the German drive just twenty-five miles from Paris at the Battle of the Marne. This turning point in the war led to a stalemate and four years of murderous trench warfare on the western front. The stalemate may have intensified German pressure on the Ottoman Empire to enter the war as well.

The wartime Ottoman Empire, as Sarah feared, was a less hospitable place for the *yishuv*. Soon after the Ottoman Empire entered the war in November 1914, Djemal Pasha urged the Ottoman government to prevent "foreign" Jews within the empire from engaging in settlement activity, to bar further Jewish immigration, and to change the names of the Jewish settlements to the names of nearby Arab villages.

In particular, Djemal hated Zionists, whom he considered a potential catastrophe for Palestine. Two Zionists—David Ben-Gurion (later Israel's first prime minister) and Itzhak Ben-Zvi (later Israel's second president)—offered to organize a Palestinian Jewish army to defend the Ottoman Empire. To show his appreciation, Djemal Pasha, now the commander of the Ottoman Fourth Army and de facto ruler of Syria, deported both men. Nonetheless, the two continued to campaign in the United States for the creation of a pro-Ottoman Jewish army.

The rest of the Ottoman government in Constantinople, concerned with world public opinion, especially in the neutral United States, was not as enthusiastic as Djemal Pasha was in taking harsh measures against Palestinian Jews. According to historian Yuval Ben-Bassat, the government in Constantinople "stressed that Jews should not be treated categorically as collaborators of the enemy and that every effort should be made to preserve their support and to encourage them to embrace the attitude of the general public in Palestine vis-à-vis the Ottoman state." To say that the Ottoman government was humanitarian-minded, however, would be grossly inaccurate. Soon, with Enver's approval, Talaat Pasha would set in motion the destruction of the Armenian community, numbering some two million people, in the Ottoman Empire.[10]

One young Palestinian Jew would not have dreamed of defending the empire as David Ben-Gurion did. To Avshalom Feinberg, who apparently avoided service in the Turkish army, the war was an opportunity for Jews to gain a homeland in Palestine by actively helping the British defeat the Ottomans. The Ottomans' repressive measures against Jews only reinforced Avshalom's conviction, especially after he personally experienced those measures.

In early 1915 a sheik from an Arab village near Avshalom's settlement of Hadera sought to gain favor with the Ottoman authorities by claiming that Jews from Hadera had illegally loaded wheat onto disguised British ships. The accusation was not just false but bizarre. To meet supply needs, the Ottoman army had confiscated from Jewish farmers their draft animals, crops, farm equipment, and even barbed wire. The *yishuv* could no longer produce enough food to meet its own needs, let alone give any to the British.

In a driving rainstorm, Ottoman soldiers surrounded Hadera and randomly arrested thirteen young Jewish men, including Avshalom Feinberg, on charges of "open armed rebellion against the authorities in exercise of their functions during a state of war." They beat fifty other Hadera Jews with sticks in an unsuccessful attempt to elicit confessions to the sheik's charge. The Turks marched off the arrested men, amid the weeping of their families and neighbors.[11]

Avshalom managed to get away in the chaos. He found a horse and galloped to Zichron, where he told Aaron Aaronsohn about the arrests. While Aaron considered a strategy for rescuing the Hadera men, Avshalom railed against the Jewish leaders, who had discouraged the *yishuv* from supporting the British out of fear of reprisals. "We can't let idiots dictate our policy. Our worst enemy is the Turk. Anyone who doesn't have a rabbit's heart would be proud to spy against them, if it would help to bring the English."

Aaron sent Avshalom back into the storm and left immediately for Beirut, where he had extensive contacts in the Ottoman bureaucracy from his agronomic work. Characteristically, Avshalom returned to Hadera so that he could be arrested by the Ottomans and join the increasingly dispirited, if not depressed, young men under arrest and keep up their morale. "To the devil with all this sentiment," Avshalom told them after his arrest. "You have to be ready for the worst. If the time has come for us to die, we'll die."

One of the Jews replied, "But if we do die, we must die for justice, not because someone told a lie about us."

Avshalom gestured at the Ottoman soldiers. "From this you expect justice? For thinking it you deserve to be hanged."

The Jews were taken to Jaffa and kept there overnight; their destination was Jerusalem. Avshalom came down with malaria. A close friend, a Hadera Jew named Liova Schneersohn, managed to obtain a cold compress to put on Avshalom's feverish forehead.

"Put a sea of ice on my head," Avshalom demanded. "My blood is boiling. All the East is boiling in me. . . . I am a Jew of the East. I can understand the mystery, the beauty, the gaiety of the East. . . . I hear the song of the Bedouin, the song he sings on the night watch, and it says much more to me than the music of your Wagner and your Beethoven."

"Avshalom, my friend," said Liova, "don't get so excited. The compress is falling from your head."

"Get away from me, you cold man of the north. We'll show all the world what our people can do, . . . we from the land of Israel, the new ones, the unknown until now. Don't you feel that a new generation is born? Don't you hear it coming with slow steps, angry, vengeful?"

Avshalom then confided his plan to Liova. "Listen, there is something I want to tell you. I've wanted to tell you for a long time. Don't think I am talking from fever."

Avshalom had no interest in acquiring a Jewish homeland acre by acre. "We can't defend ourselves against the Arabs. We haven't any arms. . . . It's impossible to remain idle now. We must make contact with the English, somehow or other. Surely we can find brave men amongst us, who will answer the call. . . . We will go and make contact with the enemy. With their help we will get arms. We will reveal to them the secrets of the country. We will organize the freeing of Palestine."

Avshalom was nothing if not dramatic. "If they catch us on the borders, or here in Palestine, they'll sentence us as spies and hang us. Good. They'll hang us. They'll shoot us. Even if the whole yishuv suffers for this, we must do it. . . . Whoever doesn't want to join us can stay home! They are already preparing to condemn us to death. And for what? If we must die, better to have died for something we have done, as my father used to say. And remember, courage and daring are the decisive things in life."[12]

As to their current predicament, Avshalom believed that time was running out for the Hadera Jews. Given the irregular train schedules,

Aaron needed considerable time just to reach Beirut and arrange a meeting with his old friend Azmi Bey, the *vali* of Beirut (the governor-general appointed by the sultan), who had jurisdiction because Hadera was in the *vilayet* (province) of Beirut. Such a meeting was risky business, however, even for a man of Aaron's stature. Azmi Bey had a Van Dyke beard and a "cruel and dissipated face," in the words of an American then living in Beirut. He fanatically hated foreigners and, according to local rumor, had carried out political assassinations before becoming *vali*. Azmi lived in constant fear of his own assassination and always had a revolver within reach. And even if Aaron's appeal succeeded and the *vali* agreed to free the Hadera Jews, given the unreliable telegraph service, transmitting the *vali*'s order by telegram to the Ottoman military authorities in Jerusalem would take time.[13]

To Avshalom the outcome depended on whether the *vali*'s telegram or the Hadera men arrived first in Jerusalem. While the danger was real, Avshalom may have been melodramatic because the Turks would not likely hang the Hadera men as soon as they reached Jerusalem. In general, in dealing with traitors, conspirators, and spies, the Turks first held trials and then hanged the defendants.

Aaron was skilled in dealing with cutthroat Ottoman potentates. He was known to have powerful Jewish friends in the United States, whom the Germans and Ottomans wished to keep neutral, and his scientific talent was a valuable resource for the empire. The *vali*'s telegram arrived first.

The Hadera men were released and sent home. Until the arrests of the Hadera men, Aaron had believed that the interests of the Palestinian Jews lay in not taking sides in the Ottomans' war with Great Britain. Now he was more inclined to agree with Avshalom.[14]

In Constantinople Sarah had limited, albeit troubling, information about the precarious position of the Palestinian Jewish community, including the increasing shortage of food. Looking out her window, Sarah watched Turkish soldiers from Djemal Pasha's Fourth Army marching through the streets while accompanied by detachments of German soldiers. (She could not have known that they were on their way to attack the Suez Canal.)

Mail was censored by the Ottoman authorities, who had commandeered the postal service for military needs. Under the postage stamps on some of her letters, Sarah wrote tiny notes about what she knew of military matters that might have been of interest to her family, especially Aaron. In a letter to Rivka, she wrote, "I know you are interested in plants as ever. So don't be surprised if you find some interesting specimens under the boules." The Hebrew word for stamp is *bul*, while in French the word *boule* is often used as an abbreviation for "boulevard."[15]

The letters themselves would not have interested a military censor because they principally concerned Sarah's increasing despair over her isolation from family and friends. In August 1915, a year and a half since leaving Zichron, Sarah received a letter from Avshalom's sister Tzila. Sarah wrote her back on August 8.

I am very happy to hear from you, I think of you very often, I was sorry to hear that you are ill, and hope you will recover soon, inshallah! . . .

I would love to tell you something interesting about my life, but actually there is nothing about it that would interest you. My life is monotonous and boring and I am lonely. I very rarely meet people, I am indifferent to everything and nothing makes me happy. I look forward to the happy day when we return to Palestine and settle once more amongst our beloved ones; for me the house here is but a temporary one. . . . If you think, my dear, that I know what is happening with our families in Palestine, I am afraid you are very mistaken; they write nothing to me, which makes me very sad. . . . There is no sign of life from Rivka, either, I have no contact with her; I am completely fed up with this life away from the family, believe me. . . . I would give so much to be with Rivka and the rest of the family now!

After Sarah had finished writing the letter, but before she had mailed it, a postcard arrived from Alexander and Rivka with unexpected news. Sarah added a postscript to her letter:

> They write that they are on their way to America. What does that mean? All of a sudden, without writing anything about it in previous letters. I don't understand this. I am so curious and can't wait to get more details. They are risking a lot by traveling such a long way with "Palestinian papers." Their journey surprises me very much; what is your opinion?

The last Sarah appears to have heard previously about her brother Alexander was that he had been inducted into the Turkish army, and her sister, Rivka, as far as she knew, was in Zichron with their father.

> For me it is truly awful, who knows if I will ever see that little girl again. Leaving home and saying good-bye to Avshalom was probably very hard for her. The nest is empty now and my poor father is left alone. I pity him. I cannot go on writing because my eyes are dripping tears and my heart aches.
>
> Hope for better days, good-bye. May God protect them on their way. Forgive me my nonsense. Kiss you Tzil'ka.
>
> Yours, Sarah[16]

That fall Haim planned an extended business trip to Germany. Sarah decided to return home for the winter. But it was no simple matter for a young woman to undertake a trip from Constantinople to Palestine, more than a thousand miles away even by the most direct route. Sarah would have gone alone, if she had to, but having a companion would make it less likely that she would be sent back to Constantinople by Turkish railway officials, who would conceivably deem it unacceptable for a woman to attempt such an arduous and lengthy trip by herself. In November Sarah heard that Yitzhak Haus, a member of Ha-Shomer (the Watchman), a Jewish self-defense organization in Palestine, was in Constantinople to negotiate the return of the group's members who had been exiled from Palestine to a remote area of Anatolia. Haus had been unsuccessful in his mission; indeed, he had barely escaped arrest. He planned to return to Palestine soon, and when Sarah went to him and begged that she be allowed to accompany him, Haus agreed. They obtained the necessary traveling permits and booked their train tickets.[17]

Given the unpredictability of train schedules in wartime, Sarah likely left the house the morning of her departure even before the muezzins had called out the first *adhan* (call to prayer) from the minarets. At the Haidar Pasha train station on the Bosporus Sea, Sarah mingled with Turkish soldiers boarding troop trains destined for the multiple fronts along the thousands of miles of the empire's besieged borders.

Sarah and her companion found seats. The train pulled away from Haidar Pasha and slowly picked up speed. For such a journey, a young woman traveler like Sarah might have worn a headscarf, a homemade cotton dress, a wool jacket, black stockings, and ankle-high shoes tied at the top with black laces.[18]

To return home to Palestine, Sarah first had to traverse the huge Anatolian plateau. Since the Ottoman Empire's entrance into the war a year earlier as an ally of Germany's, few travelers had been where the train was taking Sarah.

The train carried Sarah into a vast pastoral landscape, where an unimaginable slaughter, the Armenian genocide, was taking place. It was the first, but hardly the last, such event of the twentieth century. As Sarah set out by train that November to return home, the butchery was at or near its peak.

4

What Sights Her Eyes Have Seen

At the time of his induction into the Turkish army in 1914, Sarah's brother Alexander was twenty-seven years old. Tall, handsome, and erudite, Alexander looked like an Oxford graduate student. In 1910 on Aaron's advice, Alexander had gone to the United States, where he worked for the Department of Agriculture.[1]

After returning to Palestine in 1913 Alexander helped lead a self-defense organization as a rival to Ha-Shomer. Called the Gideonites, the group favored military discipline, secret initiation rites, and melodramatic vows of eternal brotherhood. They armed themselves with revolvers, shotguns, and rifles and wore an assortment of garb, with one sporting a kaffiyeh, another donning an old military uniform. In a developing generational divide, the Gideonites—the project of children of the First Aliyah—angered the more recently arrived socialist-minded immigrants of the Second Aliyah (1904–14) who had formed Ha-Shomer. The later immigrants were typically younger, unmarried, and more idealistic; many believed in the equality of the sexes and opposed the use of Arab labor. To the Second Aliyah immigrants, the First Aliyah immigrants lacked an ideology and European sophistication and manners. One socialist leader sarcastically observed that while the Gideonites had performed some "useful functions"—such as cleaning up the runnels, or water ditches used for irrigation ("imagine, the grandchildren of the Baron cleaning out the runnels")—the young men of Zichron were socially ill-mannered, living "the same empty life, lacking aspiration or ideals."[2]

Alexander's career with the Gideonites ended in August 1914 when the Turkish *mouchtar* (headman) came to Zichron with a list of men to be mobilized now that war had broken out in Europe. Alexander was then in the process of applying for U.S. citizenship. The American consul in Haifa, however, was unsympathetic to this foreigner's request for the consulate's assistance in avoiding induction into the Ottoman army. Along with several other young Jewish men from Zichron and nearby settlements, and several hundred Arabs and Christians, Alexander reported to the garrison town of Safed in the northern Galilee.[3]

The fashion-conscious Alex, when not wearing a Gideonite uniform, favored gold-buttoned blazers, yachting caps, and knotted scarfs; now he had to wear a green khaki Turkish uniform and a peculiar headgear that was a cross between the German spiked helmet and a turban. During the day Turkish army officers drilled Alexander and his fellow recruits in the courtyard of an abandoned mosque that served as their barracks. At night in the courtyard, the Arab recruits danced for hours in a great circle around an Arab who squatted on the ground and played a bamboo flute. A self-proclaimed poet sang improvised verses. "Tomorrow we shall eat rice and meat," the poet cried. The Arabs cried back, "Yaha lili-amali" (My endeavor be granted).

Alexander complained to his paunchy commanding officer that he and his fellow Jews could get no sleep because of the Arabs' singing and dancing.

"You are serving the Sultan. Hardship should be sweet."

"I should be more fit to serve if I got more rest."

"Look at me!" said the fat Turk waving his hand around the tent and glancing meaningfully at Alexander. "Here I am, an officer of rank, and I have not even a nice blanket."

"A crime! A crime! To think of it, when I a humble soldier have dozens of them at home! I should be honored if you would allow me, . . ." Alexander let his voice trail away. Soon the fat Turk had blankets, and Alexander and his Jewish companions were sleeping in an inn in Safed that was kept by a Jewish widow.

One morning not long after the Ottoman Empire entered the war, the Jewish and Christian soldiers were called out of the regiment. The Turk officers disarmed the men, took away their uniforms, and put them to work building a road between Safed and Tiberias on the Sea of Galilee. Alexander attributed their demotions to the Turks' desire to "conciliate and flatter the Mohammedan population" and isolate potentially disloyal minorities.

The road gang ran short a man when a Christian soldier disappeared. As Alexander pieced the story together, the Turks had arrested the soldier and probably executed him. The soldier's offense was shooting his sister for having been raped by a Turkish officer. Purely as a practical matter, the Christian soldier could redeem the dishonor and the family bloodline only by killing his sister, for had he shot the Turkish officer, the soldier's entire family would have been slaughtered. By now Alexander had seen enough of Turkish army life.

With his remaining funds, Alexander bribed half a dozen officers, from corporal to captain, to obtain a medical discharge. Since Alexander was in robust health, the doctor struggled to invent an ailment. He finally wrote down that Alexander "had too much blood." Alexander returned to Zichron to find the village full of Turkish soldiers and a curfew after sundown in effect.

The Aaronsohn family held a council. Sarah was apparently safe in Constantinople, but Rivka was at risk in Zichron. The family decided to send Rivka to Beirut, where she would stay with family friends at the American-sponsored Syrian Protestant College (now the American University of Beirut). Shortly after Rivka left Zichron, a Turkish officer on horseback, followed by thirty cavalrymen, rode up to the Aaronsohn home and demanded that Alexander take them to the village arms cache. Alexander refused. The Turks arrested him and three village elders and took them to a prison. Alexander was bound, forced to his knees, and had his shoes removed.[4]

A Turkish soldier whipped his bare feet with a pliant green rod, a torture sometimes called *falaka* (bastinado). The rod makes a whistling sound before striking the feet and instantly drawing blood and causing excruciating pain. After countless strokes, Alexander lost consciousness without having disclosed the location of the arms cache. The Turks, exasperated, announced that they would arrest the young women of Zichron and hand them over to Turkish officers if the hidden weapons were not produced. When the Turkish forces finally left, the young women were still there and Alexander had been freed, but Zichron no longer had any weapons with which to defend itself.[5]

Part of the Ottoman war strategy, supported by their German allies, was to fight under the banner of jihad. Calling for a holy war, the Turkish pashas hoped, would rally Muslims within the empire and inspire uprisings in southern Russia and in Egypt. Twenty-nine Islamic legal scholars met in Constantinople and issued fatwas authorizing jihad that the sultan then approved. On November 14, 1914, the call for a holy war in the name of the sultan was proclaimed in public to a huge, approving crowd outside the Mosque of Mehmed the Conqueror. Religious leaders read the following to their congregations in the mosques:

> Oh, Moslems! . . . Obey the commands of the Almighty, who in the Koran, promises us bliss in this and the next world; embrace ye the foot of the Caliph's throne and know ye that the state is at war with Russia, England, France, and their Allies, and that these are the enemies of Islam. The Chief of the believers, the Caliph, invites you all as Moslems to join in the Holy War![6]

In December 1915 Enver Pasha sent the Ottoman Third Army into the Caucasus Mountains of Russia. He ordered his men to leave their heavy packs behind for the sake of speed. The soldiers would supply themselves by plundering the Russian villages in their path. ("Our supply base is in front of us," Enver assured them.)[7] Enver's troops carried no fuel, tents, or bedding and took only flatbread for rations.

A major snowstorm struck the Third Army a few days before Christmas. Temperatures plunged, routes through the mountains became impassable, and at dawn, men's bodies were found frozen around the remnants of wood fires whose warmth had been inadequate to keep them alive. Of the one hundred thousand Turkish soldiers of the Third Army sent into the Caucasus, only eighteen thousand broken, starving, and frostbitten men returned. There had been no Muslim uprising, and Enver Pasha himself barely escaped capture. The defeat was such a disaster that it was "forbidden to speak of it," wrote a German general. "Violations of the order were followed by arrest and punishment."[8]

In January 1915 under the green banner of jihad, Djemal Pasha led the Ottoman Fourth Army into the Sinai Desert. Its objective was the British-held Suez Canal, a vital artery for tens of thousands of soldiers moving from India and other British and French colonies to the western front and for British merchant ships traveling from the Indian Ocean to the Mediterranean. The loss of the Suez Canal would have been a calamity for the British Empire.[9]

The main body of the Fourth Army, with ten thousand camels carrying its supplies, marched through a harsh desert with almost no roads, few sources of water, and sparse vegetation. The army marched at night when it was too cold to sleep and rested during the day, following a route through the central Sinai Desert. On that route, sand lay on a limestone base, which offered firmer support for the soldiers, the camels, and the galvanized iron pontoons for crossing the canal that the Turks dragged with them.[10]

The British had earlier received a report of an Ottoman force of tens of thousands assembling in Damascus and Jerusalem and then making its way to Beersheba in southern Palestine, the Fourth Army's jumping-off point. The British initially dismissed the report, but then their reconnaissance planes reported Turkish troop formations moving through the desert.

The Suez Canal, which ran from Port Said on the Mediterranean Sea to its southern terminus on the Red Sea near the city of Suez, was then a hundred miles long. Forty-nine miles were impassable for the Fourth Army because of natural barriers, such as marshes, and because British engineers had flooded low-lying sections. That left about fifty-one miles of the canal to be defended. Along those stretches, the British withdrew to the canal's western bank, leaving behind dogs chained at regular intervals on the east bank. Reconnaissance planes could not detect troops forming for a night attack, but the British thought the guard dogs would bark and alert them.

Taking advantage of the cover offered by a sudden sandstorm, the Turks moved their forces into position for an attack on the canal near Ismailia, halfway between the Mediterranean and the Red Sea. The Turks reached the canal late at night, but the guard dogs on the eastern bank didn't bark. The soldiers were following strict orders, as one recalled, not to "make a single sound walking across the sand." The Turks managed to launch several pontoons and, by daybreak on February 3, had begun assembling the pontoon bridge. A group of overexcited Libyan jihadist volunteers, who called themselves the Champions of Islam, began shouting slogans to each other. Then the dogs started barking.[11]

The western bank exploded in a hail of machine gun fire and artillery. The water of the canal where the Turks were trying to assemble their pontoon bridge, as one soldier recalled, "churned like a kettle of boiling water." British planes flew in and dropped bombs, and British gunboats came up the canal and began shelling the Turks. The pontoons were blown out of the water. Without a bridge, the attack failed.

The Turks, suffering relatively light casualties, withdrew after only one day of fighting. Their camels fared much worse. Around seven thousand were lost. Some fell to enemy fire; the others starved due to inefficient Turkish supply officers. Only the sterilizing qualities of the desert contained the stench and disease of the camel carcasses. The expected uprising of thirteen million Muslims in Egypt never materialized because the British had the foresight both to declare martial law in Egypt when the Ottoman Empire entered the war and to promise that Britain and its allies would do the fighting against the empire without the Egyptians' assistance (the promise was later broken).[12]

To explain why disheveled, bloody, and exhausted Turkish soldiers were flooding into Palestinian towns, Djemal Pasha blamed the weather for the Fourth Army's withdrawal. "A terrible sand-storm having arisen, the glorious army takes it as a wish of Allah not to continue the attack and has therefore withdrawn in triumph."[13]

The victory confirmed the British belief in the inferior fighting qualities of the Turks (and in their own innate superior ones), even though the desert crossing by Djemal's Fourth Army was a considerable military accomplishment. After the victory at the Suez Canal, subsequent British arrogance toward the Turks was excessive even by British standards. Prime Minister Herbert Asquith wrote of the Turks that "the poor things & their would-be bridge were blown into smithereens, and they have retired into the desert." The British concluded that they were one victory from putting an end to the Ottoman Empire and perhaps even bringing the war to a successful conclusion. The fatal blow would be struck by a powerful naval assault through the Dardanelles Strait that would capture Constantinople.[14]

The Dardanelles Strait separates Europe from Asia. Starting from the Aegean Sea, the strait runs a narrow, twisting, northeast course for thirty miles and opens into the Sea of Marmara. Constantinople lies at the northeastern end of the Sea of Marmara. Myth, romance, and armies have converged at the Dardanelles throughout history. Leander plunged into and swam the Hellespont (the Greek name) each night for an assignation with Hero, priestess of Aphrodite (one night Leander drowned, which caused Hero to deliberately drown herself). On his way to attack Thermopylae, Xerxes crossed the strait on a bridge of hundreds of boats; and later, Alexander the Great crossed the strait on his march to India.[15]

The Dardanelles campaign began on February 19, 1915, when a British and French fleet shelled Turkish positions in the southern approaches to the strait. By March with the aid of small British demolition units, the fleet had cleared the Turkish forts up to the passage called the Narrows. At that point the strait tapers to less than a mile in width, with high bluffs on either side.

British spirits were high, if not exuberant, at the prospect of victory. Winston Churchill, the First Lord (civilian head) of the Admiralty, told the prime minister's daughter, "I think a curse should rest on me because I am so happy. I know this war is smashing and shattering the lives of thousands every moment—and yet—I cannot help it—I enjoy every second I live." During the campaign to capture Constantinople, the British government printed silk handkerchiefs to celebrate the end of the Ottoman Empire.[16]

In Constantinople morale collapsed. State archives and gold reserves were removed from the city, a special train was made ready to evacuate the sultan, and the well-to-do sent their families to the interior of the country and made plans to follow them. The great monuments— including the Hagia Sophia, the epitome of Byzantine architecture— were wired with dynamite to keep them out of British hands. Signs denouncing the Ottoman government began appearing in the streets.

The British did not seem to appreciate that, precisely because Constantinople was such a prize, the Dardanelles had become the single most fortified area of the Ottoman Empire with German assistance. German gunnery experts served with Turkish gun crews in batteries on both sides of the strait. The Turks had laid lines of mines, including state-of-the-art German mines, in the Narrows.[17]

On March 16 U.S. ambassador Henry Morgenthau, on the invitation of Enver Pasha, inspected the Turk fortifications on the Dardanelles, including at the Narrows. Enver thought the inspection would convince Morgenthau that the British naval offensive would fail. Morgenthau later wrote, "My first impression was that I was in Germany. The officers were practically all Germans and everywhere Germans were building buttresses with sacks of sand and in other ways strengthening the emplacements." While Morgenthau was dubious about whether the Turks and their German allies could hold the strait, he was struck by the fanatic light in the eyes of the Turkish soldiers. Their morale was boosted by hearing, even above the din of the preparations for battle, the Muslim prayer that had preceded centuries of battles with the infidels: "Allah is great, there is but one God, and Mohammed is his prophet."[18]

During the February bombardment, the Turkish defenders had noticed that when Allied ships reversed course after bombarding Turkish positions, they almost always turned to starboard. Now gambling that the Allied ships would continue to make starboard turns, the Turks had laid in the Narrows a string of mines parallel to the shore in a location that the ships would have to traverse when making a starboard turn.

On March 18 the strait was calm, winds were light, and the Allied ships had good visibility. The first of three squadrons of Allied ships entered the Narrows and blasted away at the Turkish fortifications on the bluffs. The return fire from the Turkish defenses grew feeble and irregular. As the first squadron completed its run, it reversed course to make room for the second wave of ships and, in doing so, made a starboard turn directly into the mines laid parallel to the shore. Three warships sank and three more were heavily damaged. The mood of the British command changed instantly. The Allied fleet commander, Adm. John de Robeck, commented that "I suppose I am done for" and cabled Churchill that the British army would have to continue the campaign from the land.

No one in the Allied fleet realized that only a single line of mines had been placed parallel to the shore and that, had the attack continued, the minesweepers could have cleared a path through the Narrows. Without serious opposition, the Allied fleet could have steamed through the Narrows, across the Sea of Marmara, and taken Constantinople, changing the course of the war. In fact, knowledge of how close the Turks came to defeat was so widespread in Constantinople that Sarah Aaronsohn, in tiny handwriting under a postage stamp on one of her letters, reported to her brother Aaron that the Turks had all but run out of ammunition when the British fleet withdrew.[19]

In London Churchill was stunned by de Robeck's abdication of the campaign to the army and demanded that the fleet continue the engagement. Churchill was overruled. The British army took over the campaign and, in April, mounted amphibious landings on the Gallipoli Peninsula on the European (western) side of the Dardanelles. The fiasco in the Narrows could be attributed to bad luck, but at Gallipoli the Allied forces found themselves fighting well-dug-in, tenacious Turkish troops. Their commander, Mustafa Kemal—later known as Atatürk, the founder of modern Turkey—had told his soldiers, "I don't order you to attack; I order you to die. In the time which passes until we die, other troops and commanders can take our place."[20]

The Gallipoli attack was a failure. Britain and its dominion allies suffered more than two hundred thousand casualties without making significant territorial gains beyond a few blood-soaked beachheads. Gallipoli also cost Churchill his position as First Lord of the Admiralty and damaged his reputation, which did not fully recover until his stirring leadership in World War II. The British campaign in the Middle East had bogged down in stalemate, just as on the western front, with consequences for the Middle East—and for Sarah Aaronsohn and her family.[21]

In the early spring of 1915, however, no one in the Ottoman Empire could have foreseen the British disaster at Gallipoli. To that point the Ottoman Empire had suffered defeats on three fronts: in the Caucasus, at the Suez Canal, and in Mesopotamia, where British and Indian troops had captured Basra (now part of Iraq). An Entente navy had blasted its way up the Dardanelles and come close to reaching Constantinople. With snow melting in the Caucasus, a Russian offensive seemed likely against the defensive positions that the Turks were frantically trying to rebuild. In those frightening circumstances, the besieged pashas began to perceive enemies within the empire's borders and not just outside of them.[22]

Talaat and Enver Pasha regarded the Armenians in the empire as a particularly dangerous internal threat. Armenians in Russia had fought against the Turks in the Caucasus, and in Constantinople the Armenian subjects of the Ottoman Empire had not hidden their enthusiasm for a British victory. They gathered each day at the waterfront, as an Armenian priest recalled, to witness "the majestic British fleet pass toward the Bosporus, its mission to save the Armenians of course."

Sometime between February and March 1915, Talaat Pasha, with Enver's support, set in motion the annihilation of the Armenian community in what most now call the Armenian genocide. The general assembly of the Turkish national party, Union and Progress, developed a plan that "secretly sentenced to death" the Armenian people. A local party chapter summarized the directive: "Without mercy and without pity, kill all from the one month old to the ninety-year old." An exception was made for beautiful Armenian brides and virgins, who were to be sent to Turkish harems.[23]

On April 24, 1915, considered the start of the Armenian genocide, the elite of the Armenian community of Constantinople—including political leaders, educators, writers, and clergy—were rounded up, tortured, and then hanged or shot. The Turks were students of torture who applauded the discovery of a new method as though it was a scientific breakthrough; some had studied the records of the Spanish Inquisition to refine their skills. Djevdet Bey, known as the "horseshoer of Bashkale," was widely hailed for nailing horseshoes to the feet of his Armenian victims. Imprisoned Armenians, upon being left in their cells between torture sessions, poured kerosene from the prison lamps over their heads and set themselves on fire. The savagery was further inflamed by the Gallipoli landings on April 25. Following the landings, Ambassador Morgenthau met with Enver Pasha and came away with the impression that "the fact that the Australians and New Zealanders had successfully effected a landing had aroused their [the Ottoman rulers'] most barbarous instincts." During the Armenian massacres, Morgenthau vainly pleaded with the Woodrow Wilson administration to intervene to stop the butchery. In 1916 anguished over the slaughter and unable to tolerate dealing with the men responsible, some of whom boasted to him about their skill at torture, Morgenthau resigned his ambassadorship.[24]

Once the Armenian leadership had been eliminated, the Turks arrested Armenians en masse, marched them out of their towns, and, with the assistance of local mobs and bandits, attacked the Armenians with axes, hatchets, pitchforks, and hoes. The dead and the barely living were thrown into freshly dug ditches and covered with lime. Dirt was shoveled on those still alive until their cries—"for the love of God, shoot us so that we can be delivered"—could no longer be heard. The murderers returned to the towns in the clothes they had looted from the victims. Throughout Anatolia, Turkish peasants in sandals wore formal jackets and sported gold chains and watches.

The Turks cut the knee tendons of Armenian children so they could not walk, crucified teenage girls, and dashed small children against rocks. In 1916 an American consular official visited the region near Aleppo and saw burial mounds stretching to the horizon, and he estimated each mound contained two hundred to three hundred corpses. The last stages played out in the Syrian province of Der Zor, where shuffling columns of men, women, and children were sent into a scorching, featureless desert. Even today Armenian bones can still be found there. By some estimates, the Armenian death toll reached 1.5 million.

An Armenian poem recalls the suffering:

They gathered the Armenians in a cave.
They covered them with lime, set fire and burned them
Oh mother! Oh mother!
Our state was terrible,
When we were in the desert of
Der Zor.[25]

Sarah's train crossed the Anatolian plateau. A traveler on such a trip ordinarily saw only scenic vistas: vast steppes, wheat fields, ancient stone walls, and terraced valleys. But on this train, Sarah stared out the window at burning villages; heaps of bodies on both sides of the tracks; emaciated Armenian families staggering in the roads with Turkish soldiers kicking, beating, and shooting the stragglers; and packs of dogs feeding on the decomposing corpses of dead Armenians. At one stop thousands of typhus-stricken Armenians waited on the tracks and the sidings in the hope that they might be permitted to board a train. The engineer of an incoming train deliberately rolled the train over the Armenians, crushing dozens. The engineer jumped out of the train, rubbed his hands together, and gleefully said to a friend, "Do you see how I have smashed maybe fifty of these Armenian swine?" Sarah fainted. When she came to, two Turkish officials berated Sarah for her lack of patriotism.

The journey took three weeks because Sarah and her traveling companion often lost their seats to Ottoman military personnel and had to get off their train. While waiting in remote villages for another train, Sarah listened to Armenian women describe how they had been raped multiple times, their husbands had been beaten to death, and their children had succumbed to disease and starvation. Sarah could not escape the carnage. As she could not hide anywhere in a landscape strewn with bleached skeletons, she could only pray that she might go blind. Instead, Sarah's journey gave her a stark vision of her own people's grim future in the Ottoman Empire.

Sarah's journey ended in northern Palestine, where her brother Aaron met her in a carriage and took her home to Zichron. He wrote in his diary that night, "Today, just as before, she is the same splendid girl we have always known. Her trip lasted three weeks exactly, and what sights her eyes have seen! She has known exhaustion, suffered from want, and in front of her very eyes has seen the Armenians tortured by the Turks."

Sarah was overjoyed to be home, but she was not entirely the same. Sarah, the hardy child of a settler family that lived in an unforgiving land, appeared to be suffering from post-traumatic stress. As Aaron later wrote, "She was never hysterical before but since that trip whenever any allusions are made to Armenians in her presence, she gets into a fit of hysteria."[26]

5

They Must Attack Immediately

Avshalom Feinberg was away when Sarah returned from Constantinople. Aaron told Sarah that Avshalom had gone to the Sinai Desert to report on locust swarms from Egypt; he had left just a few days before Sarah's arrival in Zichron.

She was skeptical. "I won't believe that boy is safe until I see him with my own eyes."

Sarah had brought Yitzhak Haus home with her to Zichron. Haus stayed a few days at the Aaronsohn family home while recovering from the trip. Rahel Yanait, who worked in the Atlit research station, came to visit her friend Haus, stayed for a few days, and met Sarah for the first time.

Rahel, then in her early twenties, had emigrated in 1908 to Palestine from Russia. She left Palestine for several years to obtain a degree in agricultural engineering at the University of Nancy in France. Rahel returned to Palestine, eager to promote Jewish agriculture, but first she hoped to gain practical experience under the tutelage of the legendary Aaron Aaronsohn. Rahel went to work part time without pay at the Atlit research station, learning to handle shoots and saplings and studying the pathology of plant diseases under the guidance of one of Aaron's assistants. She occasionally boarded at the family's home in Zichron.

In Atlit Rahel made the mistake of showing Aaron her thesis on Palestinian geology. He leafed through the pages and dropped the thesis on the ground. "So? And you really think you have carried out a piece of research? It's only a miscellany of statements made by people who came to Palestine for a short time. . . . If you really want to gain knowledge, put aside the books, walk across the length and breadth of the land, observe nature, test the quality of the soil, learn everything you can about plant species and varieties." The next day Rahel and several other young workers took seats in the station's horse-drawn carriage and toured the countryside. Aaron walked alongside, lecturing as though he were in a classroom, identifying the species and varieties of plants, reading out loud for them the stories told by the rocks, and greeting trees like old friends.

After her return from Constantinople, Sarah came into Rahel's room and sat down in a chair. Rahel was struck by how Sarah's blue eyes were alive with humor and delight at being home. Sarah told Rahel about her isolation in Constantinople from her family and friends, about her youth in Zichron, and about Avshalom Feinberg—his enthusiasm and poetry, his wildness and unpredictability. She invited Rahel to ride with her and Aaron over the countryside on horseback; Sarah talked about many topics but did not bring up the Armenians.

One morning Rahel was working in the Atlit station's nursery when a carriage pulled up at the station. Sarah bolted from it and ran toward the wheat fields where Aaron was working.

"Avshalom! Avshalom!" To Rahel, Sarah's cry was primal, "as if from a wounded lioness." Rahel asked one of Aaron's workers Yehuda Zeldin, a Russian émigré, what had happened.

"As you know, Avshalom works under Aaronsohn on locust extermination in the south," Zeldin replied. "He must have gone too far out and been captured by the soldiers."

Rahel was puzzled. If Avshalom had been arrested for exterminating locusts, then surely Aaron would have no trouble getting him back. But Yehuda Zeldin only knew part of the story.

Aaron now had no choice but to reveal the secrets to Sarah about the spy ring—and the real reason that Avshalom had gone into the Sinai and why he hadn't come back.[1]

In the late spring of 1915, when Sarah was still in Constantinople and as the British military debacles in the Dardanelles and Gallipoli unfolded, Aaron and Alexander Aaronsohn and Avshalom Feinberg had gathered in the Atlit research station. The three men used only homemade candles for light. The windows were shuttered and the station's watchdog,

Azmavet (Deadly Fierce), had been unchained to prowl and presumably alert the three by barking at any intruders. Aaron, Alexander, and Avshalom talked in low voices about the war in the Middle East that, as they saw it, was going badly.

Until then Aaron had believed that it was only a matter of time before the British would drive the Turks out of Palestine, if only to protect the Suez Canal. Although shaken by the Hadera arrests and near hangings, Aaron was not as fully convinced as Avshalom that they should spy for the British. They were subjects of the Ottoman Empire, and spying for the British, the enemy, would be an act of treason that would endanger the entire Jewish community.

The British defeats had shocked Aaron, who realized that the British really didn't understand the Ottoman Empire. In Aaron's view the British should have attacked in Palestine, where the Turk defenses were much weaker, and not where they were the strongest, first in the Dardanelles and then at Gallipoli. Aaron's fear was that a Turkish victory in the war would lead to even greater repression of the Palestinian Jews.

He paced back and forth as he worked through the risks of, in effect, betraying his own country by helping the British. Aaron, unlike Avshalom, was not a romantic with boundless passion and desire for action but a scientist who reached conclusions based on empirical data and a deliberative process. In the Atlit research station, Aaron finally endorsed Avshalom's plan to spy for the British. "Today American ships are sailing in the Mediterranean, and we still have contact with the outside world, but soon they'll be taking their ships away from here and we'll be cut off from the world, an easy prey to the Turks. The English must be convinced that in their own interests, they must attack [Palestine] immediately, while the Turks are still disorganized, and the population is able to help them." The three men could provide the intelligence for such an attack. They knew Palestine, its terrain, the roads down to the goat paths, the location of Turk fortifications, and where the patrols were lightest.

It was a huge gamble for Aaron. At a relatively young age, he had attained worldwide recognition for his scientific achievements, gained influence within the Ottoman Empire, and had the support of some of the most prominent Jews in the United States. Now he was about to risk it all, not to mention his life, to spy for the British Empire, an unsavory enterprise for which he had no training or experience.

"Nobody can say we are doing this for money." Aaron wanted a saving grace that would make spying more palatable. "Leave that for Arab spies. We needn't expect honors for our work either. Nobody is more conservative in this than the English, and I don't see them showering honors on spies, no matter how great their services." Aaron added, with more prescience than he possibly could have known, "We can't even be sure that they will have confidence in us. They may think us capable of betraying them just as we are of betraying the Turks. We do not do this for our vengeance either. We do it because we hope we are serving our own cause."[2]

But first they had to link up with the British forces in Egypt. It was a difficult undertaking because the three men were behind enemy lines. The war between Britain and the Ottoman Empire had left them only two available routes—a crossing of the Sinai Desert, which the Turks and their Bedouin allies constantly patrolled, that was feasible only in winter and a passage on a neutral country's ship across the Mediterranean, where the British were blockading the Ottoman coastline. They picked the sea route and decided that Alexander would go to Beirut and, accompanied by Rivka, board a ship to Egypt. Alexander and Rivka would pose as husband and wife and thereby attract less attention.

Alexander and Rivka thus were chosen as the first emissaries to the British. Alexander spoke fluent English and, more important, was at risk if he stayed in Palestine. Alexander had recently accused Fewzi Bey, a senior Turk official, of various depredations, including stealing cattle and crops from the Jews and plundering the Arabs. In one instance, he had carried off a Bedouin bride from her wedding (after applying the *falaka* to the groom until he uttered three times, "I divorce thee," which sufficed under religious law to end the brief marriage). The Turkish authorities investigated Alexander's allegations. Even though the evidence of Fewzi Bey's guilt was overwhelming, they decided that because he was a close associate of Djemal Pasha's, Fewzi Bey was too well connected to prosecute. Instead, they rewarded Fewzi Bey with a commission in the region's religious militia. Fewzi Bey vowed revenge against Alexander, so it was thought prudent for him to leave Palestine. As to Rivka, the Syrian Protestant College was closing for the summer, and it was not safe for her to return to Palestine. Thus began the first of six attempts by the three men to reach Egypt and persuade the British to accept their services as spies against the Ottomans.

Alexander put on his Turkish army uniform, found a donkey, and set out for Beirut. He brought with him bread, dried figs, and chocolate, and he drank from the small pools and springs by the roadside. He traveled at night and in daytime hid with the donkey in caves or small valleys. After five nights Alexander reached a forest of pine trees, beyond which was Beirut. The forest was fragrant with clean, resinous smells. At a Turkish military checkpoint outside the city, Alexander boldly saluted the officer in charge, explaining that he was the orderly of a German officer who was surveying the nearby countryside. After smoking a cigarette with the Turkish officer and commiserating on how the war was going, Alexander went on his way.

In Beirut he left the donkey to its own devices, went to a friend's house to exchange his uniform for civilian clothes, and then proceeded to the Syrian Protestant College, perched on a hillside over the Mediterranean. For her own protection, as recounted, the family had sent Rivka to the college, considered one of the leading educational institutions in the Middle East, where she took classes and wrote to her family that she was lonely and homesick, much as Sarah was in Constantinople. "The evenings are extremely distressing. My heart weeps, and my imagination leads into a desert of devastation and wilderness."[3]

Alexander shocked Rivka by unexpectedly appearing at the college. After hearing Alexander explain the mission that Aaron had in mind for them, Rivka concluded that her brothers were mad. She was eventually convinced by his argument that the family would be relieved to know that Rivka had left Beirut. The college itself was under considerable pressure from Ottoman authorities and would no longer be a safe place for Rivka when classes resumed. In fact, the Ottoman authorities shortly disbanded the student union, appropriated a campus facility for courts-martial, and confined students and faculty members from "enemy" countries to the campus—in effect, putting them under house arrest.[4]

Alexander and Rivka acquired forged Spanish passports and, pretending to be a married couple to attract less attention, bribed their way through the Turkish bureaucracy to obtain the necessary travel permits. Then they talked their way onto the *Des Moines*, an American cruiser carrying Italian and Greek refugees to Rhodes. In August 1915 Alexander and Rivka reached their destination of the ancient Egyptian port city of Alexandria. At some point on this journey, Rivka and Alexander sent a postcard to Sarah in Constantinople that they were on their way to America. Their news caused Sarah, as recounted, to write Avshalom's sister: "What does that mean? All of a sudden, without writing anything about it in previous letters. I don't understand this." Rivka and Alexander apparently wanted Sarah to know that they had left Palestine but were appropriately cautious about revealing that their destination (at that point) was Egypt.[5]

Alexander presented himself to British intelligence officials, who ignored him. To get their attention, he published articles in the *Egyptian Gazette*, an English-language newspaper, about economic conditions in Palestine and Syria, the damage done by locust invasions, and Turkish defenses. British intelligence officers read the articles, and on August 18 Alexander was ushered into the presence of Capt. Stewart Newcombe.[6]

Eight months earlier, on December 22, 1914, a functionary at British headquarters in Cairo had entered a notation in the General Headquarters War Diary: "Organisation [of] Military Intelligence Department proceeding under Captain Newcombe R.E. with five other officers sent from home. Badly needed." One of the officers was 2nd Lt. T. E. Lawrence (today remembered as Lawrence of Arabia). After reaching Cairo he wrote, "There wasn't an Intelligence department it seemed and they thought all was well without it: till it dawned on them that nobody in Egypt knew about Syria."

The advance guard of intelligence officers was under the command of Capt. Stewart Newcombe, a thirty-seven-year-old professional soldier with dash and verve. Newcombe had served in France and at Gallipoli. (Later in the war, he would be captured by the Turks at the Third Battle of Gaza but would escape with the help of a woman named Elsie Chaki, whom he had met years before while recovering from smallpox in a Constantinople hospital.) Reporting to Newcombe was a collection of idiosyncratic, flamboyant, and ambitious young officers, some from *Downton Abbey*–type upbringings. Newcombe's chief was Lt. Col. Gilbert Clayton, a seasoned bureaucratic operative who controlled both military intelligence and a separate civil intelligence operation for British civil authorities in Cairo. Lawrence called him "the perfect leader for such a band of wild men as we were."[7]

Two of the intelligence officers were members of Parliament (MP). One MP, Capt. Aubrey Herbert, had been such a strong and successful advocate for Albanian independence before the war that, out of gratitude, Albania offered him the Albanian throne (which he declined with regrets). The other MP, Capt. George A. Lloyd, was an heir to the Stewarts and Lloyds steelworks and appropriately snobbish. Lt. Leonard Woolley, a professional archeologist before the war, had conducted the principal excavation of the Hittite city of Carchemish. A later arrival, Capt. Philip Graves had been the *Times* (London) correspondent in Constantinople before the war and developed a passion for entomology, especially anything to do with Middle East butterflies. He was the resident expert on the Turkish army. The youngest of the group was Second Lieutenant Lawrence, then in his midtwenties. He had worked for Woolley on the Carchemish excavation and was now drawing military maps, coding and decoding telegrams, interviewing prisoners, and writing reports. Captain Herbert thought Lawrence "an odd gnome, half cad—with a touch of genius."[8]

The British buildup of forces had turned Cairo into part military encampment and part red light district. Beggars, native guides, water sellers, street vendors, and prostitutes mixed with the tens of thousands of soldiers from Britain and its possessions. The British commandeered the best Cairo hotels, including the Grand Continental Hotel, where the newly arrived intelligence officers stayed. Facing Opera Square and the Ezbekiya Gardens, the Grand Continental's terrace with palm trees, wicker chairs, lounges, and attentive Egyptian waiters in red fezzes had attracted grandees and tourists in peacetime. Now it was filled with British officers in shorts with sunburned knees and diplomats and journalists in sweat-stained tropical whites, all seeking a cool colonial respite from the hectic city. The intelligence officers worked out of British headquarters in the adjacent Savoy Hotel, an exotic social hub in war or peace.[9]

Ordinarily British officers in Cairo adhered to military spit and polish, coming and going in their crisp khaki drill tunics, shiny brown leather shoulder straps, and Sam Browne belts while carrying polished swagger sticks and fly whisks. But the newly arrived intelligence officers, whom Lawrence biographer Scott Anderson suggested might have more resembled "some kind of Oxbridge peer-review panel than a group dedicated to the black arts of intelligence and counter-espionage," went about in brazenly unmilitary style. Lawrence, whose hair was "well ruffled," wore a uniform "minus belt with peaked cap askew"; Herbert was described as "being, after Lawrence, the untidiest officer in Egypt"; and even Newcombe, the one professional soldier, "wore slacks without a belt."

Lawrence and his colleagues did not confine themselves to intelligence gathering but were soon immersed in British military and political policy. They were remarkably successful in helping to achieve British war and postwar ambitions in the Middle East, at least in the short term. Judged by the chaos in the modern Middle East, for which they, especially Lawrence, helped lay the groundwork, the long-term result is another matter.[10]

It was Alexander Aaronsohn's bad luck that given the many unconventional intelligence officers whom he might have encountered in Egypt, his first (and only) audience was with Captain Newcombe, who happened to be in Alexandria when Alexander arrived. MP George Lloyd regarded Newcombe as "an intelligent, narrow-minded and jealous man."[11] Considerable allowances should be made for the fact that Lloyd was an Etonian from an upper-class family (the condescending Lloyd also thought Newcombe to be "underbred"). Newcombe nonetheless may have been the least imaginative of the intelligence officers in Cairo and therefore the least able to grasp the intelligence prize that Jewish spies behind Turkish lines could offer the British.

In his fluent, American-accented English, Alex explained to Stewart that he and his brother Aaron, an agronomist in Palestine, could supply a wide range of vital intelligence about Turkish military strength, deployments, and fortifications in Palestine. His proposal was bizarre enough, and it didn't help that Alexander had a German-sounding name. The conversation ended when an already skeptical Newcombe asked in a patronizing manner what these would-be spies wanted in return for their services. Alexander explained that they were not seeking money or favors; all they wanted was to help the British defeat the Turks.

Alexander's offer to risk his life as a British spy for no compensation convinced Newcombe that Alexander was either a lunatic or a spy for Turkey and Germany. Newcombe ordered Alexander to leave the country. Returning to Palestine was not an option for Alexander and Rivka. They left for the United States, where they planned to raise money from American Jews for the relief of the *yishuv*.[12]

Ignorant of Alexander's failure, Aaron had already begun gathering intelligence. He was aided in his endeavor by the locusts.

Djemal Pasha, having suffered a defeat at the Suez Canal, now found himself losing a war against locusts. Periodically locusts in great swarms had attacked Palestine and elsewhere in Syria. In one such attack, witnesses claimed to have seen locusts eating the eyes of babies for the moist fluid in their eyeballs.

But the attack in early 1915 was the worst in anyone's memory. One swarm of millions of self-guided projectiles less than three inches long and armed with sharp-edged mandibles took two hours to pass over Jerusalem. The locusts ate the bark from the trees, which were left resembling white skeletons; denuded the fields of anything that grew; attacked farm animals, driving them mad; and when there was nothing else to eat, sometimes resorted to cannibalism. Female locusts covered the ground, bore into the soil, and deposited their eggs. Once they hatched, another great air armada rose from the earth.

The Arabs called the locusts *djesh Allah* (God's army) and put up no resistance; essentially, they surrendered. In the Jewish settlements, bells were rung, the equivalent of today's emergency siren, and the settlers waved sheets, pounded on pots, and set fires. Aaron Aaronsohn knew this was a hopeless way to fight locust swarms, and such methods would only guarantee that there would be no harvest that year. Hunger was widespread in Palestine.[13]

In March Djemal Pasha summoned Aaron Aaronsohn to his office in Jerusalem. Djemal was a near-hunchbacked, stumpy man with a cropped black beard, black hair, pale face, and glaring, remorseless eyes that darted from one object to another. His unpleasant, ferret-like laughter bared white teeth. U.S. ambassador Henry Morgenthau thought Djemal resembled the Roman ruler Mark Antony in his profligacy and vanity. Djemal's postwar autobiography has dozens of references to "conspiracies" or "plots" and not without reason. A typical passage reads, "My agents displayed the greatest zeal. They continuously brought me news of a conspiracy which aimed at the overthrow of the Ministry and the deaths of Talaat Bey and myself." Djemal's mood seemingly determined whether, on any given day, those in his presence would be punished, even if they did not oppose him.[14]

Djemal once had summoned twenty Arab elders from the town of Nablus and then, while they trembled in fear, worked through a tall stack of papers on his desk. A former journalist, just appointed as a top aide to Djemal, was present. Finally Djemal turned to the elders. "Are you aware of the gravity of the crimes you have committed against your sovereign state?"

"In God's name, forgive us," the baffled elders pleaded.

"Do you know what the punishment is for these crimes?" he raged. "You deserve to be hanged."

Djemal then said, "Yes, hanged—but give thanks to the merciful generosity of the Sublime Porte. I will be satisfied, for the moment, to exile you and your families to Anatolia. You may retire." The elders, overcome with relief, prostrated themselves in prayers of gratitude, and abjectly left the room. Djemal turned to the aide, who was shaken by what he had just witnessed on his first day at work. "What do you expect?" Djemal asked rhetorically. "Here, one has to behave this way."[15]

Seeking a Jew's assistance in the fight against locusts was likely the last thing Djemal wanted to do. But the foreign consuls had told Djemal that only this Jewish agronomist could stop the locusts and avert, among other catastrophes, the starvation of the Ottoman Fourth Army. In March 1915 Aaron in Jerusalem arrived at Djemal's headquarters, a German hospice built by the kaiser for German pilgrims and clergy visiting the Holy Land.

Aaron spoke fluent Turkish, but Djemal, a Francophile, insisted on speaking in French to show off his command of that language. The conversation did not begin well. Aaron used the occasion, not just to explain the techniques for fighting locusts, but also to complain about the Ottoman military's requisitions from the Jewish communities. The Jewish farms had been the most productive in Palestine, Aaron explained, but now they had no fuel for the irrigation pumps, no animals, and no farm equipment. Many of their workers had been forced into Turkish labor brigades and the Jewish communities—

"I wonder, Aaronsohn," interrupted Djemal, impatient with this insolent Jew's laundry list of complaints, "what you would say if I had you hanged."

"Your Excellency," responded Aaron, "the weight of my body would break the gallows with a noise loud enough to be heard in America." Djemal could hardly miss the allusion, not just to the heavyset Aaron's weight, but to the political influence of his supporters in the United States, which the Germans wanted to remain neutral. Later in the conversation, Djemal made more threats, and Aaron responded by quoting Themistocles's admonition to Eurybiades when he had raised his staff: "Strike but hear me."

Djemal was intelligent enough to know that he had no choice but to listen to Aaron. At some level too, Djemal, who suspected Jews of disloyalty, might have felt a mild kinship with this particular Jew. Unlike the cold and imperious German military advisers who laughed only from behind clenched teeth, Aaron was not a foreigner. He made his home in Djemal's country and knew it better than many Ottoman officials. Instead of hanging Aaron, Djemal appointed him to take command of the locust eradication program. He even put at Aaron's disposal the resources of the Turkish army, the police, and the postal, telegraph, and railway services.

Aaron knew that the locusts had to replenish their forces as hunger drove them in a relentless migration from territory to territory, and the key to stopping them was to destroy the locust eggs before the larvae hatched. Aaron expanded the staff of the Atlit research station by fifty men and women and taught them how to dig trenches and use chemicals and controlled fires to destroy the locust eggs, thus preventing another round of locust swarms. The young Jewish locust warriors, who wore semi-military uniforms, visited Turkish military facilities plagued by the locusts, chatted casually with Turkish soldiers, traveled the roads that the Turkish army used to move equipment and soldiers, and kept detailed notes of everything they saw. This information included observations on Turkish army units, communications, camouflage, and economic intelligence.[16]

The Ottoman-Turkish government also conscripted its subjects into the war against locusts by compelling all persons between fifteen to sixty years of age to collect twenty kilograms of locust eggs or face a fine for each uncollected kilogram. When locusts attacked Cyprus in 1881, for example, 1.6 billion cases—each containing a considerable number of eggs—weighing an estimated total 1,300 tons had been gathered and destroyed.[17]

But in Jaffa Jews were fined or beaten if they didn't collect locusts and give them to Turkish military officers, who then sold them to the Arabs. The Arabs, who regarded the locusts as a delicacy, squatted around charcoal fires, roasting and eating piles of them. Aaron, infuriated, resigned in protest as Djemal's chief locust exterminator. By now he had concluded that the current swarms of locusts would not reach mature sexuality, and there would likely be no follow-on hatch. Meanwhile, Aaron's locust fighters had gathered detailed information about Turkish military installations and transportation networks.[18]

Aaron and Avshalom, with no word from Alexander and Rivka, decided that Avshalom should make the next attempt to contact the British. Avshalom obtained a forged Russian passport, grew a beard, and donned a hat and glasses. In Haifa he managed to talk his way onto the *Des Moines*, the same American ship that Alexander and Rivka had boarded in Beirut on their way to Egypt. In the evening, with his ship far out in the Mediterranean, Avshalom shed his disguise as he stared at the American flag. He wrote later, "I think the beautiful stars of the flag were never saluted with so light and grateful a heart and with such artistic antics, for I got rid of all the accessories with which I had provided myself—a baroque hat, incredible eye-glasses, and a momentary seriousness of mien." In Egypt Avshalom missed Alex and Rivka by three days. He discovered that Alexander had been unsuccessful in arousing British interest in their spy ring, had been ordered to leave, and had gone to America with Rivka.[19]

Avshalom found his way to an intelligence officer, Lt. Leonard Woolley, the Carchemish archeologist. It was as good fortune that Avshalom met with Woolley in Egypt as it had been bad luck that Alexander's contact was Captain Newcombe. Then in his midthirties, Woolley was a maverick in the British army, like Lawrence. Woolley loved literature, was at home in the Middle East, and had a taste for adventure. He seemed to regard wartime service as a sabbatical from archeology and intelligence gathering as a lark. While working as an archeologist before the war, Woolley had been asked by the British army to gather information about a railroad that the Germans were building in the Taurus Mountains in what is now southern Turkey. As Woolley later wrote, "I thought that would be great fun—it wasn't our job but it would be amusing." (Woolley came back with blueprints for the entire line.) Lawrence described the affable Woolley as "sweet to callers in many tongues, and keeps lists of persons useful or objectionable."[20]

Woolley listened to Avshalom with genuine interest. He found Avshalom likable, intelligent, and sincere. But personal affinity alone did not persuade Woolley to accept Avshalom's offer to put the spy ring in Palestine at the disposal of British intelligence. The British were concerned about signs of another Turkish offensive against the Suez Canal. Jewish spies in Palestine might be of help after all.[21]

Woolley appears to have told very few colleagues about his new recruit and put nothing in writing to memorialize that Avshalom was now a British spy. This might have been due to Woolley's maverick style or perhaps Woolley wanted to preserve deniability should Avshalom turn out to be working for the Turks. Whatever the reason, it left Avshalom dependent on Woolley to follow through on a commitment that, Avshalom must have assumed, was shared by British intelligence in Egypt.

Woolley arranged for a British ship to take Avshalom back to Palestine and drop him at Atlit. Under British procedures, a ship sailed near the coast and put a surfboat with an agent and crew into the water. If the sea was calm enough, the crew rowed the surfboat close to the beach, dropped an anchor, and let out the line until the boat had swung stern to, and a few yards from, the shore. That position allowed both the agent to wade onto the beach and the crew a faster escape if the Turks spotted them. If the seas were rough and anchoring wasn't an option, the crew sometimes ran the boat through the surf and onto the beach. This often meant taking on water that could sink or capsize the boat, and there was always the risk that the surfboat would ride the waves directly into a Turkish patrol on the shore. In rougher conditions, the surfboat stayed beyond the breaking waves, and the agent had to jump into the water and swim to the beach through heavy surf. If the agent wasn't a strong swimmer, a stout crewman swam to the shore with the agent on his back. In very rough seas, the captain called off the landings.[22]

It was "a most nervy business," in the words of one British officer who regularly dropped agents along the Mediterranean coast of the Ottoman Empire. The Turks sent out patrols and pickets to spot suspicious vessels from the shore; German submarines roamed the Mediterranean, which was both unforgiving and unpredictable; and the spy ships frequently had to drop the agents on a moonless night to avoid detection. Picking up an agent was even harder. The pickups required an arranged date and time, allowing less flexibility if the conditions were poor, and the use of agreed ship-to-shore signals, which were not always easily spotted from either the ship or the shore. "We get men in, but they never seem to come back," a senior British intelligence officer observed. In April 1915 an intelligence officer noted the drop in the enthusiasm of agents for surreptitious landings: "I know that at least two . . . have been caught and I fear both have been hanged, so that no one is very keen on going."[23]

The *Aenne Rickmers*, a seven-thousand-ton former German cargo boat, had been commandeered to drop Allied agents along the Mediterranean coast in Palestine, Syria, and Beirut. Its motley crew was more appropriate for a Mediterranean tramp steamer than for a ship of the British navy. The beefy, pipe-smoking Capt. Lewen Francis Barrington Weldon of naval intelligence was Irish, the pilot and mechanics were French, the mates and crew were Greek, one engineer was Maltese, and the ship-to-shore boat was rowed by Arabs. The *Aenne Rickmers* carried two seaplanes that flew reconnaissance missions, transported Turkish prisoners of war, and once took on board three hundred Armenians, including refugees and men who had been fighting the Turks. The senior Armenian fighter carried aboard the ship a parcel wrapped in a cloth. He proudly presented it to Captain Weldon, who opened the parcel and found a Turk's head, freshly hacked from its body.[24]

The *Aenne Rickmers* was ordered to take Avshalom to Palestine and land him on the beach at Atlit. Avshalom told friends in Egypt that he could carry letters from them to their families in Palestine, but only one, Raphael Aboulafia in Alexandria, seemed interested. Raphael was from Rishon LeZion and once had been the post office manager in Tel Aviv. A taught-faced, dark-looking man with a carefully trimmed mustache, Raphael had fought on the British side at Gallipoli, where he was badly wounded.

Avshalom wrote to Raphael before leaving Egypt: "Perhaps the others haven't any confidence, but I can tell you that in another ten to fifteen days, mail will be coming and going between us. I shall be returning in six to eight weeks. You know my address, of course! c/o Lt. C.L. Woolley, Esq. Headquarters, Port Said."[25]

Avshalom sent several letters to Rivka from Alexandria, evidently in care of one of the research station's American trustees, such as Henrietta Szold, to deliver to Rivka in the United States. In one letter, Avshalom explained to Rivka why he had gone to Egypt. He barely mentioned the threat Jews faced from the Ottomans; instead, he wrote about Aaron.

Why did I go? You can understand it better than anybody. You know—and maybe you are the only one who really knows—how much I love Aaron. But you cannot imagine how I felt since you have [all] left. Arale, the poor boy! The brain of a genius, the strength of Hercules, the spirit of a hero and the heart of a child, of a little baby. He is left all alone now. All the mothers have left him, each one went in her own way. The good and the only mother went to heaven, mother Sarah left for her own happiness, mother Rivka went into the unknown. . . . The miserable prisoner sits there in the dark, with no information, no news, no calls. I don't want this!

Who will give us water from the well of Bethlehem? I feel that after all I had the ability to penetrate the enemy lines, to draw from the good well and come back. And if not I—then who?

Avshalom added that "I always knew that when I do something for Aaron, I do something for our homeland that he loves more than anything. . . . Forgive me, my only one, for leaving, but for all those things, I had to go."[26]

In another, much longer letter, Avshalom used an affectionate nickname for Rivka: "Today is your birthday, little Ubi, may you be excited with many more good and pleasant years." Then he launched into a panoramic, stream of consciousness narrative; a mix of fantasy, dreams, and poetry; an homage "to the girl that is so far away, across many seas, across vast lands, somewhere there in America." He rode a horse with a snowy white mane over white sand, a stream, a bridge, a hill, past hay from the summer harvest and by a cemetery with its "black pits and its white grave stones." Rivka was not in America—"No. This cannot be"—but in Palestine. He pulled up on his horse before Rivka, and she stood up with "an 'angelic smile' of such brightness that only the babies and the innocent share."

But Avshalom was still in Alexandria, the smells rising from the street, "the stench of the drunk and the whoredom," angry at himself for thinking that he could "have visions in such conditions. You fool!" He wrote of Rivka's empty room in Zichron, that it had been "my room from the day you left, Ubi," the room of "hopes and frustrations and of towers and chambers built in an instant and dissolving like the morning mist." He wrote of the "girl who went so far away (so far away!)." He wanted to know only that she was "happy enough there to forget us from time to time." She had to live her life in America and not "our life." She mustn't exhaust herself from unnecessary longing and useless worrying, and she must write him that she was "grabbing and gobbling up every bit of happiness" that life could offer ("and don't write lies, do you hear me?!").

Avshalom wrote about his doubts: "Can it be that all my work is worthless. I need so much a dear voice to encourage me when I am about to give up." With a hint of jealousy, he dwelled on Rivka's existence among "new interesting people. Well educated men with good manners, and lots of glamour." But they should take care, he warned, for America was not that far away, and whatever the miracles of their medicine, "they won't be able to equip them with new necks if I break a couple of old ones."

> I have always loved you and will go on loving you forever, without ever stopping; if you understand that today when my mind is utterly set on our homeland and our great future, your name and your face are for me the symbols of this land and its future; they make me stronger and encourage me to keep going; if you understand that your happiness is necessary, so a man of strong will could happily sacrifice everything for these great goals; if in the darkness of these lines you can see all that—then you have understood everything![27]

Aboard the *Aenne Rickmers* for the return voyage to Atlit, Avshalom was in high spirits and carried presents for his family and Aaron as though he had been on a holiday trip. He charmed the ship's polyglot crew with his gaiety and enthusiasm. The vessel reached Atlit in early November 1915. Under a moonless sky, on a calm sea, Avshalom was rowed ashore by two undisciplined Syrian Arabs, whose talking Avshalom could not silence. Once on shore Avshalom hid the presents in bushes for later retrieval and walked to the Atlit research station. He woke up Aaron and told him of the British commitment to work with the Jewish spies.[28]

Ten days later, as arranged with Captain Weldon, Avshalom returned to the beach, along with his colleague Menashe Brunstein, a childhood friend of Alexander Aaronsohn's. Avshalom planned to hand to the British both the intelligence that Aaron's locust workers gathered and his own report. While there were indications of a possible new Turkish offensive to capture the Suez Canal—new hospitals were under construction in Jerusalem and Nazareth—Avshalom had learned of high desertion rates and widespread sickness among Turkish soldiers. He also discovered that the Turks would have difficulty supplying such an offensive because of their slow transport trains. The official time for a train trip between Jerusalem and Beersheba was ten hours; however, in practice it was twenty to twenty-five hours. A train officially took sixty-three hours to travel from Aleppo to Beersheba, but the trip actually required more than ninety hours, even without taking into account congestion delays due to the change in track gauge at Rayak. Until now Avshalom had hidden the information, in the form of scribblings in notebooks and on odd pieces of paper, in haystacks or in buried tin boxes.[29]

Avshalom sat down, smoked a cigarette, and listened to the breaking waves. Above the beach, on a thin promontory of rock and sand, loomed the ruins of a Crusader castle. Below the crumbling castle ramparts sat the Jewish crusader ready to take back Jerusalem. The British ship was to appear on the horizon exactly half an hour after the moon set and give a signal with a light. Avshalom would return the signal with his own, prearranged one. Then sailors in a surfboat would come to the beach, where Avshalom would hand them a leather pouch with the intelligence reports.[30]

In Arab poetry, night is the time when a poet suffers the worst torment, enduring an interminable darkness. So it was that night for the poet Avshalom Feinberg, for no agreed-upon signals flashed, no surfboat came. In those endless hours before the sun rose, it might have seemed to Avshalom that the stars had permanently affixed the darkness to the sky.[31]

6

The Wait

There had been a mix-up over the signals. A British ship had come, signaled, failed to observe the pre-arranged signal, and sailed away. According to one account, the British had changed the signal, sending word ahead of the ship to Avshalom via one of their Arab spies. Acting on the premise that the less competition the greater the reward, the Arab spy did not inform Avshalom of the change in the signal, resulting in Avshalom's flashing the wrong signal into the darkness. The British and the Jewish spy had also blundered by failing to have in place a backup plan for making contact.[1]

Avshalom returned to the Crusader castle night after night. The nights of lying on the beach at Atlit took a toll on Avshalom, who was less afraid of death than of inaction. His friend Liova Schneersohn, who had kept a compress on Avshalom's feverish forehead in Jaffa after the Hadera arrests, was in Avshalom's company during this depressing period. They drank brandy together, but it didn't help Avshalom's mood. "He doesn't speak about the Egyptian events anymore," Liova wrote in his diary. "Yet every night they wait on the shore for the sign that should come from the sea."[2]

Avshalom decided to set off again for Egypt, but this time he would go through the Sinai Desert by camel. "I don't want [Woolley] to think that the first young Jew in his service betrayed him," Avshalom insisted.[3]

Avshalom's plan was foolhardy, if not suicidal, but Aaron could not dissuade him. Liova didn't even attempt to talk him out of going. "Avshalom and his plans!" Liova wrote. "He is sure he will succeed. He keeps it vague, he didn't tell me how and when he is planning to set off for his new adventure. He doesn't really know what the consequences will be. Him and his fearlessness. But who knows?"[4]

The desert of the Sinai is one of the world's cruelest. T. E. Lawrence wrote that in the summer the Sinai was "blisteringly hot," and its winter was "cold with the unbridled cold of a country over which the wind can rage in unchecked fury." A traveler such as Avshalom had the choice of three routes. In the north, an ancient path, a few miles from the Mediterranean, veered from oasis to oasis through sand dunes with scrub vegetation. In the middle, where Djemal Pasha had sent the Ottoman Fourth Army to attack the Suez Canal, the route crossed rocky hills. In the south is the narrowest crossing, where a primitive pilgrim road ran through jagged mountains.[5]

Avshalom chose the northern route. He would pass through the Turkish lines dressed in the semi-military outfit of Aaron's locust brigade, explaining to any Turks he might encounter that he was there to eradicate locusts. He would then disguise himself as a Bedouin. And after that, assuming he survived, he expected to reach the British lines.

Avshalom was accompanied by a friend named Efriam Cohen. They left Rishon LeZion on December 18, 1915, riding hard on camels. But Cohen had trouble keeping up and turned back. After two days and nights of riding alone, Avshalom encountered a Turkish patrol near the Suez Canal. Avshalom could not produce a *vasika*, an Ottoman-issued special permit for travel in the Ottoman Empire. He hadn't taken one, thinking the British might conclude that he was an Ottoman spy if they found Turkish documents in his possession. Avshalom could only offer the lame explanation that he was in the desert to study locust migration patterns. The Turks arrested him.[6]

Avshalom was taken to Beersheba in southern Palestine, where specialists in extracting information from prisoners would torture him. Afterward Avshalom would be tried in court and hanged as a spy. Jews in Beersheba alerted Aaron, who immediately arranged to circulate gold among the prison officials. Since Avshalom was suspected of being an enemy spy in wartime, a significant quantity of gold was required to delay a trial and hanging.

A network of Avshalom's relatives and friends, mainly young Jewish men who admired him, went to work. One was Avshalom's cousin

Naaman Belkind, who would have followed Avshalom into a house on fire. Naaman was the son of Jewish immigrants who had helped found the settlement of Rishon LeZion on a thorn-covered hilltop on the coastal plain south of what is now Tel Aviv. A Baron Rothschild–supported settlement, Rishon LeZion proved unsuitable for wheat and barley but was accommodating to grapes. Wine-making became the settlement's economic base.

Naaman Belkind worked in the wineries in Rishon LeZion. Non-observant Turkish officers and the ones who liberally interpreted the Koran often stopped there. Bartender style, Belkind listened and nodded sympathetically to their complaints about army life, and here and there he asked a deft question. Soon the Turks were talking openly about the Jewish spy caught in the Sinai Desert.[7]

Another acquaintance of Avshalom Feinberg's, twenty-five-year-old Yosef Lishansky, knew his way around Beersheba and was skillful in wielding baksheesh. Yosef smuggled messages in and out of Avshalom's cell. In one Avshalom wrote to Naaman Belkind: "Tell Aaron that my morale is high. They've examined all they have to examine, and now I'm writing poems in French. Don't worry about Mother. She is the youngest and bravest of all. You can tell her anything, but Sonia Belkind [Avshalom's aunt], and my sister Shoshanah, best not to tell anything."[8]

So in January 1916 when Sarah pulled up in a carriage at the Atlit research station and frantically sought out her brother, Aaron told her about the spy ring and that Avshalom was a Turkish prisoner and would likely be hanged as a spy. The news of the spy ring likely startled Sarah; it could hardly have relieved her anxiety about Avshalom.

Aaron then had to swallow his considerable pride and find a way to persuade Djemal Pasha to spare Avshalom's life. But Aaron could not simply go to Djemal Pasha, hat in hand. Djemal would quite happily reject a direct appeal after Aaron's insolent behavior in resigning from the locust program.

Fortunately for Aaron—and even more so for Avshalom—a new outbreak of locusts occurred. Aaron heard that Djemal had summoned a local agricultural committee to propose a solution to the locusts. Aaron persuaded the committee to advise Djemal that, once again, he needed the miracle worker Aaron Aaronsohn to stop the locusts.[9]

Djemal and Aaron met in Haifa on January 9, 1916. Aaron agreed to resume his post as director of the locust eradication project, but, he explained to Djemal, he could not do it without his indispensable assistant, Avshalom Feinberg. Most inopportunely, his assistant was about to be executed due to a foolish mix-up by the Turks in Beersheba. Djemal agreed to Aaron's terms, including again giving him both access to Turkish military bases and special, military-level priority in using the telegraph and telephones. Avshalom was released the next day.

Avshalom, with a beard and in good cheer, appeared in Zichron. When Liova Schneersohn heard the news of Avshalom's release, he wrote in his diary, "The boy is lucky. . . . Who knows what else to expect from Avshalom, what new crazy plans he might come up with to renew the contact?"[10]

Sarah and Avshalom went to Damascus to reunite with Aaron, who was still at Djemal's headquarters. Each had been through an ordeal: Sarah had witnessed a genocide, Aaron had made the wrenching decision to betray his country and spy for the British, and Avshalom had barely escaped a hanging.

Rumors of terrible atrocities against the Armenians had been circulating, but Sarah's account, which she first gave to Aaron on her return from Constantinople and now to Avshalom, was staggering, astonishing, and ultimately galvanizing. But the men had a dismal record of attempts to set up an intelligence connection with the British. Alexander Aaronsohn had tried and failed, and Avshalom had tried twice, by sea and desert, and failed as well. They were not about to give up, however, and agreed that Avshalom would make another attempt. This time he would travel to England, by way of first Constantinople and then neutral Romania.[11]

Sarah returned to Zichron while Aaron and Avshalom stayed behind in Damascus to manage the locust eradication. At home Sarah encountered Liova Schneersohn. The two had met before Sarah went to Constantinople. Liova thought Sarah hadn't changed, but their conversation mainly concerned the Armenians, making an impact on Liova. "On her way here she saw things with her own eyes," Liova wrote in his diary, virtually repeating Sarah's refrain. "How terrible are these Turks. If we don't manage to get rid of them before it's too late, they can do to us what they did to the Armenians."[12]

On January 29, 1917, Avshalom wrote to Sarah from Damascus. "Before, I was blissful because you were here, yet miserable because you came; and now you are gone and I am happy that you are not here and the goddess of longing is whispering in my ear." He and Aaron had ridden horses through a snowstorm, "mentioning you every moment."[13]

Starting in Damascus and continuing after she returned to Zichron, Sarah wrote a series of letters to her husband, Haim Abraham, in Constantinople. Historians have suggested that Sarah's marriage to Haim was loveless. Sarah's letters to Haim, in fact, are warm and affectionate, if somewhat formal and lacking her lighthearted, lively style.

On January 23, 1916, while still in Damascus, Sarah wrote Haim about spending time with Aaron and Avshalom, whom she affectionately refers to at one point as the "crazy one":

My dear Haim,

I am here in the company of Arale and Avshe. We are only staying here for a short time. Aaron was summoned because of the locust issue. You will be surprised to know that the crazy one is with us. . . .

We sent you a telegram. I assume that it should have arrived by now. In any event, you will know later what is going on here. . . .

The whole family is well. We received letters from Rivka in America. She lives a nice and happy life there, as she always does, you know her. . . .

I try to make the best use of my time, so as not to get bored. I already miss you. I still haven't received your response to my telegram and I am already quite annoyed by this. Today marks eight weeks since we parted. Do you miss me? I do miss you a lot. I would like to see you, talk with you and kiss you. What are your thoughts about my returning? The nicest thing would be if you came to meet me here, I mean during Passover, and we returned together. . . .

I kiss you and ask you to write to me more often and in detail.

Yours,
Sarah[14]

Sarah allowed Aaron and Avshalom to append notes to her letter. Avshalom wrote in one corner of the letter, "I swear to you, you won't see her for a long time. The sky was wintry, and now it's bright again." Aaron wrote, "You are permitted to come and see her, but send Sarah to you? Don't even think of it. We love her very much here."[15]

On February 12 from home in Zichron, Sarah wrote to Haim about conditions in Palestine. "There is poverty everywhere and all is sadness. People seem lifeless. Nonetheless I try to spend my time in a fine way. A few times a week I go horseback riding." She described the locust outbreak, inquired how Haim's business was doing, and wrote that "if I am going to plan to leave and return home then we need to start the correspondence about it already. I think that right after Passover I will look for an opportunity to return." Sarah asked her husband to send her money because "money here is very scarce."

Let's talk clearly. I want to be home. I am very bored. By the time I come back, five or six months will have passed since the day I left. That's a long time. In ten weeks it's Passover. What do you think? How and when should I return? Write to me often and in detail. How are you planning to send me the money? . . . I am not telling you the exact amount, just send me a sum that would suffice until I return home.[16]

Three weeks later, on March 7, Sarah wrote Haim that those around her (she doesn't say who) were pressuring her not to return to Constantinople even though "I miss you and miss our home." She insisted that "I already see myself at home although people here do not want to hear about that and hope that I don't leave, but I am seriously considering returning at the first opportunity." She added, "I spend my time longing and thinking about you, my friend."[17]

On March 20 Sarah again wrote Haim. This letter appears more pessimistic about the prospects of their reuniting. Sarah had heard rumors that Haim had left Constantinople. If the rumors are true, she writes, "then I don't know whether to return home after Passover or wait. I am afraid of the possibility that we will have to remain separated, and who knows for how long and under what circumstances?" Money was still a problem. "If I had some money then I could return even before the holiday, but I told you in my previous letters how hard it is to find money here." Sarah ended the letter: "I am impatiently waiting to hear from you. I am fine. I miss home and want to be back in your arms. I am afraid, God forbid, that we won't be able to meet very soon. . . . I wish you all the best, success in business and warm kisses from the lips that have missed you for so long."[18]

When Sarah left Constantinople the previous November, she had planned to return after the winter. Sarah's letters suggest that she was still open to doing so. Then why didn't she go back? One historian suggested that Sarah had to write affectionate letters, even if she didn't feel affection, lest the censors become suspicious. This theory depends on the questionable premise that the Ottoman norm for spousal correspondence was unfailingly warm and loving.

Rather, as demonstrated by Sarah's 1914 letter to Rivka about the couple's plan to someday live in Palestine, Sarah's affection for Haim appears genuine. In these four letters written between the end of January and March 1916, Sarah wants to plan with Haim a time and means for her return, but evidently the lack of money, the difficulty in communicating, and the possibility that Haim had departed Constantinople prevented her from doing that.[19]

Avshalom had gotten as far as Constantinople on his third attempt to seek out the British when Aaron recalled him. Working through the problem of convincing the British that the Jewish spies in Palestine had valuable intelligence, Aaron concluded that the greatest obstacle likely had been that his brother Alexander and Avshalom were simply not well known. Only he had a reputation that might convince the British that they were dealing with serious men; therefore, he must be the one to contact the British.

Aaron planned a circuitous journey to England via Constantinople, Berlin, and neutral Denmark. Once in England, he believed, his scientific credentials and fame would surely gain him a hearing at the highest levels of British intelligence. Aaron's plan was to leave as soon as the locusts had been eradicated, which would not take much longer. At the approach of spring, the hatch had failed. The locusts had been declining without laying large amounts of eggs.[20]

Part of Aaron's plan was that Avshalom would run both the Atlit research station and the growing spy network, and Sarah would help him.

In the spring and early summer of 1916, before Aaron left for England, the aspiring young botanist Rahel Yanait seemed not to realize that strange things were happening at the Atlit research station. She went on a carriage excursion along the seacoast with Sarah and Aaron, who frequently whispered to one another. Rahel didn't find it odd when Sarah suddenly waved her handkerchief at a vessel out at sea. Once she came upon Aaron penciling letters and numbers on a beam over a doorway and fully accepted his explanation that it had to do with meteorological research. She awoke one night to the sound of a gunshot but fell back asleep. The next morning, Aaron asked Rahel if she had heard any shooting. Before she could reply, he explained that several cows from a nearby Arab village had wandered into the research station's grounds, precipitating a quarrel between a station watchman and the cowherd. Finally, to drive the cattle off, the watchman had fired into the air. Rahel did not question Aaron's story.

Rahel, who was somewhat naive and trusting, did not realize that the Atlit research station had been turned into an espionage headquarters. Aaron, Avshalom, and Sarah were recruiting spies, gathering and hiding intelligence, and hoping to establish contact with the British.

The vigil for a British spy ship had been abandoned after months of waiting at the beach on moonless nights. Then in March 1916 a British ship dropped a messenger near Atlit. When he reached the shore, he crossed the coast road and approached the research station, intending to deliver a note from Lieutenant Woolley and to take back a response from Avshalom. But Azmavet, the station's guard dog, began barking, and the frightened messenger hastily tied the note to a plough and fled. Aaron went into the yard, saw the note, and realized what had happened. To create a distraction in case the messenger had not yet reached the beach, Aaron fired shots into the air and shouted that Arab cattle must be kept away from the station. The message read, "The friends would like to hear how you're doing, they haven't heard anything from you for a long time."[21]

Rahel noticed that Sarah had stopped coming to see her in the library and that Aaron was increasingly absentminded and restless. She heard from workers in the laboratory that Aaron was planning to go abroad. That surprised Rahel because Aaron had seemed consumed with his scientific work and the anti-locust campaign. One evening Aaron came to the laboratory and courteously said good-bye to Rahel without explaining where he was going. Now Rahel was nervous, wondering whether she would be permitted to continue working at the laboratory.

The next morning a young man approached Rahel in the library. Even though she had never seen him before, she knew from his air of energy and authority that he was Avshalom Feinberg. He did not introduce himself.

"I am now responsible for the station and library, and your work here is finished."

"But I am not employed here," Rahel protested. "I want to go on studying in the library and the herbarium. Aren't they intended for the public?"

"Public or private. They're now under me. Aaronsohn has gone, and I'm responsible."

Rahel left the Atlit research station that day. She went to her sister's home in a nearby settlement, lay down on the couch, faced the wall, and cried. Years later Rahel learned that Aaron, Sarah, and Avshalom had been running a spy ring from the research station. "Now, in the perspective of time," Rahel wrote in her memoir, "I can see it clearly: I was no longer wanted, either by the elder brother or the sister or by Avshalom. They had resolved to get rid of me. This was why Sarah, too, kept away from me. . . . But though it is so clear today, how humiliated I was then by their inexplicable conduct, and how hard it was for me to leave the library in such a way!"[22] Rahel's memoir doesn't acknowledge that, by sending her away, the Aaronsohns and Avshalom may have saved her life.

Meanwhile, getting out of the Ottoman Empire was not easy to do in wartime and required all of Aaron's resourcefulness. Aaron began by meeting with Djemal Pasha in Damascus. He explained to Djemal that he could develop a lubricating oil from sesame plants, which were plentiful in the empire. Lubricating oil was essential to the war effort; however, it was growing scarce, as attested to by the constant shrill shrieks throughout Syria from axles without oil. Aaron told Djemal that before he could manufacture the oil, he needed to confer with scientists in Germany. Djemal readily issued a *vasika* for Aaron so he could travel to Constantinople and there obtain a visa to go to Germany.

Before Aaron left, Avshalom told him what would happen when he finally reached England. "You will arrive and you will find no one there."[23]

The months after Aaron's departure were an odd interregnum for Sarah and Avshalom. Part of their time was devoted to managing the growing spy ring. Avshalom had recruited relatives and acquaintances. Among them were Avshalom's cousins, the Belkind brothers. Naaman Belkind had helped Avshalom in Beersheba, and both he and his brother, Eitan— bold young men with ready-for-anything glints in their eyes—joined the spy ring. Another Avshalom recruit was his acquaintance Dov Blinkov, a Ha-Shomer member who had lost his right eye in a fight with Arabs. Avshalom brought his brother-in-law, Nahum Wilbushevitz, an engineer, into the spy ring as well. In his midthirties Nahum, who sported a mustache that stretched past his laugh lines, was one of the oldest members.

Avshalom also recruited friends from his home town of Hadera, such as Liova Schneersohn from the Hadera arrests. Liova's brother, Mendel, joined, and so did Nissan Rotman, an earnest-looking young man with a modest mustache who had emigrated from Russia to Palestine as a child and grew up in Hadera. Before the war Nissan worked at the Atlit research station, where he met Avshalom and became one of his devotees. One of Avshalom's most important recruits was Yosef Lishansky, who had delivered messages to and from Avshalom in his jail cell in Beersheba.

Aaronsohn family members, acquaintances, and employees were recruited as well. Before the war Sarah's brother Zvi had worked as a railway contractor. He was her only sibling still in Palestine—Alexander and Rivka had gone to the United States in 1915, Samuel had also left for the United States that same year, and Aaron was on his way to England—and recently he had been helping to manage the research station. He was among the first to join. Sarah's cousins David Sokolovitz and Reuven Schwartz, both from Zichron, also became spies. Another recruit was Menashe Brunstein, whose parents were among the first settlers in Zichron. Menashe was a childhood friend of Sarah's brother Alexander and later a member of Alexander's self-defense organization, the Gideonites. A man with a grim expression, Menashe had gone with Avshalom to the Atlit beach and had waited in vain for the British spy ship. Re'nam Nazzer, another spy, was a Maronite Christian from a Lebanese family. He had been born in Haifa and worked as a wagon driver at the research station.[24]

None of the recruits had any background in espionage, but a few had paramilitary experience from their membership in the settlements' self-defense organizations. Others had served in one army or another. Raphael Aboulafia from Rishon LeZion had joined the Zion Mule Corps, a Jewish military unit in the British army, and, as mentioned, was badly wounded at Gallipoli. Yitzhak Halperin from Zichron had served in the Turkish army during the Balkan wars. Engineer Nahum Wilbushevitz had been serving in the Turkish army since the outbreak of the war. After joining the spy ring, Nahum was sent by the Turkish army to Damascus, where he was responsible for the system supplying water to Turk forces there. Moshe Neumann, recruited by Sarah in 1917, was a doctor in the Turkish army and stationed at an important railway junction.

Most recruits were young, in their twenties and early thirties. Some recruits were so young that Sarah and Avshalom worried that their parents might object. The volunteers chafed under Turkish rule and, like Avshalom, whom they greatly admired, were restless for action. Some even walked with a swagger. Many had shooting, riding, and desert travel skills that equaled those of the Arabs; and they were more at home in Palestine than were the Turks, for whom they had only contempt. Palestine was the sole home most of these young men had known or could recall, but unlike their parents, they did not think of themselves as living there by leave of the Ottoman Empire. As well, it was difficult for young Jewish men to enter the home of the legendary Aaronsohn family, sit down on a sofa in front of the regal Sarah Aaronsohn, listen to her quietly explain what would happen to the Jews of Palestine if Britain failed to defeat the Ottoman Empire, and then decline to join her group. Sarah's presence was a message to these young men: she, a woman, was risking her life to defend their people, and they could do no less.

A handful of women also joined the spy ring. Tova Gelberg, a close childhood friend of Sarah's from Zichron (her father worked as a barrel maker in the winery), became a member. Tova had dark hair parted in the middle that she severely tied back in a bun, like an American woman pioneer on the Great Plains. Also joining was Farida Lulu, an honest, plain-looking woman who was the kitchen manager at the Atlit research station. A few women, including Avshalom's sister Shoshana, served on a part-time basis. But Sarah may have been the only woman in the organization with status, which, at this point, was largely due to the fact that she was Aaron's sister.[25]

Eventually the group would comprise two dozen or more spies throughout Palestine and in Damascus, making notes about Turkish military positions and troop strengths, chatting casually with Turkish soldiers, and stealing documents from the Turks. The spies passed the information and documents on to Avshalom and Sarah, who were assisted by Tova Gelberg, a fast writer. Sarah took stolen documents to Tova, who copied them quickly so the documents could be returned before anyone noticed their absence. Avshalom and Sarah wrote intelligence report after report, but they had no one to whom they could deliver their reports.[26]

Sarah and Avshalom also managed the research station at Atlit and supervised the workers who tended the fields and livestock, the fig trees from Smyrna, and the whitewashed mulberry trees from California. Between the agriculture and spying work, Avshalom and Sarah evidently spent a good deal of time together and wrote letters to each other when they were apart. For the first time in their relationship, Rivka was not present, and while there is little suggestion of a romance in their letters, Avshalom and Sarah unavoidably grew close as might be expected when two young people share both a common cause and their problems.

Sarah's letters to Avshalom from this period, presumably written when she was in Atlit or Zichron and he was in Hadera, suggest that she was struggling in various ways. As part of her agricultural work, Sarah planned to make a molasses-like syrup from grapes, called *dibs* in Arabic, and sell it to raise funds. It didn't go well because the carts of grapes were delayed in arriving at the Atlit research station. She wrote Avshalom:

> The situation with my work is as follows: today, or, to be more precise, tonight, at 11 o'clock, I quit the dibs work. . . . The grapes were already rotten and damaged when I got them in the evening. . . . I had to make some wine with what was left. I don't want anything to go to waste (the wife of Haim), but I am absolutely fed up with it, and I decided to solve the dibs question once and for all. It is not nice to rebel in the middle of work, especially when they anticipated a certain amount of dibs.

The "they" were apparently customers, but enough was enough, as far as Sarah was concerned. "You can imagine how tired I am if I have made this decision. . . . Forgive me dear, if I am disturbing you in the middle of your work, but, with no tools, no wood and no good help, it's very hard to go on."

Sarah suggested that Avshalom might persuade a customer to manufacture the dibs for them, but the "day and night" work was more than she could handle. Plus, a shipment of aubergines (eggplants) had arrived. "Tomorrow I might sleep longer than usual and maybe take a rest. I got the aubergines—God wouldn't leave me alone, and now I have more work to do, it's a pity they are not of the best quality."[27]

Part of Sarah's difficulty in coping with her work at Atlit was that her health was not good. "Zvi [her brother] has already informed you that I am sick and cannot come," she wrote Avshalom in one letter. Another time, Sarah wrote Avshalom that "I want to spend time with you when I am healthy and not sick. I do everything, eat and go out for walks. I have already forgotten that I was sick."[28]

Sarah suffered from recurrent blisters on her feet. Avshalom wrote, "I always want to see you young, happy, refreshed and without 'dove eyes' (I find it more poetic than Huhneraugen) on your feet." *Hühneraugen*, literally meaning "chicken eyes," is the German term for "corns" or "blisters." Avshalom evidently was pleased with his poetic "dove eyes" variation on the German word for blisters.[29]

If Sarah suffered from poor health during their wait for word from Aaron, Avshalom endured frustration. He wrote notes to Lieutenant Woolley that he had no means to deliver. In one, he wrote, "My teeth are ground down from worry about whose turn is next." In another, he explained to Woolley that Djemal Pasha would go after the Jews once he had finished with other minorities. "Our turn will come one fine morning, when a moment of ill-will, or a fluttering butterfly, or a sunbeam, or any other poetic reason pushes the great commander to implement his cherished plan."[30]

By the fall of 1916 Avshalom and Sarah were running out of money. By now, they had expected Aaron to reach England, then go to Egypt and arrange for more spy ship visits, and be back in Atlit by the end of October. In September, though, Sarah and Avshalom received a message from Avshalom's younger sister, Tzila, who was studying in Berlin. Aaron, then in Denmark, had instructed Tzila by telegram to write Avshalom and Sarah that the station's American trustees would be wiring them three thousand dollars. Tzila also wrote that Aaron was on his way to America to see friends. It may have been Aaron's way of misleading any German spy who intercepted the letter about his true destination, which was then England. Or Tzila may have bungled when writing the letter. Either way, Avshalom interpreted it literally.

"He's left us here to fight it out alone," Avshalom told Sarah.

Another cause of Avshalom's frustration was that the intelligence that their spies had gathered was becoming outdated. What's more, the money from the American trustees, if it was sent, never reached Atlit. The pleasant evenings that the two spent at the home of Sarah's brother Zvi, playing with Sarah's young nephew and niece, no longer distracted Avshalom.[31]

On December 16 Avshalom sent a letter from Atlit to Sarah in Zichron, addressed to "Sarati, my lovely." Avshalom was in a bad mood. Everyone had been reassuring him, he wrote, that Aaron was coming back to Palestine from England. "I pray to God that it is so, but I am doubtful, what can I do? Until now, my heart has not deceived me, I wish this time it does." He and one of the spies, Nissan Rotman, had just gotten into a fight over money. "What should I do with him? This fool is a born communist and is unable to understand the simplest things: 'What is mine—is mine, what is not mine—is not mine.'"

Avshalom rebuked Sarah for not taking better care of herself and was not kind about it.

And what about you girl? Still coughing? And still "blowing the horn," and not sleeping? Have you got a fever, too? When will there be an end to these things, too, oh mighty God?! Thanks to your habit of taking "good care" of yourself, which we are both aware of, you will destroy yourself, as simple as that. . . .

According to my calculation, Aaron arrived there [Egypt] a month ago or even earlier and still there's no sign of him nor a single penny, at the same time the situation here is so terrible that I am afraid to explain it even to the closest people so as not to discourage them completely![32]

Avshalom and Sarah had no way of knowing that four days earlier, Aaron, after meeting with British officials in England, had arrived in Egypt on a British passenger liner. He was now doing his best to convince British intelligence officers there to link up with the Jewish spies in Palestine.

7

Aaron Aaronsohn's Journey

Aaron had left Palestine in mid-July 1916, accompanied by Liova Schneer-sohn as his assistant. To go from Zichron to Constantinople took a week. The tracks and roadbed were in poor condition, and the train had frequent mechanical breakdowns. Once, Aaron, Liova, and the other passengers of a stalled train had to get out and walk or ride in carts to the next station, where they waited for another train. Another time Aaron and Liova ended up in a wagon pulled by three horses that had no brakes and whose reckless driver veered perilously close to the edge of a cliff. Sarah's trip had taken much longer, but she had repeatedly lost her seat to Turkish soldiers and had to wait for trains in remote stations.[1]

Unlike Sarah, Aaron did not witness the relentless slaughter of Armenians; by now, fewer were left for the Turks to kill. But between Beirut and Damascus, Aaron observed conditions that were horrendous enough, especially among the Arab and Christian populations: "babies in the streets, crying for food and dying in the arms of their starving mothers." On reaching Damascus, he described these scenes to Lt. Col. Ali Fuad Bey, the chief of staff of the Ottoman Fourth Army. "You are a healthy, strong fellow," replied Fuad Bey. "You are not going to be mollified by the crocodile tears of a half dozen hysterical, mendicating women."[2]

Aaron and Liova arrived in Constantinople on July 22. Notwithstanding Djemal Pasha's support for his "scientific" mission, it took Aaron almost a full month to obtain the permits necessary to travel to Germany. He explained to the German consulate that he planned to meet with distinguished German scientists and discuss matters that could help the war effort. The consular officials expressed their appreciation.

While waiting in Constantinople, Aaron had dinner with Sarah's husband, who either had never left the city, as Sarah had heard, or else had returned after an extended absence. Aaron visited Sarah's neighborhood, which to his eyes looked shabby and rundown. In August 1914 Sarah had described her homesickness for Zichron despite having a "fine house," but that letter had also talked of money problems. She and her husband may have been forced to move to a less appealing home and neighborhood, where, as mentioned in Aaron's diary, Sarah lived "for more than a year" until she left Constantinople in November 1915.[3]

The German consulate finally issued a visa to Aaron. But Liova Schneersohn's visa application ran into trouble. Liova had traveled to Constantinople with a Spanish passport using the false name of Haim Cohen of Haifa. The Constantinople police, evidently at the request of the German consulate, asked the authorities in Haifa for information about Haim Cohen; unsurprisingly, Haifa did not respond. Aaron enlisted his Constantinople contacts, including the chief rabbi, to help Liova obtain a visa but without success.

Aaron could wait no longer. He told Liova to remain in Constantinople, to check periodically with the U.S. Embassy for messages from Aaron, and to relay them to Avshalom and Sarah. Liova lived in a small, stuffy room in the home of a Jewish wine merchant from Rishon LeZion while waiting for a message from Aaron. "I am alone in this big, foreign city," Liova wrote in his diary.[4]

Aaron departed Constantinople on August 21. Days later, he reached Germany, where he saw the impact of the war in Europe on the German home front. Between the British blockade and wartime requisitions even wealthy Germans were running out of food. In Berlin Aaron engaged in cordial conversations with German scientists but imparted no information of any use to the German war effort. On September 16, after several weeks in Berlin, Aaron crossed into neutral Denmark.

Once in Copenhagen Aaron contacted the British legation and explained that he had information of importance to British intelligence. Aaron's persuasive powers and stature convinced the British minister to contact his superiors in London. The minister's bureaucratic intuition was that, however preposterous Aaron's story of a Jewish spy ring in the Ottoman Empire, the Jewish scientist was best sent to London, where British intelligence officials could deal with him as they saw fit. Telegrams were sent back and forth between London officials and the minister, out of which a plan emerged for getting Aaron to England.[5]

Aaron had successfully fooled Turkish government bureaucracies and German consular officials into allowing him to go to Germany under the guise of conducting and sharing scientific research. But his focus and discipline had a potentially dangerous lapse while he was in Copenhagen. Weighing on Aaron's conscience were the American trustees of the Atlit research station who had no clue that Aaron had turned the station into an espionage headquarters. Aaron had little difficulty lying to Turkish and German bureaucrats, but deceiving his American trustees and supporters was a different matter. An experienced spy would have understood the need to mislead spouses, family, and friends because his safety, and perhaps theirs, depended on doing so.

In a Zionist office in Copenhagen, Aaron wrote a letter in English to Judge Julian Mack, the federal judge in Chicago who was one of his closest American friends. The letter, which Aaron titled "The Confession," was intended for the trustees of the Atlit research station. In it, Aaron revealed that he was helping the British side and described the efforts to contact the British, including Alexander's failed attempt and Avshalom's missions and near hanging. Emphasizing that he was not spying for money or "honors," Aaron explained his involvement in the sordid enterprise:

As long as our lives, at least, were safe under the Turkish misrule, I did not feel it right to take a hand in the destruction of the Turks. But when it became clear to me, above the shadow of a possible doubt, that our lives depended on the caprices of a Djemal, or any other Turk suffering from sadism, then I felt the strong duty to draw the conclusions, and that I did. I went over mentally to the "enemy" from that moment. . . . I undertook to work with them. To do all in my power to rid our country of the Turkish scourge.

Aaron assured the trustees that "all our Jewish people in Palestine would approve of me. I do not like to have them share the responsibility, but I am sure of their moral support." At the end of the letter, Aaron asked the trustees to "please express your opinion in all frankness," although he did not say how or where they might reach him.

In Copenhagen Aaron had encountered Judah Magnes, the former rabbi at Temple Emanu-El in New York City and a trustee of the Atlit research station. Aaron asked Magnes, who was about to return to the United States, to deliver "The Confession" to Judge Mack. Aaron also gave Magnes a separate letter for Judge Mack with precise instructions on how to break the news to certain trustees. Referring to Henrietta Szold, a leading American Jewish figure, he wrote: "I am afraid that it will be such a shock to her. . . . Maybe give her the news in homeopathic doses [so] she may have some time [to] recover her balance."[6]

Aaron had relieved his guilt, but he had put at risk the lives of Sarah and Avshalom and their growing network of spies. The surprise and consternation of his American supporters would not likely be contained to them, and word of Aaron's espionage could spread. Agents of Germany, often Americans of German descent, operated in the United States. Many German Americans were sympathetic to Germany, bars along the New York waterfront were filled with out-of-work German immigrants who wished they were fighting for their homeland, and major cities had "Little Germany" neighborhoods. German diplomats and military attachés in the United States even recruited saboteurs on the theory that sabotage would force American soldiers to remain at home to protect factories and defense plants instead of their being shipped off to Europe.[7]

After reading "The Confession," some of his research station trustees and supporters were deeply angry at Aaron. Louis Marshall, a prominent lawyer, told Judge Mack that Aaron was engaged in treachery and criminal activity. The most supportive was Albert Loeb, a Sears, Roebuck & Company executive in Chicago, and his wife Anna, whom Aaron had thought "would more easily understand my case." The Loebs had taken Rivka in after she reached the United States. She called them "Popsy and Mopsy" and wrote that they were "angels in human form.

Parents cannot do as much for their children." That the Loebs had heard Rivka's stories of the travails of the *yishuv* might partly account for their reaction.[8]

In the end Aaron was lucky. His letter apparently escaped notice by German spies in the United States. But the episode illustrates that Aaron's decision to seek out the British himself was a prudent one, not only because his stature might finally gain the cooperation of British intelligence, but also, simply put, he was not a good spy. He had no business running a spy network in enemy territory, a task that depended on the calculated, cold-blooded use of deceit and trickery. Of course, at this point, it wasn't clear whether Avshalom Feinberg, who was governed more by impulse than by prudence and calculation, or the inexperienced, good-natured Sarah had that talent either.

On October 19 Aaron boarded a Scandinavian America Line passenger ship in Copenhagen. He paced the deck until, three days later, the ship reached the British port of Kirkwall in the Orkney Islands of Scotland. There, by prearrangement, a charade was enacted in which British authorities "arrested" Aaron to convince any spies on the docks that he was not a British agent. He was taken to London, which was under a blackout because of the German zeppelin airship raids that had turned some neighborhoods into smoking ruins. The impression Aaron had was of a gloomy, fog-ridden city at war. Aaron checked into a hotel, where he registered as an American under the name of William Mack, and the next day presented himself to Scotland Yard.

Waiting for him was Basil Thomson, the head of Scotland Yard's Criminal Investigation Department. Thomson, a keen-eyed investigator, could have stepped from an Arthur Conan Doyle novel. He had arrested and interrogated high-profile spies, including the nude dancer and alleged German spy Mata Hari. Thomson was intrigued and fascinated with Aaron; someone out of the *Arabian Nights* had appeared at Scotland Yard in the form of a confident "educated Jew" bringing tales from the East. In his memoir Thomson called their meeting one of the "most romantic incidents in the War experience of Scotland Yard." Thomson, evidently convinced that Aaron possessed valuable information about the Ottoman Empire, sent him to the War Office.[9]

Aaron was out of the Ottoman Empire and battle-torn Europe. "For the past few nights I have slept in peace, untroubled by nightmares," he wrote in his diary. But during the time he spent at the War Office, Aaron might have had the impression that Basil Thomson was the only British official who had any interest in his offer to put a spy ring in the Ottoman Empire at British disposal.

The War Office in Whitehall was in a huge Edwardian Baroque building that had become so nightmarishly crowded after the outbreak of the war that, according to an official history, it resembled the "Liverpool Street station on the evening of a rainless Bank Holiday." Boy Scouts, who were used as office messengers, darted here and there, demanding that senior officers follow them to meetings where their presence had been requested by higher-ranking officers. In this tumult Aaron was passed off from one military or diplomatic functionary to another and was listened to politely at one fruitless meeting after another but with no results. Avshalom's prediction—"you will arrive and you will find no one there"—seemed prescient to Aaron.[10]

Part of Aaron's problem was the perceived implausibility of a Jewish agronomist from Palestine, no matter how well credentialed, running a spy operation for the British. Another obstacle was genteel British anti-Semitism. Aaron wrote a military intelligence report for British intelligence officials: "In July [1916] there was not a single coast defense gun between Gaza and Beirut . . . the coast is lightly patrolled between Haifa, Tyre, Sidon and Beirut . . . the general arrangement appears to be a system of weak posts and patrols with very small local reserves at intervals of about 20 miles." An intelligence officer with the War Trade Intelligence Department conceded that the report was "very correct" while noting that Aaron was a Zionist and "of the Romanian type of Jew." The intelligence officer went on, "Of course, we do not know the object of his visit to this country, but he might be just as observant of these things here as he has been in Turkey and a purveyor of information of the conditions in England if he should get back to Turkey."

Aaron also wrote a memorandum, titled "Pro-Armenia," that described Sarah's experience on her train trip in late 1915. This memorandum was circulated in the Foreign Office but only after some passages had been deleted. One was Aaron's criticism of Germany's failure to stop the Armenian massacres. The other was Aaron's prediction that the Turks would deal in a similar fashion with other minorities in the Ottoman Empire, including the Jews.[11]

Aaron began taking long walks in London for exercise and to relieve his anger at the British officials who treated him so skeptically. Ever the meticulous observer, Aaron noted in his diary each walk's precise distance, which on most days was twelve miles or more. On one walk he encountered an "old lady" giving a shaky salute to passing British soldiers and concluded that she had probably lost a son at the Somme.[12]

Aaron had arrived in London near the end of the Battle of the Somme in France. The battle had begun nearly four months earlier on July 1, 1916, in glorious weather. The opening Allied artillery barrage of 3,500 shells a minute was heard two hundred miles north of London. Then, along a twenty-five-mile front, British and French soldiers charged out of their trenches at what Winston Churchill later described as "undoubtedly the strongest and most perfectly defended positions in the world."[13]

By sunset more than twenty thousand British soldiers were dead, including a thousand officers. It was the bloodiest day in the military history of Great Britain. In the first few weeks of fighting, the Somme was accompanied by a home front fervor that approached religious intensity. By the time it had ended on November 18, more than ninety-five thousand British soldiers had died at the Somme, and Britain was running short of the manpower for its military needs. The gains at the Somme had not been remotely commensurate with the casualties. Between July 1 and the last day of the battle, the British line had moved forward only six miles. It was still three miles short of Bapaume, the first day's objective. Public morale, if not broken, was bleak.[14]

In mid-November Maj. Walter Gribbon, a British intelligence official and Aaron's liaison in London, invited Aaron to his office. Gribbon explained that Aaron's military intelligence report had been well received by British intelligence in Cairo. In two days Gribbon told Aaron, a P&O liner would take him to Egypt. The news might have cheered Aaron but for the lack of specifics. Subsequently Gribbon's subordinate informed Aaron that, once in Egypt, he would be permitted to board a spy ship that would take him to Atlit although he would not be allowed to go ashore. Instead, Aaron could signal whoever was watching from Atlit to come on board the ship.

It was more than Aaron could bear. "After losing three [weeks] of waiting," he wrote in his diary, "to leave now in haste without being promised anything, to go out on a wild goose chase?" He angrily confronted Gribbon: Aaron found it unacceptable that "on the one side were people who were risking everything, who were working wholeheartedly, while the people on the other side who were receiving everything, were promising nothing and what was more, treating [him] with suspicion."

"I give this advice as a friend," said Gribbon, who then told Aaron to go to Egypt and see what he could accomplish there. In effect, Aaron had to trust that things would work out.

On November 24 while traveling under the name of William Mack, Aaron boarded the ss *Karmala*. The ship carried a four-inch gun and, for part of the voyage, was accompanied by a small submarine. "First we shall get to Egypt, renew the contact," he wrote in his diary, "and start work." Aaron meant to have it out with the British in Egypt. "Then . . . whether our friends are happy or saddened, we shall speak in different tones."[15]

On December 12, 1916, the ss *Karmala* reached Port Said at the northern end of the Suez Canal. Aaron was met at the ship by Charles Boutagy, a Christian Arab who worked for British intelligence. While the passengers disembarked, Boutagy called Aaron by his real name ("our friends' first blunder"). A British intelligence official furnished Aaron with a travel permit to go to Alexandria. There he was handed over to Capt. William Stanley Edmonds of a separate intelligence agency, the Eastern Mediterranean Special Intelligence Bureau.[16]

Edmonds initially struck Aaron as "not only very intelligent but very shrewd as well." But Edmonds and his colleagues refused Aaron's repeated demands to be taken by ship and dropped on the coast of Palestine. Edmonds also declined Aaron's request for reimbursement of the 1,500 pounds he had spent to travel from Palestine to London and then to Egypt. Edmonds did offer Aaron a stipend of one pound a day, but it was hardly enough to cover his hotel bill. Aaron rejected the offer as insulting. Aaron fumed in his diary. "I have encountered nothing but distrust and reticence, smallness and pettiness. I must try and control my nerves so that I can establish another connection with Absa [Avshalom]. Then he can continue the work if he wants to. . . . I am not going to continue working under such conditions."[17]

The British had brought Aaron all the way to Egypt, but they didn't fully trust him. One problem was that he had no one to vouch for his credibility other than Lieutenant Woolley, who was no longer able to do so and had left no record of his contacts with Avshalom. That summer Lieutenant Woolley's superior had ordered Woolley to take leave on one of his spy ships, the *Zaida*, as a kind of vacation. Woolley protested that he didn't have the time. "Nonsense, you've got to take a holiday, it'll do you any amount of good, [and] that's an order."

In the Gulf of Alexandretta, the *Zaida* hit a mine and sank in less than thirty seconds, but Woolley managed to get off the ship. He and the other survivors clung to wreckage until a Turkish vessel picked them up. Woolley spent the rest of the war in a Turkish prisoner of war camp. Thus, the one man in Egypt who could confirm the existence of a Jewish spy network in Palestine, from the British point of view, was conveniently unavailable.[18]

In a ploy that especially infuriated Aaron, Captain Edmonds proposed that Aaron write a letter for the British spy ship to deliver to his Jewish spies in Palestine. Might Aaron have a "special message to convey"? Aaron was adamant that unless he was on board the spy ship, he would terminate his dealings with British intelligence. He would not permit the British to send "some blunderer" ashore and risk the lives of his spies in Atlit. "If we do not trust you," Edmonds told Aaron, then "you don't trust us either." In the end both sides compromised. Aaron would be allowed to go aboard the ship but would not go ashore. A messenger would take ashore Aaron's instructions and, to assure Avshalom and Sarah that Aaron was on the ship, some of his personal items.[19]

The day before Christmas, Aaron boarded a small, former fishing trawler named the *Goeland*. He brought with him supplies, including condensed milk, cocoa, coffee, and coal oil, for the British to drop off at

Atlit. Capt. Ian Smith, the senior British intelligence officer on board, informed Aaron that the provisions would not be allowed aboard. When Aaron insisted that his people in Atlit might be starving, Smith replied, "Let them starve, what do we care?"[20]

The *Goeland* reached Atlit the afternoon of Christmas Day 1916. Aaron, who had left Palestine six months earlier, was almost home. A figure came out on the station's balcony. Someone, after all these months, had kept a vigil, which moved Aaron. He might have identified the person had Captain Smith brought a sufficiently powerful set of binoculars, as Aaron had requested before they sailed. Captain Smith insisted to Aaron that the binoculars on board, Goerz x8 field glasses, would be adequate. They proved weak, and Aaron could not identify the person on the balcony.

The wind picked up, and lightning flashed in the sky, possibly making it easier to identify the *Goeland* as a British ship. Thus, the *Goeland* sailed out to sea. It returned as the weather improved somewhat, and the crew lowered a boat. Captain Smith rejected Aaron's pleas to be allowed in the boat and go ashore. Aaron gave the messenger a penknife and a magnifying glass that Sarah would recognize. The boat rowed away from the *Goeland* but returned after an hour because the sea was still too rough. The *Goeland*'s officers gave up, and the ship returned to Port Said. It had been heartbreakingly close. Had there been slightly calmer seas, the boat might have landed and delivered a message to Avshalom and Sarah that Aaron had succeeded in contacting the British.[21]

In early January 1917 the British asked Aaron to relocate from Alexandria to Cairo, where he would stay in the Grand Continental Hotel. The idea was that Aaron would meet and work with, among others, British intelligence officers at the headquarters of the Egyptian Expeditionary Force and in the Arab Bureau. Since the start of the war in the Middle East, British forces had fought on widely separated fronts, including at the Suez Canal and the Sinai Desert, at Gallipoli on the Dardanelles, and in Mesopotamia (Iraq). Separate command hierarchies had developed, including one through London and another through the British colonial administration in India, whose sphere of influence included Mesopotamia.

The result was a classic English muddle, with some agencies working in ignorance of what others were doing while the most informed agencies sometimes did their best to undermine the more ignorant rival agencies. The Arab Bureau was originally conceived as a grand coordinating body. But by the time of its formation in mid-1916, fierce objections by, among others, the viceroy of India had watered down the Arab Bureau's authority until it was just another bureaucratic player. At the time of Aaron's arrival in Cairo, T. E. Lawrence, later credited with leading the Arab Revolt, was assigned to the Arab Bureau.[22]

Aaron's knowledge of Palestine and his spy ring should have been welcome in Cairo, especially at the Arab Bureau, but the British remained suspicious of Aaron, while he barely disguised his contempt for them. In Aaron's view the Cairo officials lacked precise information to exploit their gains in the Sinai, their maps were inaccurate, their thinking was obtuse, and their bureaucracy was impenetrable. Throughout much of his stay in Egypt, Aaron wrote scathingly about the British officers he had the misfortune to work with: "More than twenty times I felt like throwing up to their face what I thought of their complete and irremediable inability to understand the situation. A hundred times daily I curse the moment when we decided to work with them . . . better [to] commit suicide than to continue under such conditions with people whom we thought were our friends."[23]

He and Captain Edmonds "had a heated and disagreeable argument . . . which, unfortunately has been customary of late." Jewish officer Capt. Norman Bentwich was "neither shrewd nor quick—two indispensable qualities in the enterprise which he wants to conduct." Aaron's nemesis on the spy ships, Captain Smith, was "always an idiot." Aaron's biographer, Ronald Florence, observed that his frustration was due in part to his lack of experience with "a huge enterprise with a complex agenda in which his own project—no matter how important—was only one of many priorities."[24]

Nonetheless, the British made another attempt to establish contact with Sarah and her spies. On January 20 Aaron set out again to reach Atlit on a trawler named the *Chauveau*. Captain Smith was again in command, but this time he brought with him a more powerful set of binoculars. Aaron, a proud, accomplished man, was told to eat in the hold with the crew and not with the officers, as once more, as he put it, he was forced to "drain the cup of insults." But after a few hours at sea, bad weather forced the *Chauveau* to turn back.

Four days later Aaron's mood brightened after a meeting with Maj. Wyndham Deedes of the Arab Bureau. "He is now in charge of the Intelligence Service," Aaron wrote, somewhat overestimating Deedes's authority. "He is more American-like in his methods of work and I hope things will go better with him." Deedes was responsible only for political intelligence, not military intelligence, but his authority included recruiting agents in Palestine. Deedes, then in his midthirties, had descended from several centuries of landed gentry and, after graduating from upper-crust Eton, had joined the British army to fight in the Boer War. (He demurred to a question about his experience in that war by saying, "Well, anything was better than Eton.") In this world war, he had seen service at Gallipoli before his posting to Egypt. Lawrence wrote that Deedes was "a very excellent man. I like him best of the bunch."[25]

But Deedes was unusual even by the eclectic standards of British intelligence personnel in Cairo. Deeply religious, Deedes believed that Christians had to atone for their historic sins against Jews by helping to establish a Jewish state in Palestine. After the war he became known as a Christian Zionist. It's doubtful that Deedes shared those sympathies with the Jewish agronomist, but he might have shown a deeper appreciation of Aaron's objectives than his colleagues had.[26]

A year earlier then commander of the Egyptian Expeditionary Force Gen. Sir Archibald Murray had proposed an "active defense" of the Suez Canal that ultimately turned into an offensive to push the Turks out of the Sinai and later out of Palestine. Today the term would be "mission creep." Holding a defensive line closer to Palestine would require a smaller force than would holding a defensive line at the Suez Canal, and Murray's forces were shrinking due to troop transfers to the western front.

The Sinai Desert is 120 miles wide from east to west along the Mediterranean coast. Murray's strategy was to send a large British force through the Sinai along the coastal route and eventually establish a British base at El Arish, a strategically located town of mud huts on the Mediterranean about 100 miles east of the canal. From there the British could attack the flank of any Turkish force sent along the central route that Djemal Pasha had used in his failed 1915 attack. The maneuver would also have the beneficial effect of relocating tens of thousands of British soldiers from Cairo, where "thousands of officers [were] hanging around the hotels" and enlisted men were contracting venereal disease at a rate four times that of British soldiers on the western front.[27]

The British forces used both modern technology in the form of airplane reconnaissance and bombardment and old tactics out of bygone ages such as dashing horse and camel charges. Strategic calculations on both sides were driven by water. Oases, however, could be taken but not always held; the salinity in the water in some oases caused the British soldiers to become ill (the Bedouins appeared to tolerate the water); and stretches of the desert where the British planned to advance had no water of any kind.

The British and their allies in the Sinai fighting, notably Australia and New Zealand, had to find other means to supply their forces with water, as well as provisions and munitions. The British used dhows and barges to bring water pipes and tracks for light trains down the canal to the town of Quantara. The Royal Engineers and tens of thousands of men of the Egyptian Labour Corps, mostly native Egyptians, worked in temperatures that sometimes reached 122 degrees Fahrenheit while beset by hordes of stinging flies. They laid track and water pipelines eastward across the northern Sinai behind a protective line of trenches that were constantly being dug and re-dug (with considerable difficulty in the sand) to stay in front of the pipes and tracks. The desert ahead of the trenches was patrolled by Australian and New Zealand mounted brigades. The track and water pipeline–laying procession advanced at the painfully slow rate of four miles per week.

The Turks attacked British railheads, the British ambushed Turkish formations, the patrols from both sides clashed in the northern Sinai, and the forces fought battles on sandy terrain that shifted during the fighting. In August 1916 the British defeated the Turks in a major battle at Romani, about twenty-two miles east of the Suez Canal. By December Murray's forces and their railhead had reached the wells of Mazar, forty miles from El Arish. On December 21 nine days after Aaron arrived at Port Said from England, the Turks retreated from El Arish under threat of bombardment from British ships offshore and attacks by British infantry, which achieved the campaign's principal objective. On December 23 Australian and New Zealand horse and camel mounted brigades attacked Magdhaba, where Turkish forces posed a threat to the British rear. Magdhaba had to be taken by sundown, or the thirsty soldiers and their mounts would have to withdraw to El Arish for water. In the early afternoon, a combined horse and camel charge breached the Turkish lines and took the town.[28]

The British now had more than two hundred thousand troops in the Sinai theater who were supplied daily by rail, pipe, and camel with 1.2 million gallons of water. The desert campaign was over. Palestine lay in front of them like a giant oasis. "[It was] delightful country, cultivated to perfection and the crops look quite good if not better than most English farms, chiefly barley and wheat," recalled a British officer who led a reconnaissance patrol into Palestine. "The villages were very pretty—a mass of orange, fig and other fruit trees. . . . The relief of seeing such country after the miles and miles of bare sand was worth five years of a life."[29]

But after crossing the expanses of the Sinai Desert, the British forces now faced a comparatively narrow gateway into Palestine if that, in fact, became the next objective. The gateway was the twenty-five miles between Gaza on the Mediterranean and Beersheba in the Negev Desert. Breaking through the Gaza–Beersheba gateway would give the British direct access to the main roads in southern Palestine, including the roads to Jaffa, Jerusalem, and Hebron. Fully understanding that, the Turkish forces set up a new defensive line between the two towns. In London the British government dithered over whether to attack Palestine.[30]

The Turks were largely gone from the Sinai, but the Bedouins were still there. The Bedouin men, who had dark complexions and thick dark hair, wore black tunics and kaffiyehs held in place with an *agal* of camel wool. Professionally these shepherds and herdsmen also plundered travelers and caravans, a practice they regarded as simply collecting customs duties owed by those trespassing on their land.[31]

In the Sinai more Bedouins served with the Turks than with the British. In 1915, 1,400 Bedouins from the Negev had joined the Turkish attack on the Suez Canal. By one estimate, overall several thousand Bedouins served with the Turks during the Sinai Desert fighting, many from the Ibn Rashid tribe and the adventurous camel-dealing Egeil tribe. The Turks used the Bedouins as scouts and spies who would provide disinformation when the British caught and interrogated them. With their feet clad in open sandals and carrying rifles and sharpened lances, the Bedouins moved freely back and forth across the front lines on horseback or by camel.

Some Bedouins viewed the fighting between the British and the Turks as both a spectator sport and a looting opportunity. One British war correspondent observed Bedouins gathering to watch a cavalry charge near the town of Rafah "with the same coolness as if it were field day in peace time." Perhaps that was why the Bedouins were there that day, but another British officer recalled that they often "prowled round the edges of the battlegrounds ready to tear uniforms and boots from the fallen, and even to dig up and strip the [British and Turkish] dead."

Mobility was the great strength of the Bedouins. They used it to slip away from a stronger enemy as though vanishing from the face of the earth or to attack a weaker foe without warning. The wind might have stirred up only a wisp of sand behind a dune, or it might have been Bedouins.[32]

8

One of Your Men Came across the Desert

In early January 1917 Avshalom wrote another note addressed to Lieu-tenant Woolley. The note was to be kept at the research station in the event Woolley sent another messenger because Avshalom would not be there. He did not intend to remain in Atlit or even in Palestine. "I have decided, come what may, to cross the desert, and to reach you. I must run my last race, and I beg you to note that I do this in the ser-vice of His Majesty, George Vth, King of England who, in my mind, is already crowned King of Palestine and Mesopotamia. You will hear further details from my friends at the Station, who tomorrow will be your comrades in arms."[1]

Avshalom had confided his activities in Nili to his longtime friend (and Jaffa café brawling companion) Baruch Ben-Azar. Baruch had worked in Aaron's 1915 locust campaign, during which he also had met Sarah after her return from Constantinople. Decades later in his oral history, he recalled Sarah's insistence that the Turks would destroy the Jewish community just as they had the Armenians'. Baruch served as an Atlit beach watcher, waiting for British ships that, on his watch, never came. One night at the Atlit research station, Avshalom told Baruch that he planned to cross the Sinai Desert to Egypt while accompanied by fellow spy Yosef Lishansky.

Baruch tried to talk Avshalom out of going. Their arguments became so heated that Avshalom pulled out a gun.

"Get ready for a pistol fight."

"I won't pull out my gun against you."

The station's bell rang, signaling that it was time to tend to the cows, and the argument ended. Sarah's room was next to the room that Baruch and Avshalom shared. Baruch encountered Sarah, whose eyes were red. She told Baruch that "she hadn't closed her eyes the entire night because she heard us arguing, and couldn't decide which one of us was right."[2]

Yosef Lishansky purchased two camels and found a Bedouin guide. The two men planned to set out from Ekron, west of Jerusalem, where Lishansky lived. Avshalom left from Hadera by carriage to rendezvous with Lishansky in Ekron. He stopped in Tulkarem to mail a letter to Sarah. Avshalom reported that the first part of the trip had been terrible, the road to Tulkarem was in poor shape, and the carriage had broken down. "I am still not sure that it wasn't a nightmare." He hoped to be with Yosef in a few days. After that he could no longer send or receive letters.

Avshalom's letter lacked any of his customary playfulness. "We need to look forward to the future, which appears to me to be not bad at all. Patience and diligence can achieve anything and I hope to see you in February or at least send good news to you." He mentioned a few personal and business matters that he wanted Sarah to take care of: to divide the half tin of tahini (sesame seed paste) at the Atlit research station with Avshalom's mother, to take the emptied tin to the warehouse and claim the deposit, and to please remind Apelrot, the station's accountant, to go to Haifa and obtain the funds needed to purchase wheat. He was sure that Sarah "will arrange my papers like I asked you to do."

> What else? It's impossible to write everything. I just miss you very very much and I am terribly worried because I know that you don't love me enough to remember that you have to take care of yourself, if not for yourself—then for me. I would be very grateful to you if you did so. Don't run, don't get cold, don't get upset and especially now, when I am not there to shout at you, and to stop you.
>
> Enough. Goodbye my lovely. Be a good girl. A thousand warm kisses. Love you always . . .
>
> Avshalom

P.S. Tomorrow, my lovely, it is your birthday. A thousand kisses and greetings to you. I am certainly happy that you were born, and I wish that from now on—you were happier or at least wished to be happy.[3]

Avshalom appeared at Lishansky's home in Ekron at a difficult moment for Yosef and his wife, Rivka. The Lishansky family had recently moved to Ekron, rented a house, and purchased a cow to provide milk for their two young children—a daughter, Ivria, and a son, Tuvia. Now Yosef told Rivka that he intended to cross the desert with a man named Avshalom Feinberg. Rivka vaguely recalled seeing Avshalom at a dance when she lived in Hadera.

Yosef and Rivka's angry argument was witnessed by Ivria, who was then about four or five years old. "I did not realize yet what it was all about," Ivria recalled as a grown woman, but she never forgot her parents' "grim expressions," as though they were two enemy soldiers on a battlefield. Shortly, a tall Jewish man, dressed like a Bedouin, walked into their home. He did not introduce himself to Rivka and spent his time talking with Yosef out of her hearing. Yosef said good-bye to Rivka and his children and left with Avshalom Feinberg.[4]

Avshalom carried a supply of dates. Rich in sugar and spoil resistant even in the summer heat, dates are the ideal desert food. For centuries Arab travelers in the desert brought with them only a bag of dates, which was sufficient to sustain both the traveler and his or her horse or camel for lengthy periods. Ordinarily a traveler could eat dates growing on the date palm trees in oases, but the oases on Avshalom's route might be held by isolated Turkish units in the desert or by unfriendly Bedouins. The unverified story is that at their farewell meeting, Sarah had given dates to Avshalom as a small contribution to the success of his journey.[5]

Sarah had seen first Aaron and now Avshalom set off to reach the British. At least until Avshalom's return, Sarah, who had been frustrated by the challenges of manufacturing dibs from grapes, was now the leader of the spy ring.

In the afternoon of January 25, 1917, twelve days after Avshalom and Yosef Lishansky had left Ekron, Aaron entered the Continental Hotel in Cairo. At the foot of the hotel's grand staircase, he encountered his liaison, Captain Edmonds.

"You are the very man I am looking for," Edmonds said to Aaron. "I have been looking for you all morning. You must go immediately to Port Said. One of your men came across the desert."

Aaron went to his room for some belongings. He jotted a few notes in his diary. "It appears that the man who has arrived is Yosef Lishansky. Is he wounded I wonder? Why do they send me to him instead of sending him here? These gentlemen are so uselessly and so unfortunately mysterious!" Aaron left by train for Port Said a little after six o'clock in the evening and arrived just before midnight. A carriage met him at the station and took him to Lishansky, who was suffering from gunshot wounds. Once they were alone, Yosef told Aaron why he and Avshalom had gone into the desert and what had happened to them.

Avshalom and Yosef had made good progress after leaving Ekron on January 13, reaching Beersheba less than a week later. Once in the desert, they and their Bedouin guide traveled at night and slept during the day. Avshalom's and Yosef's Bedouin disguises worked; whichever Turkish army units they encountered ignored them. They reached the vicinity of Sheikh Zowa'id, not far from Rafah, now in British hands.

The night they neared Sheikh Zowa'id was misty with no visible stars. Their Bedouin guide got lost, claiming that he had no reference points in the flat, barren desert or in the black sky. The three men spent the night next to their camels. At dawn they hoped to spot a British outpost.

But when the sun rose, thirty to forty mounted Bedouins emerged from the desert and began shooting at them. Yosef was shot in one leg and fell. Then Avshalom was hit. Yosef managed to crawl to Avshalom, who had been badly wounded and was unable to speak. Avshalom grasped the hem of Yosef's Bedouin gown and pointed to the horizon, a gesture that meant Yosef should get away. Yosef hugged and kissed Avshalom. Yosef got up and ran until another bullet hit him in the shoulder. He fell to the ground and lost consciousness. An Australian patrol found him and brought him to Port Said.

"I didn't want to leave him," Yosef tried to explain to Aaron. Seeing the look on Aaron's face, he added that the British had "brought me here to die."

"You won't die," Aaron said bitterly. "You hugged and kissed him under a volley of bullets?"

"Yes."

"And did anyone else see how all this happened?"

"No."[6]

Aaron asked the British in Port Said to send a patrol to find Avshalom's body. The request was not a matter of sentiment but prudence, since the discovery of Avshalom's body might expose the spy ring in Zichron. That night Aaron wrote in his diary, "Absa fell in the desert—shot through the back! Absa in the hands of Bedouin bandits! Absa—our 'Knight without fear and without reproach' ignominiously assassinated."

Aaron left Yosef to get some sleep and briefly dozed off in a hotel room. He abruptly awoke at 5:00 a.m. and made another entry in his diary. "So Absa, the brave, was shot by vile, rapacious Bedouins—he fell dying into the hands of those whom he despised most. And to think that the best we could wish for him and for us all was that he had been disfigured and buried without the least trace being left."

He went to see Yosef, who was in terrible pain. Aaron pleaded vainly with the British to move Yosef to Cairo, observed the dressing of Yosef's wounds by a British military doctor, and then went to the Port Said train station. He boarded a train for Cairo that he had to himself for part of the trip. "I could remain alone with my sorrow." He reached Cairo on the afternoon of January 26 and went to see Maj. Wyndham Deedes, whom Aaron had met two days earlier and found to be "more American-like in his methods of work."[7]

In front of Major Deedes, Aaron broke down, sobbing without shame. Deedes was a hard man with a thin frame, bony face, and sharp widow's peak. He was an ascetic in his habits and had an icy personal reserve. Even so, Deedes was moved by Aaron's grief.[8]

By now hundreds of thousands of young British soldiers had died in France and Belgium and at Gallipoli. Beneath their patriotism, sense of duty, deference to authority, and sacrifice, the British had suffered a broken heart. Deedes spoke of the dead British soldiers and listened sympathetically to Aaron, whose heart was also broken.

Grief was not Aaron's only emotion. He angrily blamed the British for Avshalom's death, raging against their delay in contacting his Jewish spies in Palestine and how it had led Avshalom to make the desperate trip across the desert. Deedes acknowledged the defects in British intelligence and promised Aaron that "in the future there would be no more humiliation and distrust and that everything would go well."

Deedes kept his promise. He arranged for Yosef Lishansky to receive the same care as wounded British officers. Aaron returned by train to Port Said and at five in the morning of January 28, less than a day and a half after his meeting with Major Deedes, boarded the torpedo boat *L'Arbalète*. The ship's orders were to take Aaron and Liebl Bernstein, a Jewish courier who was a strong swimmer, to Atlit.

The ship neared Atlit. At 11:00 p.m. the moon disappeared, and the surfboat, with Liebl Bernstein on board, was lowered and rowed away from the *L'Arbalète*. Twenty-five minutes later the boat signaled that Liebl had reached the beach. "My emotion can easily be imagined," Aaron later wrote in his diary. Then a furious wind blew out of nowhere.[9]

9

What about Avshalom?

On January 21, 1917, the day after Avshalom Feinberg and Yosef Lishansky left Beersheba and followed their Bedouin guide into the Sinai, Liova Schneersohn arrived at the Atlit research station from Constantinople. Through the window from the station's second floor, an observer had a view of the sea. There Liova stood watch for a British spy ship and made notes in his diary. Sometimes Sarah joined him, and they watched together.

Liova Schneersohn wore glasses, favored bow ties, and had the pale-faced demeanor of a university student whose days and nights are spent in the library. Born in Russia, Liova was a descendant of a Russian family closely identified with the Chabad movement, an offshoot of Hasidism. Chabad sought to reconcile Hasidic mysticism with scholarship; Liova's personality had elements of both. His parents emigrated to Palestine and settled in Hadera, but Liova stayed in Russia to pursue studies, in among other subjects, anarchism. He fancied himself a poet with a Russian soul and found a kindred spirit in Avshalom Feinberg, whom he had known since leaving Russia and joining his parents in Hadera.[1]

How Liova got to Atlit from Constantinople, where he had been left behind the previous August as Aaron set out for Germany, is a tribute mainly to the young man's luck. In accordance with Aaron's instructions, Liova had regularly checked with the U.S. Embassy for messages from Aaron and spent time trying to get a visa to Romania, from where Liova hoped to travel to Egypt. But the Romanian Embassy refused to give Liova a visa because, as with the German consulate, when the Romanian officials demanded more information about Haifa resident Haim Cohen, Liova's fictitious identity, none was forthcoming from Haifa.

Liova ran out of funds and sold matches in the street to raise enough money to maintain a near-starvation diet (the selling price reflected a hefty profit margin). He came up with the idea of traveling to Austria-Hungary and then making his way to Russia. In his diary Liova called it a "crazy idea," presumably not least because Austria-Hungary and Russia were at war with one another. Liova applied for a visa at the Austro-Hungarian Embassy using his forged Spanish passport. The clerk, who happened to be Jewish, looked at the Spanish passport and at Liova's Slavic Jewish features, which could not be easily reconciled. The clerk took Liova off to the side.

"Young man, if you want to live, get out of here!"

Liova took the advice. He decided to return to Palestine. One of Liova's few contacts in Constantinople was Dr. Arthur Ruppin, a friend of Aaron's then in the city who knew a German officer who was about to leave for Palestine and conduct a forest survey. Dr. Ruppin recommended that the officer take Liova with him as an assistant, citing Liova's expertise in forestry that had been gained at the well-known agricultural research station in Atlit run by the famous Aaron Aaronsohn. The German officer and Liova traveled together until they reached Damascus, where Liova slipped away and made his way to Atlit.

Sarah told Liova that she had not heard from Aaron since the fall of the previous year, that she was now in charge of both the research station and the spy ring, and that while she had lost some recruits, others were still gathering and bringing intelligence to her. Avshalom, she explained, was trying to cross the Sinai Desert with Yosef Lishansky and reach the British. Liova was stunned because he thought surely Aaron had reached England and by now might even be in Egypt; Avshalom was supposed to be in Atlit with Sarah. "After all the trouble that it took me to come back from Constantinople and here we are—Avshalom has gone! This is not what we talked about."

"Why didn't you notify us with a telegram when you left Constantinople?" Sarah asked.

"My dear, it was impossible, it would have given rise to too many suspicions. I was being watched too closely."[2]

Liova spent a few days at the Atlit research station with Sarah. They ate meager meals together of bread made from bulgur (cracked wheat), fig jam, and tea brewed from dried leaves. ("It's good that I brought some saccharin from Constantinople," Liova noted in his diary.) After a few days, Liova went home to Hadera. He was concerned that his German officer could appear in Atlit at any moment "and demand his 'lost luggage.'"

Liova's parents were relieved when their son appeared after months of having no word from him. On the night of Purim, which commemorates the salvation of Jews from the Persians, Turks came to Hadera and searched for deserters. Purim is ordinarily a festive time for Jews, but Liova had to hide in the Feinberg home, which was otherwise empty that night except for a scared housekeeper. After the Turks left, Liova slept in Avshalom's bed and half-dreamed, half-remembered how he once read Russian poetry to Avshalom and the poem that Avshalom had dedicated to him.

Liova returned to Atlit to resume the vigils from Aaron's bedroom and "just help around." He and Sarah went for walks along the coast, noting the Turkish patrols. Liova was in love with Sarah, possibly from the first sight of her, but his infatuation was conducted at a respectful distance. When she joined him on the second floor of the research station during his vigil, he may have watched her as much as the sea. "I see you sitting quiet and wonderful, with your wonderful white hands and your slim fingers," he wrote in his diary, "of such loveliness and beauty as I had never seen."

It's remarkable that Liova, daydreaming of Sarah, even noticed the ship. But he must have looked up and realized that a ship spewing black smoke from a funnel was approaching Atlit. He called out, Sarah ran up the stairs, and they watched together. He recorded the events that followed in his diary. Liova's entries, which are often quite detailed, alternate between past and present tenses, as though he had been reliving some events as he wrote them down afterward.

"The most important thing, Sarah, is the smoke. This is the sign. The smoke should be black and twisting." The ship was the *L'Arbalète*, with Aaron and the swimmer-courier Liebl Bernstein on board. The

L'Arbalète sailed close to Atlit and then abruptly turned and sailed in the opposite direction. "This is the second sign. Tonight, Sarah!"[3]

Sarah, with appropriate apologies, ushered visitors out of the research station. She told a worker to take charge of Azmavet, the station's diligent watchdog that had already scared off one British courier, and sent the worker on an errand with the dog. Several of her spies were at the research station, and she summoned others, including her cousin Reuven Schwartz and Yitzhak Halperin.

By the hour when the ship was supposed to make an approach under Captain Weldon's procedures, two groups of watchers were in separate locations on the shore near the Crusader castle. Sarah and Liova remained in the station, having blacked out its lights. Outside, the wind strengthened, and the treetops began whipping back and forth. The sounds of waves crashing on the beach could be heard from inside the research station.

Two hours went by. Then the wooden staircase shook from the pounding of several men coming up the steps. Liova jumped up and opened the door. Two of the watchers held up a third man. He was coughing and confused, trembling, wearing soaked clothing. Dripping water, he also smelled of alcohol.

"Here he is," one of the watchers announced. "Take him."

The near-drowned man looked around. He was badly frightened. "Who's here?"

"Speak, man, speak! Say everything that you were sent to say!"

"Aaronsohn . . . on the ship . . . Reuven should come." With some difficulty, he withdrew a medallion from his pocket and handed it to Sarah, who recognized it. She had given the medallion to Aaron.

Everyone fell to helping the dripping man. Some in the room massaged his legs; others shouted to "bring him tea," or anything, as long as it was hot. Someone remembered they already had hot tea brewing on the stove and fetched it.

"Who are you? What's your name?"

The man recovered enough to talk, coherently if disjointedly. He was Liebl Bernstein, and he was drunk. He used to work as a carriage driver in Petah Tikva.

"So," said Liova, suddenly remembering that Liebl had once driven him in a "diligence"—a horse-drawn, covered carriage, similar to a stagecoach—"this is the courier of good deeds, the renowned coachman Reb Liebl Bernstein."

Liebl told them how he had gotten to the beach. The British spy ship had put the surfboat, manned by Arab boatmen, into the sea. Liebl, an Arab swimmer named Abdullah, and British officers were on board. The waves breaking onto the shore were too high for the boat to risk going to the beach, and it remained beyond the surf. The British officers gave Liebl a drink from a bottle of whiskey, asking, "Do you know what that is?" Liebl stripped off his clothes; put the clothes, a revolver the British gave him, and the whiskey bottle in a leather bag; and strapped the bag to his back.

"Are you ready to jump?" asked Abdullah, who had stripped off his clothes and carried them in a leather bag on his back. "Ready," replied Liebl, whose courage had been bolstered by the whiskey. He jumped from the boat into the water and began swimming. Abdullah also jumped into the water and swam beside Liebl. The crew of the *L'Arbalète* had nicknamed Liebl, who had poor vision, "The Owl" because he wore large, round-framed glasses. Abdullah may have accompanied Liebl to make certain he located the beach.

The whiskey kept Liebl warm, and, despite the waves, the two men made it to the shore. There an exhausted Liebl drank more whiskey. Abdullah shook his hand. "You're a hero." Abdullah wished Liebl good luck, plunged into the surf, and swam back to the boat. Liebl put on his clothes and set out in the darkness for the research station, all the while shivering uncontrollably. He then encountered the beach watchers, who brought him to the station.

Liebl explained to Sarah that, when he was ready to return, he was to signal the surfboat from the beach with a flashlight. Someone brought out the intelligence reports. "No luggage, only intelligence reports," Sarah insisted. Liebl informed her that Aaron had been adamant that Sarah not try to come out to the surfboat. Sarah did not argue or protest. "Discipline is discipline," Liova thought to himself.

Liova asked Liebl, "What about Avshalom?" Liebl didn't know anything about him.

The plan was that Liova and Reuven Schwartz would swim with Liebl to the surfboat, bobbing further out. Baruch Raab, a station worker, accompanied them to the beach while carrying a shotgun. If they encountered any Turks, Baruch, whose better judgment may have been overcome by the excitement, planned to fire a shot and cry out, "Ah Rahat el bat" (The duck got away). Of course, any passing Turkish patrol within earshot would have immediately descended on them because no hunter would be out shooting ducks on that stormy night. They were amateurs, but, in fairness, they hadn't had an opportunity to train for this work.

At the beach, the three men found two naked, shivering Arab seamen who had swum ashore from the surfboat on orders from impatient British officers and who were now anxious to swim back. High, foamy waves rolled out of the dark, crashing onto the beach. To Liova it seemed "as if five story buildings are running toward us."

Reuven Schwartz took Liova aside. "We are to swim to the ship at a time like this? It's impossible. I don't intend to get drowned." Liova didn't argue with him. Consideration was given to having Liova carried on the back of one of the Arabs. That was vetoed by the now-experienced Liebl, who pointed out the risk that Liova might drown.

"Yallah, yallah, Leibl, let's go! Yallah, yallah!" The two Arabs had to shout to be heard over the wind, risking drawing the attention of any nearby Turks. The Arabs jumped into the sea and began swimming. Liebl waded in after them. The heavy intelligence pouch stayed on shore because, in this surf, its weight might drown whoever carried it. Liova shouted to Liebl, "Tell Aaron to send another ship." Liova, Reuven, and Baruch returned to the station, carrying the intelligence pouch. Liova, head down, was dejected by his failure to get to the surfboat.

"What can we do?" Liova said defensively upon seeing Sarah's surprised look. "The sea doesn't take orders from us."

They stayed up late talking. The young people, wound up by the evening's events, were embarrassed by their failure to deliver the intelligence reports. They were also concerned about Aaron's frustration, impressed by the need for luck in this new enterprise of theirs, and wondered about Avshalom. Finally they went to sleep.

At three o'clock in the morning, a stone struck the shutter of a window, rousing them from their beds.

Liova said to Sarah, "I'll go and see."

Sarah insisted on going with him. They opened the door, and there was a nearly naked man. Ghostly pale, shivering, and disoriented, he was an apparition from the sea.

"I'm Liebl."

Liebl had nearly drowned for a second time in one night. As he swam to the rowboat, he had lost sight of the two Arab seamen and was overpowered by the waves. Liebl turned around and barely made it back to shore.

The immediate task was again to restore Liebl. Baruch gave him an alcohol rubdown and warm clothing and put him to bed. Liebl stayed at the station for a few nights. Then Sarah went with him to Zichron, where her father took care of him until he could return to Egypt on a British spy ship.[4]

Perhaps the British had tried harder this time, now fully convinced by Aaron's agony that he was not a Turkish agent, or perhaps it was just luck. But a giant circle—beginning with Aaron's journey through the Ottoman Empire, across Europe, to England, and then by ship first to Egypt and then across the Mediterranean to Palestine—had been closed. In Avshalom's dying in the desert, he may have made it possible for Aaron to finally establish the link between British intelligence and the Jewish spies whom Sarah now led.

After returning to Cairo, Aaron saw Major Deedes, who told him that the Bedouins sent to find Avshalom's body had reported that there was no sign of the body or a grave. That night Aaron wrote in his diary, "So our brave knight is dead! Without even confessing it to myself, I had entertained a wild hope that he had survived. But now, we can do nothing except to complete the work for which he gave his life."[5]

On February 19, 1917, three weeks after Liebl Bernstein's swim, the *Managem*, a British steamer of 160 tons, came to Atlit. Captain Weldon was on the *Managem*, which had replaced the *Aenne Rickmers*, his last ship. Captain Weldon had brought the Arab boatmen from the *Aenne Rickmers* to his new ship.[6]

Aaron was aboard, as well as Yosef Lishansky, who had recovered sufficiently from his wounds to be dropped on the Atlit beach and join the spy ring as Sarah's lieutenant. During their time together in Egypt, Aaron realized that the wounded young man had skills that could be of assistance to Sarah.

Yosef was born in Kiev in the Ukraine in 1890, the year of Sarah's birth. After most of his siblings died from cholera and his mother perished in a fire in their home, Yosef's father, Ya'akov, left Kiev for Palestine, taking Yosef with him. The two moved in with Miriam, the daughter of Yosef's one surviving sibling, a much older brother who had left for Palestine before the tragedies.

Miriam lived in Metula in northern Palestine (today, Israel's north-ernmost town), where the air was fresh and healthy, and its water springs and fertile soil made it ideal for agriculture. Yosef's father did not adjust well to life in Metula and moved to Jerusalem. The family lost track of Ya'akov and never learned what became of him. Yosef grew up in Miriam's household, essentially an orphan.[7]

After graduating from the school in Metula, Yosef was admitted to a seminary in Jerusalem for advanced studies but lacked the funds to complete them. He moved to Egypt, where he worked on a farm run by a friend from Palestine. Returning to Metula, Yosef, a redheaded man with a red moustache, found work on farms and in almond groves and married Rivka Brishkovsky, a farmer's daughter from Beit Gan. Yosef and Rivka started their own farm, where they kept horses, and raised their two children.[8]

Yosef's physical courage, horsemanship, and weapons proficiency were never in doubt. Those assets were prized in that place and time, but Yosef irritated people with his airs of social superiority, taste for fine clothes, disdain for authority, unconcealed fondness for women, and thirst for danger as a means of self-fulfillment. He grew bored and restless with farming and tended to leave the household chores to Rivka.[9]

With Rivka's encouragement, on a trial basis Yosef joined Ha-Shomer, the settlement self-defense organization. Many of its members were from Russia, where they had joined self-defense groups to safeguard Jews from pogroms. In Palestine they wore Arab kaffiyehs and Cossack tunics and rode horses that they magnificently decorated in the Bedouin style, which favored velvet saddle covers with dangling three-tier tassels and a nose chain with tiny gold daggers attached to the lead rope. (After the war, Ha-Shomer became the nucleus of the newly formed Haganah, an underground Jewish army that, in turn, was the forerunner of the Israel Defense Forces.)[10]

Ha-Shomer was as much a lifestyle as a militia. Obedience and discipline, not among Yosef's strengths, were a prerequisite to full membership, which was conferred in a ceremony. After the members had voted to approve a candidate, he was led into the meeting between two rows of men holding rifles and administered the solemn Ha-Shomer oath: "In blood and fire Judea fell, in blood and fire Judea shall arise."

In fact, Ha-Shomer's policy was to avoid bloodshed if possible. The rules of engagement for encounters with Arab brigands follow:

> You do not seek an encounter with the thief; you chase him off, and only when you have no choice do you shoot. After all, he is out to steal a bag of grain, not to murder you, so don't murder him, drive him off. Don't sleep at night. If you hear footsteps, fire into the distance. If you feel he is a few steps away and you can fire without him falling upon you, fire into the distance. Only if your life is in danger—fire.[11]

Yosef was a Ha-Shomer swashbuckler (he even wore gold rings on his fingers). He had always wanted his first born to be a son so he could raise him in his own bold self-image. After the birth of his daughter, Ivria, Yosef decided that the best way to compensate for her gender was to teach her to be fearless. One of Ivria's earliest memories, probably from the age of three or four, was of her father holding her by one leg and whirling her through the air as he rode on a horse. Yosef devised other physical exercises and challenges for Ivria, including making her drink horse milk because, according to Arab tradition, its nutritional qualities supplied courage and strength.

Ivria adored her father. She recalled his many good-byes as he set off to guard one settlement or another, and once he rode on a camel decorated with colorful fringed robes. "He said farewell to me and immediately galloped away, like a desert wind, while the red fringes spread open behind him like a gust of flame until his image dissolved into dust like a mirage." Ivria's childhood years veered from the sorrows of her father's departures to the excitement of his return. "When Father got up on his horse and rode away, I felt as if I was becoming smaller and smaller until I disappeared [and then] I found myself again standing at the gate, expecting him. And as he approached I felt I was growing bigger and bigger, and this feeling turned into reality when he grabbed my hand and raised me to the saddle in a single yank."[12]

Yosef was given responsibility for security in the settlement of Milhamiya, later Menahamiya, the first Jewish settlement in the Jordan Valley. Menahamiya was the Wild West of Jewish settlements. It was in an area the Arabs called Sahuneh, which means "intense heat," and was therefore highly malarial. Menahamiya was isolated from the other Jewish settlements and adjacent to Arab villages and Bedouin tribes, with whom the settlers had poor relations. Yosef Gorny, a historian of Zionism, writes in *Zionism and the Arabs* that in the decades preceding World War I "there were few cases of mass violence" between the settlements and the Arab fellahin, but "the tension was always present." One source of that tension was the fellahin custom "to permit flocks to graze freely in the fields after the harvest" without regard for the legal owners' rights.[13]

Their exact motivation isn't clear, but some Arabs apparently drove a herd of cows into the settlement's cultivated fields at a time when Yosef was away from Menahamiya. Tensions boiled over. Jews tried to stop the Arabs, and a band of Arabs raided the settlement. In a scene witnessed by Yosef's wife, Rivka, a Ha-Shomer member came out from behind a building and shot and killed one of the leaders of the raid.

Ha-Shomer held Yosef responsible as he was known to advocate the severe punishment of Arab marauders. Although Lishansky wasn't present and the shooting might have been consistent with the Ha-Shomer policy of firing only as a last resort, Ha-Shomer denied Yosef membership and told him never to be seen in the area. Yosef formed a rival self-defense organization called Hamagen (the Shield) to guard settlements where Ha-Shomer did not have a presence. Yosef and the members of Ha-Shomer remained bitter enemies. Yosef's family followed him to posts at Hamagen-protected settlements, first to Ruchema and later to Ekron.

Yosef learned about the spy ring while he was in Beersheba in early 1916. A small Arab boy brought him a note sent from prison by his friend Avshalom Feinberg, who had just been arrested in his first attempt to cross the Sinai Desert and contact the British. Yosef went to the prison, where Avshalom asked Yosef to notify his cousin Naaman Belkind in Rishon LeZion about his imprisonment.

Either while he was in the prison or after his release, Avshalom invited Yosef to join the spy ring. Yosef accepted and then informed his wife. Rivka decided to leave him and take the children with her. A separation agreement was drawn up and signed by both husband and wife and by a rabbi. While playing with his daughter, Yosef gave Ivria the separation agreement and asked, "What do you think we should do with it?" Ivria, then around four or five years old, didn't like the "scribble of letters" on the paper. Aware that her father was teasing her, as Ivria later recalled, "I tore the paper to pieces, and thus put an end to the separation issue of Mother and Father."

Then, to Rivka's dismay, in January 1917, Avshalom Feinberg walked into the Lishansky home in Ekron dressed like a Bedouin. Yosef and Avshalom left and headed to Beersheba and the Sinai Desert.[14]

Aaron was on the *Managem* when the ship took Yosef to Atlit on February 19. On the *Managem*'s first pass by Atlit, Aaron could not see anyone at the research station, but a wall appeared blackened by fire. Aaron had a bad moment until he realized that the ship's auxiliary sails had cast a shadow on the wall. Then, he spotted two men on the balcony of the station's two-story building displaying a signal cloth that Aaron interpreted to mean it was safe to approach Atlit.

The ship returned that night around nine o'clock. The sea was relatively calm, although rough waves were near the shore. Captain Weldon, wearing a blue jersey, dark flannel trousers, and tennis shoes, climbed into a boat along with Aaron, Yosef, and two Arab swimmers. Some distance from the shore, the swimmers and Yosef jumped into the water. One Arab swimmer took Yosef on his back while another Arab swam alongside. Aaron soon lost sight of them in the water. Aaron had instructed Yosef to tell only Sarah about Avshalom's death and no one else.

Waiting on the beach were Liova Schneersohn and Reuven Schwartz, who had brought with them an intelligence pouch. At first, Liova and Reuven couldn't see the *Managem*; then they spotted a silhouette, a ghost-like black mass, floating in the distance with no lights or signs of sailors. A smaller silhouette—the surfboat—broke away from the larger one and approached the shore but stopped before encountering the surf. After a while, two Arab swimmers emerged from the waves and then a third figure emerged.

"Who's that?"

"A Jew."

"Who are you?"

"Yosef—"

"Lishansky?"

It was the first time that Liova and Yosef met. "I am Haim Cohen," said Liova, using his fictitious name.

"Avshalom told me so much about you," replied Yosef, evidently knowing it was Liova Schneersohn. "We shall be friends."

"What about Avshalom?"

"He is in Cairo. Aaron will tell you everything on the ship. But hurry up, hurry up, friends!"

The Arab swimmers carried Liova and Reuven to the surfboat, although only Liova, who was resuming his role as Aaron's personal assistant, would board the *Managem*. Once on the surfboat, Reuven kissed his cousin Aaron. They talked, but Liova kept interrupting.

"What about Avshalom? Where is he?"

"In Cairo," replied Aaron. "In Cairo."

Reuven got off the surfboat and was carried back to shore by a swimmer, who returned to the surfboat. Then the boat's crew took Aaron, Liova, and the intelligence pouch to the *Managem*, where the men had to climb a rope ladder up to the deck. As Liova climbed, Aaron, behind him on the rope ladder, called out, "Go, go! You are standing on English land, you are a free man!"

The *Managem* left Atlit before the sun rose. Aaron took Liova, who was exhausted, down to his cabin.

"What about Avshalom?"

"Tomorrow, tomorrow, I will tell you everything. Now just sleep."

The next day, the waves built up, and Liova became seasick. He sat on a chair on the deck in the chill dawn light. Liova clutched his Bible, a gift from Avshalom. Aaron came over to him.

"Avshalom was killed in the desert."

Liova lost all sense of his surroundings and of time, his head felt heavy, and he couldn't seem to think. He later wrote in his diary, "Avshalom doesn't leave me." As events unfolded over the coming months, Avshalom never left any of them.

Later, while Liova still sat on the deck and in a daze, a British intelligence officer approached Aaron. "By the way, what's your password?"

Aaron turned to Liova. "What name shall we use? Make sure it is short and sounds nice!"

At first Liova couldn't focus on Aaron's question. He heard himself speak Russian, "Boze moj" (My God). When he finally understood what Aaron wanted, Liova opened the Bible, randomly stabbed a finger among the pages, and counted down seven lines from his finger. On the eighth line was a phrase from 1 Samuel, "The Eternity of Israel will not lie nor repent." In Hebrew it is, "Nezah Israel Lo Ieshaker."

"Aaron, I've found the name in the Bible."

"In the Bible?"

Liova showed him the phrase. "See! Nezah Israel Lo Ieshaker. The initial letters—N-I-L-I!"

"Not bad, not bad." Aaron turned to the British intelligence officer. "Our Mr. Schneersohn has found the password: 'Nili'!"

"Oh, how nice," said the officer with a mischievous smile. "She must be a nice girl, this Nili!" Nili became both a password and, eventually, the name of the spy ring.[15]

On returning to Cairo, Aaron brought the intelligence pouch to his liaison, Captain Edmonds. The contents, as Aaron recounted in his diary, included the "first report from Absa, my notes on my trip from Haifa to Beirut, extracts from our statement of disbursements. Reports from the Station, etc." Captain Edmonds said that he wanted to keep the documents to study, which gratified Aaron.

Avshalom's report was based on information he had gathered in late November through early December 1915. Although his report by now was several months old, it offered the British a glimpse of the intelligence potential of the motivated Jewish spies in Palestine. As recounted, Avshalom had gathered information about the Turkish order of battle; the logistics and transportation infrastructure; the leaves, desertions, and reduction of Turkish forces in Palestine; and the unexpectedly long time required for rail transportation of troops and equipment from Aleppo and Jerusalem to Beersheba. According to Israeli military intelligence historian Yigal Sheffy in *British Military Intelligence in the Palestine Campaign*, "Had the document arrived in time, it would have constituted one of the best and most reassuring reports to be received by Cairo from any agent during a period of concern over a large-scale offensive against Egypt."[16]

The *Managem*'s trips to Atlit allowed Sarah and Aaron to send each other letters. In early March 1917 Sarah wrote a letter to Aaron asking for some word about Avshalom. She wasn't certain that, in fact, he was alive as no letter from him had been delivered by the *Managem*.

Sometimes I want to return home and be with [Chaim]. But usually I feel that I would rather come to you, to speak a little, to listen, to see and particularly to see our crazy one with my own eyes. Perhaps you remember how last year I said that until I see him with my own eyes, I would not believe that he is all right and is still with us, and this is what I say today as well. Why do I have this feeling? You figure it out. If it's possible, then why wouldn't he write a few words to me, the child, for he knows in what situation he left me. . . .

To our crazy one I will write next time, and ask him to write to me a little so I can answer.[17]

Sarah apparently wrote the letter in anticipation of a forthcoming visit by the *Managem*. While the exact circumstances may never be known, evidently when Yosef landed at Atlit a week earlier, he had fended off Sarah's questions about Avshalom, perhaps the way Aaron had deflected Liova's questions when he boarded the *Managem*. Around the time that Sarah wrote this letter, she and Yosef set off in the research station's carriage to pick up intelligence from the Nili spies in place, to brief them on the newly established connection to the British in Egypt, to gather intelligence on their own, and to recruit new spies (recounted in chapter 10). Shortly after they started their trip, Yosef told Sarah that Avshalom had been killed. As he later wrote Aaron, "I revealed to your lovely sister the secret of the disaster. She was very much affected by it but managed to stay strong."

Yosef's estranged wife, Rivka Lishansky, witnessed just how Avshalom's death affected Sarah. Rivka, who was then living with her children at her parents' home in Beit Gan, had a visit from Yosef, whose espionage mission with Sarah took him to the area. The visit appears to have been only a day or two after Yosef broke the terrible news to Sarah. "I wasn't too thrilled to see him," recalled Rivka, "because I didn't know what he expected of me." Yosef brought Rivka and their children to nearby Tzemach, close to the Sea of Galilee, where he had left Sarah. If Yosef thought that Rivka and her children might distract Sarah, he was mistaken. "She kept crying all the time," Rivka remembered of her time in Tzemach with Sarah. Yosef later moved his family to Zichron.[18]

After Sarah returned from her espionage trip with Yosef Lishansky, she wrote another letter to Aaron. She put both letters in the intelligence pouch to be picked by the *Managem*, the one she had written before learning of Avshalom's death and the one written afterward. The first letter had been written by a young woman who, although managing the spy ring well enough, seemed somewhat in over her head. The second letter was different because, after the initial shock of the news of Avshalom's death, Sarah had discovered something about herself that was unexpected and even troubling.

It's hard for me to even mention our great disaster in this letter. It is truly awful and there is no consolation. But one thing I must tell you; I am stronger than iron and cold as a stone. I would never have believed that I could find such strength in myself. At moments I see myself as a sort of inanimate object, for how is it possible to stay indifferent in the face of such an awful sacrifice? Maybe it is the work allotted to me, the duty, to continue the work that our dear one began. Yes, to continue is the only thing I wish for. And vengeance, great vengeance on the wild ones from the desert and even on the cruel Turks.

Sarah then addressed Aaron's request that she board the *Managem* and come to Egypt.

L [evidently the swimmer-courier Liebl Bernstein] told me that you want me to come. I would love to but with the condition that I will return, because under no circumstances can I leave Yosef on his own. We are very reliant on each other in our work and understand how to work together. He is absolutely devoted to the work which for him, too, is a holy and precious duty. He is willing to sacrifice everything in his devotion to the work.

. . . as I am writing, the ship is here again and I need to finish. . . .
Goodbye and a thousand kisses. May they [the English] continue their success because the sacrifice is too great.[19]

From Cairo Aaron wrote his American friend Rabbi Judah Magnes about Avshalom's death and asked him to inform Alexander and Rivka personally. Magnes apparently misunderstood Aaron's request; instead, in May 1917, Alexander and Rivka learned of Avshalom's death from Henrietta Szold, another trustee of the research center (who may have learned about it from Magnes).

At some point Sarah sent Aaron a letter to deliver to their brother and sister in the United States.

The loss is too great. And even if we succeed in our work, and Israel is redeemed through the sacrifice that we made—even then, my dears, I won't be consoled. Perhaps this is the lot of all those who aspire and work for their people and their land; and our dear one set off on his journey with his good will, knowing what danger he was putting himself in. However much we talk and however many tears we shed our hearts will not be lightened. The disaster is truly great so why keep rubbing salt into your wounds.

In a separate note to Rivka, Sarah wrote,

Rivka, my girl, you must be suffering more than all of us but I am with you. . . . I grieve and cry with you over our misfortune.

My girl, you have no idea how close I and your loved one became while being together. I was the only one to whom he could come to pour out his heart, his thoughts and his hopes, and I helped him very much. I encouraged him and raised his spirits and I suffer much from this disaster. But can we complain? And to whom? This is our fate, we will not see our dear one accomplishing great things, although he dreamed and suffered so much throughout his short life. But our ongoing work will always be in the memory and name of its dear founder—Avshalom.[20]

Just how "close" had Sarah and Avshalom become? Sarah's loyalty to her sister seems absolute; moreover, she was a married woman with evident affection for her husband. "Close" could mean only that she and Avshalom shared a comradeship during the difficult months in 1916 while waiting for word from Aaron. And yet, and yet—Avshalom

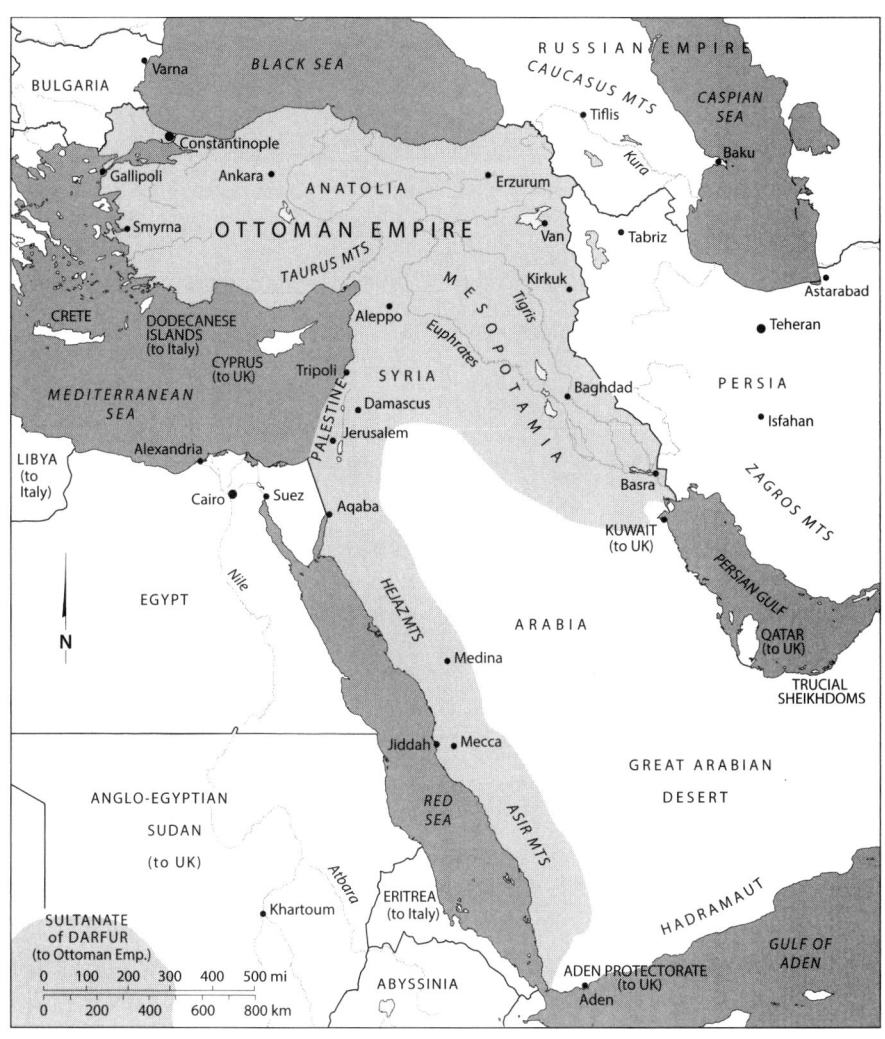

BULGARIA

Varna

BLACK SEA

RUSSIAN EMPIRE

CAUCASUS MTS

Tiflis

CASPIAN SEA

Baku

Constantinople

Gallipoli

Ankara

ANATOLIA

Erzurum

OTTOMAN EMPIRE

Smyrna

Van

Tabriz

Astarabad

TAURUS MTS

Kirkuk

Teheran

CRETE

DODECANESE ISLANDS (to Italy)

Aleppo

M E S O P O T A M I A

CYPRUS (to UK)

Tripoli

SYRIA

Euphrates

Tigris

PERSIA

MEDITERRANEAN SEA

PALESTINE

Damascus

Baghdad

Isfahan

Jerusalem

LIBYA (to Italy)

Alexandria

Basra

ZAGROS MTS

Cairo

Suez

Aqaba

KUWAIT (to UK)

PERSIAN GULF

EGYPT

Nile

HEIAZ MTS

ARABIA

QATAR (to UK)

N

TRUCIAL SHEIKHDOMS

Medina

GREAT ARABIAN DESERT

ANGLO-EGYPTIAN

SUDAN

(to UK)

Jiddah

Mecca

RED SEA

ASIR MTS

SULTANATE of DARFUR (to Ottoman Emp.)

0 100 200 300 400 500 mi

0 200 400 600 800 km

Khartoum

Atbara

ERITREA (to Italy)

ABYSSINIA

HADRAMAUT

GULF OF ADEN

ADEN PROTECTORATE (to UK)

Aden

1. The Ottoman Empire (Geographx and the New Zealand
Ministry of Culture and Heritage).

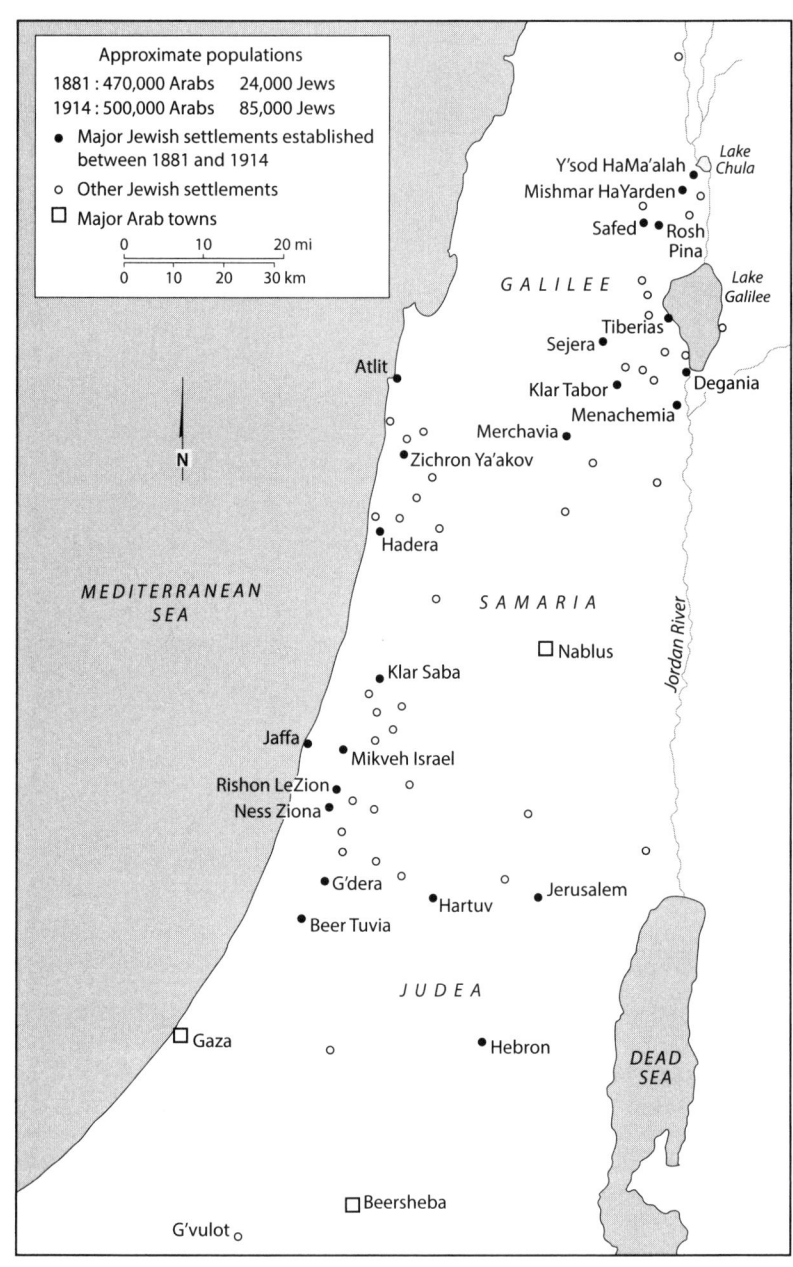

Approximate populations
1881 : 470,000 Arabs   24,000 Jews
1914 : 500,000 Arabs   85,000 Jews
● Major Jewish settlements established
   between 1881 and 1914
○ Other Jewish settlements
□ Major Arab towns

0   10   20 mi
0   10   20   30 km

Lake
Chula

Y'sod HaMa'alah
Mishmar HaYarden
Safed ● ● Rosh
Pina

GALILEE

Lake
Galilee

Tiberias
Sejera
Klar Tabor ●
Merchavia ●
Menachemia

Degania

Atlit

N

Zichron Ya'akov

Hadera

MEDITERRANEAN
SEA

SAMARIA

□ Nablus

Klar Saba

Jaffa ●

Mikveh Israel

Rishon LeZion ●
Ness Ziona ●

Jordan River

● G'dera

Hartuv

● Jerusalem

● Beer Tuvia

JUDEA

□ Gaza

● Hebron

DEAD
SEA

□ Beersheba

G'vulot ○

2. Jewish settlements in prewar Palestine (PASSIA).

3. Rivka, Alexander, and Sarah as children (Beit Aaronsohn Nili Museum Archive).

4. Sarah (Beit Aaronsohn Nili Museum Archive).

5. (*top*) Sarah's wedding in March 1914 (Beit Aaronsohn Nili Museum Archive).

6. (*bottom*) Armenian mother leaning over a dead child (Bain Collection, Library of Congress, LC-USZ62-48100).

7. Aaron Aaronsohn (Beit Aaronsohn Nili Museum Archive).

8. Djemal Pasha and a German officer (Bain Collection,
Library of Congress, LC-DIG-ggbain-18812).

9. Avshalom Feinberg
in Paris before the war
(Beit Aaronsohn Nili
Museum Archive).

10. Rivka Aaronsohn
(Beit Aaronsohn Nili
Museum Archive).

11. Alexander Aaronsohn in a British army uniform
(Beit Aaronsohn Nili Museum Archive).

12. (*above*) Sarah with Yosef Lishansky and Liova Schneersohn in Cairo, 1917 (Beit Aaronsohn Nili Museum Archive).

13. (*opposite top*) Jewish agricultural experiment station in Atlit (Beit Aaronsohn Nili Museum Archive).

14. (*opposite bottom*) Sarah cleaning the coop of the pigeon that went off course, 1917 (Beit Aaronsohn Nili Museum Archive).

15. Aaron's home in Zichron Ya'akov (Beit Aaronsohn Nili Museum Archive; photo by Yael Berkovich).

16. Aaron's bathroom preserved as it was on October 5, 1917 (Beit Aaronsohn Nili Museum Archive; photo by Golan Bar-Or).

17. General Allenby's entrance into Jerusalem, December 1917
(Carpenter Collection, Library of Congress, LC-USZ62-93094).

18. Grave of Avshalom Feinberg with palm tree on
Mount Herzl (photo by Lisanna Wallance).

19. The graves of Sarah (with the Israeli flag) and her mother, Malka, in Zichron Ya'akov (photo by Lisanna Wallance).

20. Rivka Aaronsohn in Aaron's study after the war (Beit Aaronsohn Nili Museum Archive).

and Sarah *had* spent a great deal of time together, it was wartime, they indeed were close, and they were young.

The compass needle points in both directions, so we will never know. The only certainty is that deep bonds of love and devotion—below the surface of Avshalom's poetry and playfulness and flirting—that bound the three of them had been shattered. In a letter to Sarah after her departure for Constantinople in 1914, Avshalom had written: "What connects us more than blood and fellowship is our love, is the habit of being together and the suffering we have shared. These are things that will not die. That's why the absence of one of us is like a little death for the other two."[21]

Rivka's letters to Aaron and Sarah tell of her own "terrible shock" at hearing the news. She asked Aaron for the details of Avshalom's death, explaining that "no matter how hard it will be to bear, do not be afraid for the shock, the heart is bleeding anyway and thus it will continue forever."

After receiving Sarah's letter, Rivka wrote back:

I, of course, thought that I was dreaming when I saw your dear handwriting and you can imagine what an impression your letter has made on me. Our lot today is obviously nothing but a sea of tears. What can one say at all?! You know, you can understand, as you are the only person who can see deep into my heart. You wonder how I can go on living at all, don't you? I have no idea myself. People say that I bare my sorrow heroically, but the truth is that I am weak. How come I didn't lose my mind? Didn't lose my speech? That my hair didn't turn all white? How is it that I didn't become sick and lay down, not even for a single day?!

. . . I cannot promise that I will be able to keep up my miraculous heroism when I come back home and see with my own eyes all the miserable truth of this horrible tragedy.

How is it possible that I can be home and Avshalom is not?! Why isn't he coming? I will wait and wait and grow sad and angry with impatience and he will never appear, he will never come, how can it be?! How can the light keep shining over the earth when he is not here? How and again how? . . .

A thousand kisses Sarati. I will write more.[22]

Avshalom Feinberg had no gravestone or funeral. A letter that Avshalom had written to Sarah in September 1914, however, contains a passage that could serve as his requiem. In the letter Avshalom described for Sarah a nighttime visit that he and Rivka had recently made to the Zichron cemetery to lay a wreath at the grave of Rivka and Sarah's mother, Malka Aaronsohn. "I wanted to split the wreath in two: one piece for Sarah," but "Ubi promised that sharing the thought with everybody is enough." He and Rivka had sat among the rows of white graves, encircled by the silhouettes of cedar and eucalyptus trees, as the stars flickered in the night sky. "We sat without a sound, surrounded by a great silence."

> And the heart sang its Yizkor [memorial prayer]. Bereavement of pain and longing, of ruins and ashes, remembrance of the dead and the missing, of all those who have left and took a part of our being, of all those who were and remain blood of our blood and a part of our soul, those who went away and left us incomplete, pledged to our mourning, slaves to our memory, that every day plunders a piece of our heart, a drop of our blood, a bit of life.
>
> The flow of the Bereavement washed over us and the heart, that knows all the secrets of the magic of necromancy, resurrected everyone from their graves and brought them back from great distances.

Avshalom ended the letter, "I thought a lot of you, my dear soul. I would love to try and connect with you a little, to submerge and dive deep—even if for just a moment—in your memory."[23]

10

Black Nights

The *Managem* only came on moonless nights, so the Nili spies had to make their way in the dark from the research station to the beach to greet the *Managem's* surfboat. Lanterns or flashlights were out of the question, but neither were they necessary. The Nili spies knew the terrain on the way to the beach, including the wadi with steep banks, well enough that they could have walked the route blindfolded in the daytime. The riskiest part was crossing the coast road to Haifa that the locally based Turkish soldiers patrolled. Nili had a man in Zichron who plied the Turkish soldiers with drinks and engaged them in card games on nights when the *Managem* was expected, but sometimes the soldiers still left and went on patrol. The spies also had to be watchful for the caravans of camels and their Arab herders that passed along the coast road from time to time.

Crossing at night from the research station to the beach was sometimes a strange affair. One night as Sarah and two men made their way to the beach, a cow charged out of the blackness, hurtled past them, more sensed than seen, and then disappeared into the dark. "If a cow has escaped," whispered Sarah, "a man is running after it." The three spies hid behind a rock. An Arab shortly ran by, disappeared, and then reappeared with the cow. The Nili spies had to wait behind the rock while the Arab relieved himself on the other side. The cow took advantage of its master's momentary distraction and ran off into the darkness, again chased by the Arab. The Nili spies continued to the beach.

On another night Sarah and her companions lay on the bluff overlooking the beach and waited for the surfboat. The sea was calm, the night breezeless, and sound carried a long distance. The spies heard Arab guards talking in a watermelon field about a hundred yards to their left. A few minutes after nine o'clock, a boat approached the beach. Three silhouettes got out of the boat, waded to the beach, and began walking in Sarah's direction. One stepped on a dry branch, making a sharp cracking sound that could be heard in the watermelon field. The Arabs grabbed their guns and began firing in the direction of the sound.

On the beach the three British sailors dropped to the ground. After a while the Arabs stopped firing, satisfied that it was a false alarm or that they had scared off any intruders. The British sailors lay motionless, then rose, and began running back to the boat. Sarah chased after them, further frightening the sailors and causing them to run harder. She managed to catch up with them before they pushed off from the shore.[1]

For the Nili spies, a beach rendezvous—that is, when the surfboat got to the shore or close to it—was a tense but gratifying event: the rapid exchange of greetings; the questions from the British about the Nili spies' safety and, from the spies, questions about Aaron's well-being; the handover of the intelligence bag filled with reports and letters; and the sailors passing back a pouch with letters of instruction from Aaron, newspapers, and, in the summer of 1917, provisions and gold for the relief of the beleaguered *yishuv* and for bribes. The sailors then climbed onto or swam out to the boat, which disappeared into blackness. Between March and September 1917, the British spy ship made nine rendezvous with the Nili spies at Atlit to pick up Sarah's intelligence reports.[2]

The espionage roles played by Sarah and Aaron, according to military intelligence historian Yigal Sheffy, were "optimal" in that Aaron, who understood both the needs of the British and the capabilities of the Nili spies, was the British "permanent liaison officer" to Nili, whose leader was his own sister. But Aaron had no influence over Sarah's day-to-day decision making. By the middle of the summer of 1917, word reached Aaron that, despite his instructions, Sarah was going to the beach on the nights the *Managem* was expected. Aaron reprimanded her, albeit affectionately, in a letter:

I want to smack your face for going to the shore to wait for Raphael [Aboulafia, a Nili spy on the *Managem*], but at the same time I want to kiss you for doing it. You are a brave person. Have you heard of the Arab Subayeh tribe? They owe their name to one heroine from their tribe whose name was Sabha. And until this day when someone from the tribe wants to encourage himself or his brothers he calls out: "I am your brother, oh Sabha my sister." Do you want us to be the "tribe of Sarati," "I am your brother, oh Sarah."[3]

Sarah wrote in response, "You amuse me, Arale, when you write that my face should be slapped because I go to greet visitors from the sea. Do you really think this is bravery?"[4]

On one of its first visits, the *Managem*'s swimmer delivered a letter from Aaron instructing Sarah that Yosef Lishansky should function as her deputy. In some respects it was a sensible decision because Yosef had courage and physical strength, spoke fluent Arabic, had more contacts in Palestine than the other Nili members, was experienced in paying baksheesh, was an expert at disguises, and could go places where a woman alone would attract attention. But the disadvantages were that important elements of the Jewish community, especially the settlements' self-defense organization Ha-Shomer, were antagonistic to Yosef and that he had a sometimes volatile temperament. In his letter, Aaron also listed the intelligence that the British needed, including the identification of Turkish army units and their bases, the movement of the units and troop and supply trains, and the location of heavy armaments. As important, he wrote, Sarah must report on the condition of the yishuv.[5]

In her letter in early March to Aaron expressing concern about Avshalom, Sarah had written, "As far as work is concerned, rest assured that everything will be done properly. Tuvion [the code name for Yosef] is persistent in his work, he is brave and optimistic, and I believe that this is what really matters. I try to help him as much as I can, and so does our brother [Zvi] and even our old father. Besides our family, he has his own people who are loyal to him and will help him."[6]

For her March espionage trip through Palestine with Yosef, during which she learned of Avshalom's death, Sarah wore a blue suit with a white blouse, a young pleasant-looking woman enjoying a carriage ride through the countryside. She kept careful notes of her observations, from crop conditions to Turkish troop movements. "The yield of corn between Zichron and Atlit is small because the heavy rains delayed sowing. In the Station itself the yield is very good. On the way from Atlit to Haifa, we met the Arab military coast guards, patrolling, not on the coast but on the highway."

In Nazareth Sarah and Yosef discovered a large Turkish arms dump in the courtyard of the convent of the Carmelite sisters, the Turkish soldiers in Nazareth were starving because the officers stole their rations, and, in turn, the pack animals were hungry because the soldiers stole the animals' food provisions. The spies went on to Beit Gan, southwest of the Sea of Galilee (and spent time with Rivka Lishansky and her children in Tzemach), to recruit spies. Yosef failed to win any recruits, even among his friends. The perspective of Jews in this region was that espionage was dangerous and that relations with the Turks could be managed. Why revolt against an empire when it can be bribed?[7]

The two had more success in Afula, to the east of Mount Carmel. In the Jezreel Valley, a fertile land with grand vistas, Afula was a key railway junction. Soldiers and munitions from Constantinople, Aleppo, and Damascus passed through the area on their way south and to the front at the Gaza–Beersheba line. Much of the intelligence gathering in the war involved watching trains to learn about the movement of armies and to identify targets for aerial bombardment. Train reporting in Europe was done from buildings, including homes or cottages, along the train tracks.[8]

In Afula Sarah contacted Moshe Neumann, a Jewish doctor serving in the Turkish army who worked in a twenty-bed military hospital adjacent to the train station. His responsibilities included giving medical examinations to Turkish soldiers on trains arriving from the north as a preventative measure against the spread of cholera, among other contagious illnesses. Trains had to stop two hundred meters from the station and were permitted to enter Afula only after Dr. Neumann completed his examinations.[9]

The doctor was a cautious man. He was a bachelor in his early thirties and was devoted to his mother, who accompanied him wherever the Turkish army sent him. He was also a friend of Aaron Aaronsohn, who had advised Sarah that Dr. Neumann's post was ideal for intelligence gathering. When Sarah gave Dr. Neumann a note from Aaron, he read it and looked at Sarah in dismay.

"But I'll be playing with my head if I do this!"

"You see, my head also sits firmly on my shoulders but I am endangering it all the time. If you call yourself a man, you should be prepared to do the same."

Dr. Neumann, whose political sympathies were with the British, did become a Nili spy; after a while, he even seemed to be enjoying himself. He prepared reports in Hebrew for Sarah, and his brother Mendel took them by horseback to Atlit every ten days. Neumann's first report provided a geographical description of Afula, including the locations of military installations and warehouses, and a short history of military activities since Dr. Neumann had arrived in Afula at the beginning of 1917.

Dr. Neumann invited Turkish officers to a café or his home. From them he learned the names of senior Turkish commanders, the numbers of active soldiers, the quantities of munitions available, and the health of the army's animals. Sometimes Dr. Neumann would declare one or two Turkish soldiers to be ill and send them to the hospital, where he would talk to them.[10]

Dr. Neumann's reports were detailed—he made notes during the day on a cigarette box or on the palm of his hand and then wrote the account at night—and even contained a description of the physical condition of the Turkish soldiers. In Battalion 137, which had just arrived from Lebanon, for example, the men were short statured and weak looking; all but one were barefoot.[11]

Dr. Neumann asked Turkish authorities to provide a daily schedule of incoming and departing trains so that he could more efficiently organize his days and evenings around the medical examinations; then he delivered the schedule to Sarah. Dr. Neumann reported the identification numbers of Turkish units that may have been unknown to the British and his conversations with German officers and pilots (Neumann spoke fluent German). At Aaron's request he also reported the railway line gauges so that the British might use that gauge in building their tracks and eventually run their trains on the Turkish tracks all the way to Damascus. While Dr. Neumann was a Nili spy in Afula, no British planes attacked the town.

British prisoners of war who came through Afula were given special attention by Dr. Neumann, who sometimes obtained permission to take them home for a meal. He passed along the officers' names to Sarah for her to send to the British. Important personages also came through Afula, including Enver Pasha and Djemal Pasha. Once Djemal Pasha, who was impressed by Dr. Neumann's work, provided him with a leave so he could visit Jerusalem. Djemal served Dr. Neumann coffee and gave him cigarettes. The two men talked politics.[12]

Dr. Neumann's most important intelligence would prove to be the number and capability of the German planes transported on the trains to the Gaza–Beersheba front. In one instance, he talked with a pilot and two German mechanics who were traveling on a train from Damascus that was carrying an airplane. They boasted to Dr. Neumann of the plane's characteristics, including its flying speed and the firing velocity of its machine gun. Dr. Neumann reported to Sarah what he learned about the planes that came through Afula.[13]

After the meeting with Dr. Neumann, Sarah and Yosef went to Jerusalem, where they stayed at the Hotel Fast, one of Jerusalem's best and a favorite of German officers. Yosef heard one officer talk about the number of German soldiers in Palestine. Sarah spent her time in the hotel lounge, seemingly engrossed in writing letters. She was actually writing notes of the conversations among the young German officers, at least as much as her Yiddish and more limited German allowed her to understand. Sarah later reported to Aaron, "The Germans were previously informed by Bedouin spies that the English had an army of about 100,000 men in the South, and now that they've made a count by aeroplane, they've decided that the English haven't more than 50,000 there."

In Jerusalem a Turkish army engineer who was also a Nili spy gave Sarah a Jerusalem city map on which he had marked the location of Turkish fortifications. In Sarah's report to Aaron, she enclosed the map.

I will get some more maps from him, and from other places, which will be very interesting and useful to you. We have also contacted another man, very important in the [Turkish] government, and he is prepared to work for us without getting any reward. The population [in Jerusalem] is impoverished and dispirited. Everyone here says that if the English really wanted to come, they would have come long ago. They are certain they won't come now.[14]

Yosef and Sarah stopped in Rishon LeZion to pick up information from Nili spy Naaman Belkind, who was responsible for Nili's espionage in southern Palestine. In addition to intelligence reports, Belkind gave Sarah and Yosef a letter to deliver to his cousin Avshalom Feinberg.

The issue Sarah faced was whether to tell her spies such as Belkind that Avshalom Feinberg was dead. Aaron had considered Liova Schneersohn stoic enough to bear the news, but that might not have been true for the other Nili members, many of whom were Avshalom's friends or relatives. Sarah believed that apart from the few who already knew, the Nili spies must not learn what had happened to Avshalom in the desert, lest it badly demoralize them.

Sarah concocted a story for the Nili spies that Avshalom Feinberg was now in England, training to be a pilot, and that he had no time to write. Yosef told the same story to Naaman, who disliked Yosef because he appeared to be usurping Avshalom's leadership of the spy ring. The pilot story left Belkind unsatisfied, but the deception was aided by his overwhelming preference, like that of the other Nili spies, to believe that Avshalom was alive.

As noted previously, Aaron Aaronsohn had lied his way from Palestine to Denmark, but that only involved deceiving Ottoman and German officials. He could not bear to lie to those he was close to; so driven by his conscience to tell the American trustees of the research station the truth about his activities in "The Confession," Aaron had jeopardized everyone connected to his spy network. Sarah, however, did not hesitate and deceived those closest to her about the death of the man who had mattered the most to all of them. While Aaron was much older, more experienced in the ways of the world, and seemingly tougher, with his abrasive, sometimes bullying personality, Sarah better understood espionage.

Belkind introduced Sarah and Yosef to Avshalom Fein, a Nili recruiting prospect who had heard about Sarah. Fein, then in his early twenties, had been born in Rishon LeZion. His mother had died when he was young, and then his father had committed suicide. At age thirteen he was taken in by the Belkind family and grew up with Naaman Belkind and his brother, Eitan (also a Nili spy). Fein was a neatly groomed young man with a thin nose and a fragile, troubled look in his eyes.

The prospect of meeting Sarah had left Fein trembling at the knees. "I saw a blonde woman, pretty, tall and gentle," he recalled later of his first sight of Sarah.

"He is one of the boys prepared to make sacrifices," Naaman Belkind told Sarah. "He can be depended upon."

"Good. We'll make him work hard."

Fein was put to work as a courier between Sarah and Belkind. Then Sarah and Yosef returned to Atlit and prepared a lengthy intelligence report.[15]

On March 27 the *Managem* picked up the report, which included Dr. Neumann's information about the Turkish airplanes. On board the *Managem* Liova Schneersohn translated Sarah's report into English. It was then sent by wireless radio to Cairo, likely during the ship's stop at Cyprus, where a British base had a wireless station for sending urgent field reports. The next day Aaron, Captain Edmond, and other British officers reviewed the report. Despite some "imprecisions," Aaron wrote in his diary, "they were delighted with the reports." The officers asked him "to write a note 'and put it strongly' on the Turkish lines of retreat in Palestine and how the aviators must worry them." The "note" was meant for the Egyptian Expeditionary Force commanders.[16]

The "aviators must worry them" evidently referred to the report from Dr. Neumann about the advanced airplanes heading to the Gaza–Beersheba front on Turkish trains. On March 30 an entry was made in the British "War Diary or Intelligence Summary," a near-daily summary of raw intelligence from field agents, wireless intercepts, and airplane reconnaissance from around the Middle East. This entry read: "Agent from Afuleh reports that, between March 11 and March 18, the follow[ing] moved south . . . 4 aeroplanes (12 more expected)."[17]

On March 31 the "General Officer Commanding-in-Chief, Egypt," General Murray, sent a dispatch to the British War Office. The dispatch stated that based on "reliable information," Turkish forces on the Palestine front were about to receive more advanced airplanes, which Nili or the British misidentified as the Halberstadt (it was actually the Rumpler, which had been highly effective on the western front). The dispatch "most strongly" emphasized that, with all due respect to the British planes on hand, advanced aircraft were urgently needed:

> 10 of our latest type of machine [must] be dispatched to Egypt at once. Experience in recent fighting has shown clearly that our present aeroplanes even when fought as they have been with extreme gallantry are nothing like a match for the Halberstadt. It is found, moreover, that the Martinsyde type which is good enough in a cold climate and which is at present our best machine, over-heats very rapidly in such a hot climate as this and cannot deal with the Halberstadt on anything like equal terms. I cannot urge too strongly that in my opinion the provision of 10 of the latest type of aeroplane now asked for is essential to the success of my future operations as we shall certainly lose supremacy in the air if these are not sent.[18]

As Nili's espionage intensified, so did the opposition to Sarah within the *yishuv*. Residents in Zichron and Atlit and members of the self-defense organization Ha-Shomer suspected that Sarah was engaged in secret work, which could only mean that the British were involved. The signs included Aaron's disappearance from Palestine, Sarah's lengthy trip in the research station's carriage, young men visiting her father's home but staying only for a short time, and the lights being lit in the Atlit research station on some nights but not on others.

Ha-Shomer began campaigning in the *yishuv* to "root out the evil" of Nili. The bulletin of the Hapoel Hatza'ir (Young Worker) labor party issued a veiled warning: "Our realistic policy in the existing circumstances is one of absolute civic loyalty, and any action outside of these limits must be seen as an attack on the existence of the community."[19]

Sarah wrote to Aaron that, despite the opposition within the *yishuv* to Nili, "as you can see, we keep on working and the danger is not very great. Some say the rumors have reached the government, but I don't believe it is so."[20]

11

What I Have Done, I Have Done Purely for My People and My Country

Liova Schneersohn was lonely in Port Said. He was in Egypt as Aaron's assistant, but Aaron was spending his days with British officers. Liova therefore had ample time to dream of Sarah.

Unfortunately for Liova, the object of his romantic ardor was a married woman; for all he knew, she had been the lover of his late best friend, Avshalom; and whether she had reciprocal romantic feelings for Liova wasn't clear. Liova's loneliness was aggravated by the cold and aloof attitude of many of the British officers. At one point he wrote Aaron that the British "don't understand us. . . . We are doing our work for them—but is it meant only to be for them?" Aaron didn't even bother to respond.

Through the swimmer-courier Liebl Bernstein, Aaron had asked Sarah to come to Cairo. She had agreed but, perhaps sensing that Aaron had ulterior motives, insisted that she must be free to return to Palestine ("I would love to but with the condition that I will return"). Aaron told Liova to sail on the *Managem* to Atlit and bring Sarah to Egypt, a heaven-sent errand for the young man.

On April 14, 1917, the *Managem* left Port Said with Liova on board. At nine o'clock the next morning Liova could make out houses in Zichron through his binoculars. At two o'clock in the afternoon the ship approached Atlit. "We don't see any signals," he wrote in his diary. "What happened? We don't see anybody."

The *Managem* went up the coast to Haifa, reversed course, and, at 9:00 p.m. with the ship's lights extinguished, approached Atlit. The sea was calm, so the surfboat took Liova and Liebl Bernstein all the way to the shore but landed them in the wrong location. They headed north, walking with difficulty because their route took them through rocky terrain. The night was warm and pleasant, though, and Liova heard frogs croaking. Liova and Liebl crossed the coastal road and hurried to the research station, where a light was on.

"Who's there on the balcony? Yosef?"

"Yes, yes."

"Hurry up then. What's happened to you? Where's Sarah? Why didn't you give the signals?"

The questions and answers got lost in everyone's excitement. They left the station, with Liova leading and Sarah, Yosef, and Liebl walking behind in single file.

At the beach Liova flashed a signal into the darkness, while the others lay on the sand. He sensed the presence of the surfboat before he could see it. When the boat reached the beach, the British urged the Jews to be quick because two submarines were in the area. Liova, carrying the bag of intelligence reports, got into the boat, and the others followed.

Yosef Lishansky was supposed to stay behind. Aaron's instructions had been clear: only Sarah should come to Cairo because Yosef was needed to run Nili in her absence. But Yosef had pleaded with Sarah to be allowed to go with her, and she finally agreed. They were going to be gone only three days; Yosef had worked hard, with Sarah praising him in her letters to Aaron; and the trip to Cairo was a well-deserved reward. If left behind, Yosef would be crestfallen and resentful, which could affect his work. In effect, Sarah had to choose between angering Aaron or upsetting Yosef. To make her decision more difficult, Yosef, like Liova Schneersohn, was in love with Sarah. Bringing Yosef to Cairo would put together two rivals for her affection, but leaving Yosef behind in Palestine might only inflame an already jealous imagination.[1]

The *Managem* did not proceed directly to Port Said but first made a stop at the British base on Cyprus, where the Jewish spies boarded a different ship, the *Kosseir*, which reached Port Said on April 19. Sarah came down the gangway first. She and Aaron, who had arrived by train from Cairo, stood looking at each other on the wharf. To Aaron, Sarah appeared pale if not ill. "Are you well, Sarati?" Brother and sister had last seen each other ten months earlier. In the interim, not only had they lost Avshalom, but also their lives had changed beyond recognition. Aaron was now playing a highly influential role in British intelligence, and Sarah was in charge of a spy ring.[2]

Behind Sarah was Yosef Lishansky and Liova Schneersohn. Aaron was not surprised at Yosef's presence because the *Managem* had informed Captain Edmonds via the Cyprus wireless station that Lishansky was aboard. "I felt that as long as there was a chance of continuing the work, Y. had no right to come here," he wrote in his diary before going to Port Said. But being forewarned had afforded Aaron more time to stoke his temper. Aaron, Sarah, Yosef, and Liova took the noon train to Cairo. During the trip, Aaron angrily accused Lishansky of deserting his post.

If the three wanted conversation topics to distract from the tension between Aaron and Yosef, they were certainly available. Recent wartime events would change the course, not just of the war, but of the twentieth century.[3]

By 1917 after nearly two and half years of war, the belligerents were in varying stages of domestic stress and turmoil, but Russia, which had suffered horrendous casualties, was in extremis. On March 15 in the face of nationwide strikes and mutinies in the Russian army and navy, Czar Nicholas II of Russia abdicated, and the three-hundred-year-old Romanov dynasty came to an end. The daughter of the British ambassador in Petrograd (now Saint Petersburg) reported a conversation between two Russian soldiers just before the czar's abdication: "What we want is a Republic." "Yes. A Republic, but we must have a good Tsar at the head of it!" In the end, Russia had neither a republic nor a good czar. In November 1917 the Bolsheviks, led by Vladimir Lenin, seized power and took Russia out of the war the following year.[4]

On April 6, 1917, the United States had declared war against Germany due to its unrestricted warfare against U.S. merchant ships and to the disclosure of the so-called Zimmermann telegram. The Germans gambled that even if the United States entered the war on the side of Britain and France, submarine warfare against U.S. ships carrying critical civilian and military goods across the Atlantic to Britain would be so crippling that Britain would have to sue for peace before the U.S.

military's weight could have an impact on the western front. In fact, Britain held on, and the following year, or much earlier than the German generals had calculated, the United States had a sizable army in France that turned the tide against Germany.[5]

In a war of blunders and miscalculations, the Zimmermann telegram deserves a special place. The telegram was a secret, coded cable from Arthur Zimmermann, the German foreign secretary, to the German minister to Mexico. In the event the United States entered the war, the minister was to propose a military alliance with Mexico against the United States. The minister was further instructed to promise Mexico "generous financial support" and "an understanding on our part that Mexico is to reconquer the Lost Territory in Texas, New Mexico and Arizona." The details of how to "reconquer" those states would be left to the Mexicans.[6]

British intelligence intercepted the Zimmermann telegram, decrypted it, and gave the telegram to President Woodrow Wilson. The Zimmermann telegram infuriated President Wilson and, when made public, the American people and removed any lingering doubt over going to war against Germany. The United States did not regard itself as a member of the Entente but only as a power associated with England and France; thus, it did not declare war on, or fight against, the Ottoman Empire. But the prospect of fresh American soldiers and a steady supply of U.S. arms in Europe gave the British more flexibility to pursue their ambitions in the Middle East.[7]

Another consequential event, including for Sarah, was the accession at the end of 1916 of a new British prime minister, David Lloyd George. With the western front still in a stalemate, Lloyd George wanted to boost British morale after the appalling losses at the Somme and elsewhere by capturing Jerusalem centuries after the Crusaders had been driven out. His generals, however, viewed the western front as the critical theater and were reluctant to expend military resources on an operation in Palestine.

The War Cabinet in London reassessed its strategy in Palestine but could only come up with a compromise. General Murray received instructions that while the objective was still Palestine, for the present he should stay on the defensive in the Sinai. But by the time the directive reached him, Murray had already pushed into Palestine and, on January 9, 1917, had captured the town of Rafah, which was in an indefensible location. Faced with a choice of withdrawing from a town that he had just captured or pressing forward to keep control of Rafah, Murray chose the latter. Not having much choice, the War Cabinet went along.

A battle plan was drawn up for an attack on Gaza that required taking the town before nightfall. Otherwise, British forces would have to retreat to the railhead fifteen miles away at Khan Yunis to replenish their water supply. From the British point of view, the omens were favorable. On March 11, 1917, British troops had entered Baghdad, winning a major British victory after a series of damaging defeats on the Ottoman front. In a proclamation that rings familiar today, the British assured the people of Baghdad that the British armies were not there as conquerors or enemies but "as liberators."[8]

Two weeks after the fall of Baghdad, in the early morning hours of March 26, British forces attacked Gaza with cavalry and infantry. The infantry force moved into position along the coastal road to Gaza. Thousands of marching men were joined by blue-gowned camel drivers and ambulance units atop both wagons, which were emblazoned with red crosses and drawn by six or eight mules, and camels with empty stretchers slung on their sides, below their humps—all to the accompaniment of Scottish bagpipes and the blathering gurgles of hundreds of camels.

The Ottomans concentrated on the infantry attack, allowing the mounted brigades to close in on Gaza. But a communications breakdown left the British commanders unaware that they were on the verge of victory. Fearful that their forces would not take Gaza by nightfall and would run short of water and ammunition, the British generals called for a retreat, to the amazement of soldiers on both sides.

General Murray, a cultured man who lacked the stamina for the stress of command, reported to his London superiors that he had "inflicted very heavy losses" on the Turks without directly acknowledging that, in fact, he had lost the battle. The London papers published Murray's claim that Turkish casualties were between 6,000 and 7,000 men when they were actually less than 2,500. In Cairo Aaron heard rumors of a "great victory over the Turks in Palestine." Shortly after the battle, however, a Turkish plane dropped a message that was picked up by a New Zealand officer. "You beat us at communiqués but we beat you at Gaza."[9]

Despite the setback, Lloyd George was still resolved to take Jerusalem. On March 30 the War Cabinet cabled General Murray that his objective was "the defeat of the Turks south of Jerusalem and the occupation of Jerusalem." Murray responded that taking Jerusalem meant "heavy fighting with considerable losses." The War Cabinet instructed Murray that he was to pursue the "enemy with all the rapidity compatible with the necessary progress of [his] communications," and his present force would have to suffice without reinforcements.[10]

With that less-than-all out support from the War Cabinet, Murray then ran the same play again and attacked the same Turkish fortifications at Gaza. His unimaginative tactics at the Second Battle of Gaza were even more reminiscent of those used in the western front than during the first battle. General Murray planned a set-piece frontal assault but with a reduced role for mounted forces, even though they had led most of the assaults since the Battle of Romani in August 1916. He even managed to procure eight tanks and four thousand rounds of gas-tipped artillery, the first use of tanks and poison gas in the Sinai campaign.

The Turks were prepared. After the First Battle of Gaza, Djemal Pasha had built up the trench and earthwork fortifications between Gaza and Beersheba. "I decided to hold that front and prevent the English from breaking through at any cost." The battle began on April 17, 1917, with a British naval bombardment from the Mediterranean and from artillery positioned outside Gaza. Even though the Turkish defenders had no gas masks, the gas shells were ineffective, and the bombardment, as often had been the case in battles on the western front, did not appreciably degrade the Turkish defenses. When British troops advanced, they came under heavy rifle and machine gun fire. The tanks advanced with them, but the Turks held their ground. By sundown on April 19, the day that Sarah arrived at Port Said, the British had suffered 6,444 casualties, or three times that of the Turks, and the battle was over.

By the end of June, Murray was gone, replaced by Gen. Sir Edmund (The Bull) Allenby, an aggressive and sometimes hot-tempered commander. The prime minister unequivocally instructed Allenby to take Jerusalem by Christmas as a present for the war-weary British public. At the end of July while planning a new offensive to break through the Gaza–Beersheba line, Allenby received a telegram informing him that his nineteen-year-old son, Michael, fighting on the western front, had died five hours after a shell splinter hit him in the head. Allenby's new colleagues in Palestine found him a "pitiable figure" in his grief. The war spared no one.[11]

On April 19 Aaron, Sarah, Yosef, and Liova arrived in Cairo. Sarah and Aaron went to the Grand Continental Hotel while Yosef and Liova checked in to the Metropole Hotel. They met in the evening, and once they were alone, Aaron erupted at Yosef for coming to Egypt and slammed a table so hard with one hand that he broke the glass on his wristwatch. Yosef appeared crushed. Sarah did not intervene because Aaron's rages were forces of nature, violent storms that had to be waited out.

The next morning Liova Schneersohn came to the hotel with flowers for Sarah and found both Aaron and Yosef in glum spirits, unable to speak to one another. Late in the day Sarah, Yosef, and Liova went to the cinema. After this much-needed distraction, they returned to their respective hotels, as Liova wrote in his diary, "quite relieved." Aaron, concerned about Sarah's health, arranged for Dr. Naftali Weitz, a friend in Cairo, to examine her. Dr. Weitz told Sarah to avoid strenuous activities.[12]

Sarah and Yosef planned to stay in Cairo for three days and then return on the *Managem* while the night sky at Atlit was still moonless. Aaron thought Sarah should stay in Cairo permanently because it was too dangerous for her to return to Palestine. When brother and sister weren't going over intelligence reports, Aaron had what he called long chats with Sarah, trying to persuade, if not pressure, her to remain in Cairo. Aaron evidently assumed that Sarah was the same young woman he had left behind in Palestine when he set out for England. Sarah had deferred to Aaron's leadership then.

That had changed. "She insisted that she could not stay here," Aaron wrote in his dairy. "Her duty called her to where danger existed, and I should not try and prevent her from going back. She is so simple in her greatness—and so unconscious of the nobility of her soul."[13]

Aaron took Sarah to Groppi's Tea Garden, located between the Grand Continental Hotel and the Savoy Hotel. Joining them was Peretz Pascal, an orange grower from Petah Tikva whose parents had come to Palestine with the Aaronsohns. Pascal had left at the start of the war and now resided in Egypt, although his family was still in Palestine. He was Aaron's age and a close friend and confidant. Groppi's Tea Garden was a favorite of British officers in Cairo. T. E. Lawrence liked to stop there for an iced coffee and chocolate. While Sarah had tea with Aaron and Pascal, British officers came in, whispered to one another, and perhaps found an excuse to wander near her table.[14]

Word had gotten around that Aaron's "plucky sister," as Maj. Wyndham Deedes called her, was at Groppi's. Since the receipt of the first pouch of Nili intelligence reports, British officers had gone out of their way to compliment Aaron on the high quality of his sister's espionage work. Deedes, for example, told Aaron that "we have never received such fine reports as those sent in by your organization." Although not mentioned in Aaron's diary, the British officers may also have been intrigued that one of their best agents was a woman.

Sarah's presence had roughly the same effect as though a famous stage personality had walked into Groppi's. But since it was a public venue, they were intelligence officers, and Sarah was their spy, the men's admiration was discreet. No one at Sarah's table even noticed the star-struck intelligence officers. Aaron wrote in his diary that night, "[Captain] McCury told me that he and others had come to look at Sarati while she, Pascal and I were having tea at Groppi's. People always like to see a heroine."[15]

Aaron did not give up and kept trying to persuade Sarah to remain in Cairo. In fact, he went to such lengths that he provoked Sarah into a rare outburst. The incident occurred when Sarah, Aaron, and Peretz

Pascal were in the lounge of the Grand Continental Hotel. Captain Edmonds, Aaron's liaison, came over to them.

Edmonds looked pointedly at Pascal.

"Sir, we can speak in Pascal's presence," said Aaron, "he is one of us and we have no secrets from him."

"Madame," Captain Edmonds said in French, "the High Command expresses their gratitude for the service you did England. But it's because of this service that they advise you not to return to Palestine. You are welcome here in Egypt and can stay as long as you like. What you did until now is more than enough." Aaron must have put Captain Edmonds up to this because the British officer, on his own initiative, would never have approached Sarah, who reported only to Aaron.

Sarah responded in French, speaking as much to Aaron as to Captain Edmonds.

Tell your superiors that I am grateful for their feelings and yet my only concern is with saving my Jewish brothers and sisters in the land of Israel. Had it not been for them, do you think I would be working for you? Despite the dangers, I have decided to return, and if mistakes were made and secrets were revealed, I am responsible for those and only I shall pay and not others. If you are thankful to me, provide me with the means to go back; if they are not provided, I shall seek them by myself. If I can't do it on my own, I will take my own life.

Perhaps Sarah's last threat was a calculated rhetorical flourish, albeit a somewhat ruthless one, intended to end the discussion of whether she should stay in Egypt. But it's also possible that she meant it. If so, a serious threat of suicide might hint of impulses that Sarah, despite her discipline, could not fully control, at least when someone attempted to restrain her from doing what she saw as a sacred duty. "A shiver ran down our spines," Pascal recalled later. "Should we stop her? Should we force her to stay? Is there now anything on earth that can stop her from going back?"[16]

Aaron was undeterred and kept pressuring Sarah to remain but without success. In fact, his efforts only led to tension between the two.

In the end Aaron simply succeeded in establishing that Sarah's will was stronger than his. "After a long, painful argument, I was forced to accept Sarati's sacrifice. How bravely and calmly she offered herself!"

A bright moment during Sarah's stay in Cairo came when Aaron managed to obtain a British commitment to provide relief funds for the Jewish community in Palestine. The money would have the additional benefit of restoring Aaron's stature and authority in the face of the community's opposition to Nili. "When I left the country I destroyed my influence (ruined my strength)," Aaron had told several British officers (as he described it in his diary). "It was natural that now—considering the danger on one side [the *yishuv*] and the very few tangible results on the other [meaning by the British and Nili]—they should oppose that our organization continue its work."[17]

Just before Sarah's departure, Captain Edmonds came to the hotel to pay his respects. Courage in the British army was hardly a rare commodity in that war. On the western front, British soldiers had been charging German machine guns, which cut them down like scythed wheat; had been asphyxiated in poison gas attacks; and had endured the mud-filled trenches that stretched from the English Channel to the Swiss border and cut a blood-seeping gash in the heart of Europe. The British intelligence officers in Cairo, including Woolley the archeologist, now in a Turkish prison camp after barely getting off a sinking ship, also took their own risks. Lawrence had spent part of March 1917 in the desert in what is now Saudi Arabia with the forces of the Arab Revolt, laying explosives under Turkish train tracks.[18]

Any intelligence officer, of course, finds ways to express appreciation for an agent's work in dangerous circumstances. Nonetheless, Captain Edmonds seemed to feel that Sarah was exposing herself to risks that, even by British standards, were extreme. As Aaron noted, "Edm. called to see Sarati in the afternoon. He admired her exceedingly."[19]

At 5:30 a.m. on April 22, three days after Sarah had arrived in Egypt, Aaron woke up his sister, and they went to the Cairo train station, where Yosef waited for them. Liova Schneersohn either met them at the train station or in Port Said, because he was going as far as Atlit as Aaron's representative on the *Managem* but then returning with the ship to Egypt. On the train trip to Port Said, Aaron had "heated arguments with Yosef who is wild and obstinate." But by the time they reached Port Said, the two men had calmed down.

That evening Aaron was even optimistic. "With Sarati to guide him [Yosef] will be all right. I kissed them goodbye at 4 o'clock and left them. They were in very good humor. The 6:30 train brought me back to Cairo around midnight."[20]

At some point, Liova began writing in a notebook that he titled "To Sarah." His writing was a mix of Chabad mysticism, Russian melodramatics, and the spirit of innovation in the sense that Liova wanted to remake Sarah because, in his mind, she had fallen from grace. He began by worshipping Sarah's saintliness:

I shall come and create one thing for you Sarah. A great and wonderful creation. This creation is you.

It shall be the manifestation of all the beauty that there is in you; you will be the most beautiful song, a song sang once in an eternity, a song sang in holy trembling, a song sang in purity and complete mastery of the soul.

And in this song you shall find yourself, you—the blessed saint. Every fiber of my being, all the suffering and the turmoil of my spirit I shall put in the verses of this song and give to you. To you—the only one, to you—the good one.

But to Liova, re-creating Sarah was necessary because she had become a different person in the two months after he left Atlit:

Over one dark and misty night you changed and when I returned from the sea, I saw a different you. Sarah—my good Sarah was not the same—and I was shocked. My shock has passed and now again my heart burns and my spirit sings, I know again that the rest of my life on earth is a great and beautiful song that I shall sing to you. I have understood you—while in the darkness of this life it is so hard to find the one to love and understand.[21]

These passages in "To Sarah" do not directly address why Liova Schneersohn believed that Sarah had stepped off the pedestal where he so firmly thought she belonged.

12

To Sarah

In the end, the Mediterranean Sea succeeded, at least temporarily, where Aaron had failed. Bad weather and rough waves prevented Captain Weldon from landing Sarah and Yosef. The *Managem* returned to Port Said. The ship was not built for heavy seas, and the cabins were below the waterline and poorly ventilated. Captain Weldon rarely slept in his cabin, preferring a couch in the "saloon," or common, main cabin.[1]

Aaron's diary entry for April 28 records, "All our people disembarked yesterday at Port Said—the sea was very rough and they could not land and had to come home. They will be here at 1:50 p.m. I went to the station to meet them. They have suffered terribly."[2]

It would be several weeks before the next moonless night at Atlit. Sarah and Yosef were stranded in Cairo. Meanwhile, Aaron's promotion of the Zionist cause had been given a boost by none other than Djemal Pasha.

After the First Battle of Gaza, Djemal Pasha had ordered the evacuation of the entire population of Jaffa–Tel Aviv (Gaza had been evacuated earlier). The purpose was to allow the Turkish army freedom to fight the British without having to deal with a civilian population. Included among the evacuees were thousands of Jews.

On April 19 the day that Sarah had arrived at Port Said from Atlit, Aaron wrote in his diary that "I heard of the looting (plunder) of Jewish Jaffa. Two Yemenites hung on trees are all the Jews that remained in the city. Everything Jewish was plundered—under the fatherly eye of the Turkish police." If Sarah was the source of this information, it was a rare instance of faulty intelligence on her part. No one had been hanged, and the Jews had been allowed to leave behind a dozen watchmen to guard their vacated homes and property. Aaron, however, instantly grasped the propaganda value of the Jaffa–Tel Aviv evacuations for the cause of Zionism. He met with British diplomat Sir Mark Sykes, then in Cairo, at the first opportunity and informed him of the evacuations.[3]

Sykes and Aaronsohn were an improbable pair. Sykes, "a Roman Catholic Tory baronet," in the words of historian David Fromkin, had been through the typical British upper-class marination: Yorkshire foxhunts with the York and Ainsty hounds, a succession of tutors instead of a preparatory school, a stint at Cambridge, service in the Boer War, and travels that only the wealthy could afford for their offspring. "Before I was fifteen," Sykes wrote later in life, "I visited Assouan, which was then almost the Dervish frontier. Then I went to India. . . . I did some exploration in the Arabian desert, enjoying myself barefooted among the Arabs." Sykes was the archetypal aristocratic British amateur whose mythical self-image, suggests sociologist Joan Rockwell, is that he "does everything better, with no trouble, than the lower orders do with great effort."[4]

In 1911 Sykes was elected to Parliament. In 1915 Lord Horatio Kitchener, secretary of state for war, appointed Sykes, then in the British army, to an interdepartmental committee that advised the British cabinet on the Middle East. With his outspoken, self-assured personality, charm, and driving ambition, Sykes soon became the dominant member of the committee and exercised an outsize influence on British policy.[5]

In 1916 Sykes received a momentous diplomatic assignment even though he had no significant diplomatic experience. His assignment was to negotiate the postwar division of the Ottoman Empire with French diplomat François Georges-Picot. Their now infamous Sykes-Picot Agreement partitioned the Ottoman Empire, which had yet to be defeated, between the presumptive victorious Entente powers— Britain and France (and, before its withdrawal from the war, Russia). The agreement included a map, along the lines of a child's crayoned atlas. It used colors (blue for the French, red for the British) and letters (A, French; B, British) to identify areas of direct control and spheres of influence, respectively.[6]

In the opinion of some historians, the Sykes-Picot Agreement guaranteed instability and turmoil in the Middle East that persists today.

Others, however, disparage that notion because it assumes, as historian Sean McMeekin wrote, that Sykes and Picot "were the only actors of consequence on the Ottoman theatre in the First World War and Britain and France the only relevant parties to the disposition of Ottoman territory." A remarkable feature of the Sykes-Picot exercise was that the British and French diplomats actually thought they could keep it a secret.[7]

In fact, in January 1917, not long after arriving in Cairo, Aaron learned from Capt. Philip Graves—the former *Times* correspondent and Middle East butterfly aficionado—about the Sykes-Picot Agreement's provisions for Palestine. "There is already some sort of agreement between the English and the French regarding Palestine; the British to go up to Acre and the Plain of Israel, in which way Jerusalem would remain English and Protestant, while the French would have the upper Galilee, so that Nazareth would be French and Catholic." The Palestine provision was actually more complicated than that because it divided Palestine into multiple zones. Jerusalem was to be governed by an international administration that would take charge of the holy places; the rest of the zones were divided between the French and British in the spirit of "we [the British] want the ports of Haifa and Acre, you can have the tributaries of the Jordan River north of the Sea of Galilee." Aaron wrote in his diary that the agreement described by Captain Graves "would be a misfortune for us, but we are too weak, in the meantime, to have anything to say in the matter."[8]

At the same time Aaron, who may have sensed that the Sykes-Picot Agreement was too improvised and complicated to be a final blueprint, saw in Mark Sykes an opportunity to exercise influence over the *yishuv*'s future in postwar Palestine. For his part Sykes believed that British interests would be served by cultivating the Zionists, who might influence American Jews to support a U.S. intervention in the war on the British side; and after the United States entered the war, Sykes viewed the Zionists as an ally in achieving full British domination of Palestine (and in pressing President Wilson to declare war on the Ottoman Empire, but it ultimately did not happen). All this is not to say that Sykes liked Jews personally; moreover, his view of the power of

Zionists in the United States reflected the tendency, especially by anti-Semites, to exaggerate Jews' power in international affairs. As a young man, Sykes once commented, "Even Jews have their good points, but Armenians have none."[9]

Aaron's diary entries around the time that Sarah arrived in Cairo frequently refer to Sykes. For example, on April 27, Aaron wrote in his diary, "Saw Sir Mark Sykes at 9:15. At last! We immediately broached intimate subjects. He told me that since he was talking with a Jewish patriot, he would entrust me with very secret matters—some of which were not even known to the Foreign Office." In their meeting Sykes described to Aaron how he had encouraged back-channel negotiations involving prominent Jews in England and the French minister of foreign affairs aimed at ensuring the "realization of our *Palestinian* aspirations."[10]

After hearing Aaron's account of the Jaffa–Tel Aviv expulsions and mistreatment of the Jews, Sykes sent a cable to the British Foreign Office requesting that it deliver a message to Chaim Weizmann, a leading British Zionist. "Aaron Aaronsohn asks me to inform you that Televiv has been sacked. 10,000 Palestinian Jews are now without home or food. Whole yeshuv [*sic*] is threatened with destruction. Jemal [Pasha] has publicly stated that Armenian policy will now be applied to the Jews."

A humanitarian disaster had indeed cost the lives of at least hundreds of Jews from disease or starvation. But a humanitarian disaster is not a genocide, and, in fact, the Ottoman government in Constantinople did not want any such thing. As historian Yuval Ben-Bassat pointed out in his study of enciphered Ottoman telegrams from World War I, the Ottoman government "constantly asked Djemal Pasha to provide information on the fates" of the expelled populations, including where they were sent and about their housing and medical care. The Ottoman government, perhaps more sensitive to international opinion than Djemal was, insisted that Jerusalem's leaders "avoid thrusting the Jewish population into the arms of the enemy."[11]

Aaron's report gained worldwide attention. On May 4 the *Jewish Chronicle*, a leading Zionist publication in Britain, ran a story about the expulsions with the following subheads: "Grave Reports—Terrible Outrages—Threats of Wholesale Massacre." The report, citing an "absolutely reliable source," described how Tel Aviv, "the beautiful Garden City suburb of Jaffa, has been sacked and lies in a mere heap of ruins." The *Chronicle* further stated that Djemal Pasha had announced the intention of the "authorities to wipe out mercilessly the Jewish population of Palestine, his public statement being that the Armenian policy of massacre is to be applied to the Jews."[12]

With Sykes's assistance Aaron also sent cables with similar reports, via the British Embassy in Washington, to leaders of the American Jewish community. On June 3 the *New York Times* ran a story headlined "Cruelties to Jews Deported in Jaffa—Djemal Pasha Blamed." Djemal Pasha insisted that the entire population of Jaffa, not only the Jews, had been evacuated and denied the reports of atrocities. Later, envoys from three neutrals—Spain, Sweden, and the Vatican—conducted an investigation. The Vatican and Spanish envoys found that the reports of murders of Jews and Jewish persecution were unsupported. "In many ways," the Swedish envoy reported separately, "the Jewish community of Jaffa had fared far better—and certainly no worse—than the resident Moslem population in the evacuation." But by then the Jaffa pogrom had taken its place alongside actual atrocities, such as the Armenian massacres and the Germans' pillaging and devastation of Belgium, as emblematic of the enemy's ruthlessness.[13]

Aaron exploited the initial reports without, apparently, subjecting them to the kind of rigorous scrutiny that he had demanded in his scientific work. Sarah's report on the Armenian slaughter had been the credible account of an eyewitness with no bias to exaggerate, but Aaron appeared to have no such foundation for the report that he gave to Mark Sykes that the *yishuv* was threatened with wholesale destruction. The Armenian massacres understandably colored any reports of mistreatment of the Jews, but in this case there was an element of political opportunism in that Aaron disseminated the reports to rally support for the Zionist cause.

The Jaffa–Tel Aviv expulsions also highlighted the emerging division of responsibilities between Aaron and Sarah. Aaron, empowered by the importance of the Nili spy ring to British intelligence, was focused on Zionist objectives and increasingly regarded himself as being in a position to realize them. He now wielded political influence. Sarah did the difficult and dangerous espionage work that was essential to Aaron's influence.

The propaganda had one beneficial outcome. The relief funds for the *yishuv* provided by the British government in the form of gold coins were supplemented by donations from the United States and Europe. As will be seen, Sarah later took the gold with her on the *Managem* and used it to support the Jewish communities in Palestine and to attempt to buy peace with Nili's opponents in the yishuv.[14]

The Jaffa–Tel Aviv evacuations, however, raised an uncomfortable question for both Sarah and Aaron. By June Aaron knew that the two Jews had not been hanged but apparently only had been arrested on charges of looting. If Jews had not been deliberately killed by Djemal Pasha, notwithstanding the constant threat of a British breakthrough into Palestine, then perhaps the *yishuv* was not in as much danger of annihilation as Aaron and Sarah had feared. That question was not easily answered, however, given the murderous unpredictability of the Ottoman rulers. With the outcome of the war in doubt, the Ottomans had an incentive to avoid inflaming world opinion over the treatment of Jews. If the Ottoman Empire won the war, however, that restraint would be removed. But many Jews in Palestine had a different risk calculus than Sarah did. To them, the safety of the *yishuv* depended on *not* antagonizing the Ottomans. If the British won, Jews would perhaps benefit; but if the Ottomans prevailed, these Jews believed it better not to have given them any reason to settle scores.

More than Aaron, Sarah recognized the genuine unease, and in some instances outright opposition, among Palestinian Jews about her activities. Almost upon arriving in Egypt, Sarah reported to Aaron the antagonism of groups like Ha-Shomer to Nili. Aaron seemed to think that the problem was principally due to his absence from Palestine; if he were there, then the *yishuv* would rally to Nili's cause. That line of thinking appears more attributable to the inflation of Aaron's already large ego by his growing influence in Cairo than to a healthy appreciation of the hostility Sarah faced from the people she was risking her life to protect. Aaron wrote in his diary on the day Sarah arrived in Egypt, "The opposition of our people against our work is—as might be expected—due to cowardice and intrigues encouraged by the master's absence. When I take matters in hand everything will run smoothly again."[15]

The extended Cairo visit turned into the World War I equivalent of a furlough for Sarah. Having no other option, Sarah spent time shopping, sightseeing, and going to the theater, museums, and lectures. As Sarah explained in a letter to Aaron, who was then away from Cairo, she, Yosef, and Liova planned to visit the pyramids one day, but "the gentlemen were a bit late, so we decided to go to Heliopolis. . . . Look at us, what charlatans. When the rabbi is not around the kids go wild." The next day, she explained, she planned to spend the morning shopping and, in the afternoon, finally visit the pyramids.[16]

They dressed fashionably for their outings, with Liova and Yosef in suits, vests, straw boaters, and ties—in Liova's case, a snug bow tie—and Sarah in a dark suit with a white blouse and a white hat with a broad brim. At one point Sarah and Liova decided to take English lessons and found a private tutor, an ugly old female missionary who liked to talk about Jesus. "In the beginning God created. . . . I wonder why she hasn't got a cat or a dog in her house," Liova wrote in his diary. After a while Sarah, who had neither the time nor the patience for the English lessons, stopped going, but Liova wanted to improve his English skills and continued studying with the old woman.[17]

Sarah attended social events, including with people whom Sarah called "our Zichronians"—that is, residents of Zichron who were then stranded in Egypt or self-exiled from Palestine. She was invited to teas, taken to restaurants, and spent time at the home of Dr. Weitz, Aaron's friend. "Everybody is fighting over me," she wrote in another note to Aaron. "[Dr.] Weitz wants me to stay only with him, Cohen wants me only for himself, and all the rest of them, too. I manage not to disappoint any of them." Sarah noted that no one, not even those who knew her well, asked her many questions about why she was in Cairo. Sarah must have lost weight because Dr. Weitz advised her not to have her photograph taken until "I become fat again. He finds my face very beautiful."[18]

Cairo might have been a well-deserved rest for all of them but for the lurking tension over the pending return of Sarah and Yosef to Palestine and the fact that both Liova and Yosef were jealous rivals for Sarah's attention. One evening Sarah and Liova attended a symphony concert that performed the music of Alexander Borodin and Nikolai Rimsky-Korsakov. After Liova returned to his hotel, he had a dreadful night, experiencing a nightmare, although it's unclear whether he was asleep or awake at the time.

A boy left alone in the depths of the forest, a man struggling for his life in a little boat tossed by angry waves . . . young women wearing white are dressing the wounds of young freedom fighters whose teeth are clenched in terrible silence, . . . a sentenced man walking to the gallows, calling out to his hangman, "I despise death!" Celestial hymns . . . hands stretched out to protect the secret believers . . . the hands of a priest are raised in the air to bless the crowd.[19]

During their stay, Yosef decided to look for Avshalom Feinberg's body. Sarah and Liova spent the day with Yosef as he shopped for a disguise for his trip and bought a black *abaya* (a woman's cloak), a white kaffiyeh, and a red belt. Yosef took a train to Port Said, boarded a trawler to Deir el-Belah on the coast, and then took a train south into the desert. He returned and reported to Aaron that he hadn't found Avshalom's remains. "[Yosef] said he had found the place where they were attacked and where our unfortunate friend was killed. But since then they have leveled the ground—built a railway track, made trenches—and it was impossible to find the remains of our unfortunate Absa." For his part, Liova wrote that Yosef's "journey . . . was unsuccessful. Yosef is in a bad mood. Sarah doesn't feel well. I go to the pharmacy to buy pills for her headache. This is how we spend our strange days in Egypt."[20]

Yosef's quest to find Avshalom's body had been anything but cathartic. On May 14 the day before the next scheduled departure from Egypt, he announced to Sarah, Liova, and Aaron that he had no intention of returning to Palestine. Yosef, in effect, was deserting Nili.

"Why?" demanded Liova. "What are you doing it for?"

"On principle!" Yosef shouted, without explaining what the principle was.

Liova tried to calm the situation. Yosef brooded. Aaron stormed about for a while and left for the Savoy Hotel. He was not going to allow Yosef to jeopardize Nili and the work that he had done to build credibility with the British.

At British intelligence headquarters in the Savoy Hotel, Aaron announced that he was going to Atlit in Yosef's place. Not surprising, "there was great excitement at the office," but according to Aaron, the British "were forced to accept my proposition." But the "excitement" was likely because they realized the Turks would recognize and arrest Aaron almost as soon as he set foot in Palestine and then torture him into revealing vital British secrets. In all likelihood, British intelligence would have forcibly confined Aaron to Cairo if he had tried to go to Palestine.[21]

Yosef Alhadeff, a Jewish resident in the Galilee, was in Egypt at the time. Alhadeff, who knew about Sarah and Nili and who was a Nili sympathizer, came upon Sarah and Yosef in the Grand Continental Hotel that day. As he wrote in a letter years later, "It seem[ed] to me that Sarah had been crying. She was very distressed; they were having a harsh conversation."

"I don't know what's come over him," Sarah said to Alhadeff, and she left.

"I know that this time I am going to my death," Yosef told Alhadeff in melodramatic tones. "I shall never return."

Alhadeff tried a combination of argument, praise, and encouragement on Yosef. He lauded him for all that he had done and reminded him of the importance of Nili and of the key role that Yosef was playing. "He did not deny what I was saying, but at that moment he preferred arrest and trial in Egypt to the death he feared awaited him at the hands of the Turks."[22]

Liova tried to convince Yosef to return to Palestine but got nowhere. Sarah then went to see Yosef alone. It's unclear what she said to him, but whatever it was, his mood changed.

"Look, you've got to go," Liova said to Yosef after Sarah left. "If you don't agree, I'm going to take you by force."

"I've decided to go."

Aaron didn't give Sarah any credit for changing Yosef's mind but did credit himself. As Aaron wrote in his diary, "Y, who acted like an unbalanced fool, changed his mind. When he saw that we had seriously decided to leave him here, he became reasonable again and came along with his trunks." All of them were exhausted. Aaron, Liova, and Sarah tried to be nice to Yosef, but that did little to cheer him up.[23]

The four left for Port Said and spent the night in a hotel. At one point Sarah and Liova were alone together in Liova's room, apparently discussing Yosef, who was in the hallway outside the room and trying to eavesdrop. When Sarah came out, Yosef flew into a rage at her, evidently jealous.

The next day, May 15, they went to the *Managem*. A storm had arisen in the Mediterranean. Captain Weldon approached Aaron and said, "Go to the Eastern Exchange Hotel and receive instructions there. A departure is impossible." Later Aaron wrote that "Weldon informed me that they would sail tomorrow afternoon. The storm had subsided. I gave my last instructions. Sarati's courage is above anything I had expected. She is calm and reasonable." The next morning Sarah, Yosef, and Liova boarded the *Managem*.[24]

The *Managem* approached Zichron on a clear day. The shutters on the homes could be seen from the ship, which sailed on to Atlit. The visibility was worse by the time it reached Atlit, and no one on the ship could tell if a signal cloth was on the research station's balcony. The *Managem* went north as far as Haifa, turned, and went back to Atlit, but the sea had become too rough to attempt a landing.

Captain Weldon decided to go (or was ordered) to Cyprus. There the *Managem* was ordered to leave, not for Cairo, but on another mission. Sarah, Yosef, and Liova had to disembark in Larnaca and spend ten days on Cyprus until another ship could take them to Egypt. They whiled away time sightseeing, including making visits to a moldy Turkish mosque and a salt factory. The three also came down with malaria. "I had the fever all night through," Liova wrote in his diary, "and now I am totally broken and exhausted."

Sarah, Yosef, and Liova prepared to board the British ship *Kosseir*, but the Larnaca port officials demanded to see their passports, which none of them had. One British officer, aware of Nili's importance, spoke to the harbor master while a crowd gathered on the wharf to stare at the three Jews. Eventually they were allowed to board without passports. A port official went out to the *Kosseir* on a motor launch out of concern for their well-being; he shook hands with Sarah, Yosef, and Liova and wished them the best of luck on their voyage back to Egypt. Once in Cairo, however, they would have to wait for the next moonless night to attempt yet another landing at Atlit.[25]

It was a period of introspection for all of them. After the blowup in Cairo, Sarah, Liova, and Yosef found it easier to communicate their feelings in writing rather than in face-to-face conversations.

Liova continued to write in his notebook "To Sarah." He suggested that Sarah was in the grip of dark forces that threatened her soul; she was vulnerable to these forces because she was a woman.

> You are again under the influence of other forces, forces that you are not aware of, and yet they possess you, possess you fully and you cannot stand against them.
>
> You are a woman and you give in to these forces. . . .
>
> Just be strong for a short moment and admit it to yourself! Admit it because one day you might need to stand against these forces after all and to overcome them so you can proceed along your path, a path that you don't know and yet are destined to follow. Then it is still possible, then you can still save your soul.

Liova does not expressly name Yosef Lishansky. But the following passage clearly indicates that Liova blames Yosef for (in his eyes) Sarah's loss of divinity.

> You let him into your room to speak with him, and share your goodness with him. By doing so, you do no good! And again you show

how submissive you are. . . . Such a woman you proved to be. . . . You show submission, great submission, instead of greatness of spirit, instead of kindness of the heart. Are all women like this? Not all!

I have known women who are so holy, so beautiful, so sublime.

Liova insisted that his love for Sarah was anything but carnal.

I am not the one who can give simple happiness to women. I wouldn't be able to give it to you either. I cannot satisfy the needs of simple, earthly animal love. . . . Every day I wear my white clothes, come to the altar and bow and pray . . . and praise my wonderful goddess, my Sarah who was elevated from the simple life to acquire a new world.

Just in case Sarah misunderstood the degree of Liova's moral disapproval of her conduct, he invoked Avshalom Feinberg: "I knew a man who is no longer with us, who could admire you, exalt you and raise you to an ever higher level—and even if just for the memory of this man you are so dear to me, and my heart aches for you so much." He asked Sarah to "just understand me, that's the only thing I am asking for. Just understand the man who seeks to find in love not pleasure, but sublime emotion and spiritual ecstasy."[26]

At some point—exactly when is unclear—Liova gave "To Sarah" to Sarah. She read it and then wrote a letter to Liova.

I have read the notebook that you dedicated to me, with much attention and went over it once and once again and I will surely come back to it. . . . On almost every page you write that I don't understand you. You are mistaken my friend, as you know well that I understand you thoroughly and there aren't many who can understand you like I do. But if that's what you have decided then so be it, maybe one day you will realize you were wrong. My feeling is that we are bound to understand each other whether we want it or not.

Sarah could have stopped there. But "To Sarah" had touched a nerve because she was still coming to terms with her own self-worth.

It is not in my nature to boast and I don't like to give myself com-
pliments. But recently I have come to understand that I have to
appreciate myself and put "myself" in its rightful place. And that's
why you can suddenly hear me saying that "Sarah is wise, isn't
she?" I, who always reproach myself and refuse to trust other people's good opinions of me. But I, Liova, understand many things
and sense and feel even more, only that God hasn't granted me the
talent of writing and expressing myself in words and that's why
many beautiful things and many profound thoughts are buried in
the deepest chambers of my heart, without being heard and understood by others.

The letter (as with others Sarah had written), in fact, displays her gift
for writing.

Sarah then pointed out that the person Liova described in "To Sarah"
never existed in the first place; there had never been a fall from grace
because there had been no grace to fall from. It was the closest that
Sarah came in her letter to acknowledging Liova's assertion that she had
a relationship with Yosef Lishansky, and she was unapologetic.

With you everything is built on visions and fantasies and when you
meet people like me you become frustrated so quickly. I am too real
for you, I belong too much to real life, while you are searching for
your fantasy, for those beautiful girls, clear as crystal, who you have
created in your imagination and who do not exist and are not to be
found anywhere in the real world, for this world is one big lie. And
it is good for you that you have a world of your own where you can
create everything in your own image but I, unfortunately, have to
deal with life as it is, and choose the lesser evil, so to say. You should
know that there aren't many Sarahs to be found in this world and
not even such "Bad Sarahs" as I am. This I can tell you and one day
you will see it for yourself. With every day that passes life becomes
more harsh and more cruel, and there is less and less truth in it. So,
will there come a day when the veil is dropped and the naked truth
is exposed to us? No! No!

The core of the problem, in Sarah's view, was that Liova no longer understood *her*.

And you, Liova, there was a time when you understood me. . . . when you poured out your heart to me, when you read me your writings, this was surely a sign that I have understood you, and you felt I was worth it . . . You have changed, you became so different and believe me, my friend, it is your fault and not mine, because I have remained the same, just as you saw me in those first moments; and it's just you, with your poetic spirit, with your wandering soul, who have traveled so far into the worlds you have created and kept ascending higher and higher and farther away. And now you look at me from those heights and I appear tiny to you. You have written poems and built towers, you have loved me for the greatness of my spirit, but all these were nothing but castles in the air and that's why they collapsed so soon. That's the way it always is and I have warned you about it. And if one of us fails to understand the other, then believe me that it's you who doesn't understand me. But I am strong, my mind is clear and simple, I accept things calmly, without too much agitation and that's why my flame can burn longer.

Once, there had been someone who understood her.

And if there were a few people who could understand me, there aren't many of them left. The dearest and most special one who knew and understood me so well is no longer with us. . . . I prefer not to speak of him, because the heart aches too much and silence, in this case, is a better cure than words.[27]

For his part, Yosef wrote a letter to Liova that was part apology and part confession to his doubts about their work. The apology was short: "I was too miserable, wasn't I?"

The doubts took much longer for Yosef to explain, but it came down to a single question that he had been unable to answer: "What are we doing all this for?" In fact, the more Yosef thought about the question the more complicated and unanswerable it seemed.

You will say, "What, do you want to stop? How can one stop in the middle of the work?" Then not to stop? My head is whirling with worries, till I am nearly mad. It's difficult, my friend, to grope in the dark. If I were groping alone, I wouldn't care, but many people are working for me, and I cannot reveal to them what I reveal to you. And so I am deprived of both alternatives. I am working, but with terrible pessimism about the value of the work I am doing.

Weighing on Yosef was his and Sarah's deceiving the Nili members about Avshalom Feinberg's death and their failure to do anything for the *yishuv*.

In addition, I am deceiving innocent people, who believe all I say. And how much longer is this going on? I don't think I can stand much more. We've got to get out of this mess somehow or other. Our Jews are being destroyed under our eyes, and we're not bringing them any results. On the contrary in some ways we're even harming them.

Yosef steadied himself, as though expressing his doubts on paper had been beneficial.

But I must stop writing. I'm getting upset again, for nothing, for it won't do me any good. Forgive me that you found me in this bad mood. I would like to be at Port Said already, and get the telling off that Aaron will give me, for being under his eyes once again. Poor, miserable chap. He's also justified in his anger. He also has his troubles. But am I to blame for them?[28]

Yosef's letter at least temporarily ended the tension between the two men. Thereafter they found a way to get along.

On May 16 Sarah and her two jealous companions—one a mystic, the other a troubled buccaneer—had left Egypt on the *Managem*. On May 31 after the stay in Cyprus, they were back in Egypt. Aaron wrote in his diary that "Sarati and her companions arrived in the afternoon. They suffered cruelly aboard the Managem—spent 10 days in Larnaca [Cyprus] where they caught malaria—and came back with the Kosseir. It would be cruel to send Sarati back once more. I do not see the necessity of it, now that the most precious time is past."[29]

The *Managem*'s next departure—the third attempt to return Sarah and Yosef to Palestine—was set for mid-June. In the days leading up to the departure, Sarah and Aaron conferred on Nili's activities while Aaron and Yosef continued their painful arguments. Aaron apparently did not hide his contempt for Yosef in these vehement quarrels; certainly, he did not hide it from his diary. "Had a painful argument with Yosef. His way of doing things is exasperating."[30]

In mid-June nearly two months after Sarah had left Palestine, the *Managem* sailed again. At Atlit the sea was calm. Two surfboats were launched from the *Managem*. Captain Weldon and Yosef Lishansky were in one boat; Liova and Sarah were in the other. The plan was for Captain Weldon and Yosef to go to the shore and find the Nili spies. If it was safe, then Captain Weldon's boat would return and take Sarah to the beach.

The night was quiet. Sarah and Liova listened to the water lapping against the side of their gently rocking boat. The two stretched out on the bottom of the boat and gazed at the stars.

"Why don't I feel any fear?" Sarah asked Liova. "Any fear at all. It's as if I was out on a nice evening trip, off the coast of Atlit, sailing in a little boat in complete serenity. What is it? Bravery? Or rather stupidity, numbness of the mind, and an inability to acknowledge the situation?"

Liova reassured her that, at a moment like this, it was possible to feel anything but fear.

Captain Weldon's boat, returning from the shore, where he had left Yosef, signaled Sarah and Liova and shortly pulled alongside. Liova squeezed Sarah's hand.

"Sarah."

And then, as Liova wrote in his diary, "she elegantly skip[ped]" onto Captain Weldon's boat, which took her to the shore, along with the spies' luggage and sacks containing gold.[31]

By now it was midnight. Nili spies had kept a vigil at the beach; that night Reuven Schwartz and Menashe Brunstein were waiting. The surfboat rowed up to the beach, and Sarah got out. Reuven, Menashe, and Yosef removed the luggage and gold. The three men hid the gold in a cave in the rocks that served as an emergency hideout. Sarah tried to help, but the others expressed concern that her health was not sufficiently recovered for her to carry the heavy sacks of gold. "Never mind," she insisted, "it's nothing to make a fuss about." Upon greeting her cousin Reuven Schwartz, Sarah asked about Nili's situation.

All Reuven would say was, "Bad, very bad."[32]

13

We Are Watched by a Thousand Eyes

On June 25, ten days after returning to Palestine, Sarah wrote separate letters to Aaron and Liova for the *Managem* to pick up on a forthcoming visit. Her letter to Aaron began on the sensitive topic of her refusal to stay in Egypt and her stunning response to Captain Edmonds in the lounge of the Continental Hotel in Cairo, where she threatened to take her own life if she was unable to return to Palestine. Sarah seemed simultaneously to blame Aaron for insisting that she stay in Cairo and to apologize for her outburst.

> We arrived on the 15th and luckily, it [the sea] was very quiet. We unloaded everything and had to carry it all, since there was only [Reuven] Schwartz, Menashe [Brunstein] and Yosef. I cannot list myself among the ones who did the carrying but I have helped a great deal, as much as I could. I was very happy to finally set foot on land, on our land, which I have missed so very much, while you, my dear, perhaps not understanding me, demanded that I stay. Arale, you've known me as a tight-lipped person and therefore you have never heard me express my sorrows to you. Although if I wanted to I could find plenty of things to complain about, I am reminding myself again that silence is the way of the wise and again I refrain from speaking and forgive me for these few words here. Straight and to the point is more appropriate, is it not?[1]

Her letter to Liova was more lighthearted and teasing.

To my friend Rabbi Levi
Shalom!

As a start, a few words about my arrival. I got off without a problem, and we carried all our luggage—Reuven Schwartz, Menashe, Yosef and I. You must be laughing, saying what a man I am, but even for me there was something to carry. We arrived and I was happy to set foot on our land. From the day of our arrival until now we haven't yet rested, it's hard to believe just how busy we have been and how much work there is to be done. And for the time being the work has to be carried out secretly. Here, everything was upside-down, changes in personnel and changes at work, but not as bad as we imagined.[2]

Actually, as recounted by Sarah in detail in both letters, the situation in Palestine was more than just upside-down and far worse than she could have anticipated. Jews in Zichron and Hadera were actively opposing Nili's activities; her own brother Zvi, a Nili member, was furious that Sarah had returned; even those loyal to her, including her own father, were "frightened terribly"; and family and friends of Avshalom Feinberg's were increasingly upset at not hearing from him for many months. "Our people and family members are terribly concerned and wish that we were already gone," she wrote Liova. "But we have to stay cool headed and understand the situation."

One cause of Sarah's many problems was that Nili's activities had become practically an open secret in the *yishuv*, especially after Sarah and Yosef disappeared from Palestine for almost two months. (Originally, they had planned to be away just three days.) Everyone, Sarah wrote Liova, was talking about their activities, "even the babies in their cradles." Secrecy, indispensable to effective espionage, had been all but lost.

In Cairo, or else on the *Managem*, Liova had told Sarah that he wanted to return to Palestine. In her letter, Sarah suggested that now was not the time to do so because the Jewish leaders from Hadera, Liova's hometown, would be incensed.

They know that you are also one of our workers. Your arrival would raise questions and upset the entire world. . . . If you came the purpose of your stay would be to work, to travel around and gather information. . . . That would be impossible because we are watched by a thousand eyes, and every step we make is followed both by the Jews and by the Bastards. We ourselves are not yet settled in and don't yet know what will happen. In a few weeks, if we see, Liovka, that everything is quiet then "Welcome!"

Sarah urged Liova not to judge her harshly or suspect any ulterior motives for telling him not to come, an indirect acknowledgment of his rivalry with Yosef Lishansky. Abandoning her cheerful and amused tone, Sarah then admitted, "As for myself, I am always upset and in a bad mood, and generally speaking I don't know what is going on with me, there are so many things to do and to take care of." At the end of her letter, Sarah asked Liova to send her the "little notebook"—that is, "To Sarah"—because "it belongs to me."

The yishuv's opposition to Nili had deepened. While Sarah had been in Egypt, representatives of community councils from Zichron and Hadera had gone to Sarah's brother Zvi and demanded that he account for Sarah's suspicious activities or, as she put it, "what are we up to, and where and whither we had disappeared. They claimed they knew everything, and they could not consent to play with the fate of the whole Jewish community."

Zvi told the irate Jewish leaders that the rumors were untrue. But he was a mild-mannered man, not nearly as bold as Aaron and Sarah, and had been unnerved by the increasing anger in Zichron at Sarah. Zvi discontinued his own espionage work and may have discouraged other Nili members from spying. After Sarah's return, Zvi demanded that she and Yosef go back to Cairo. Zvi's attitude may have been due to long-simmering resentment over the fact that two of his brothers, Aaron and Alexander, had started a spy ring without initially telling him; and, like many, he could not abide Yosef Lishansky. Indeed, Zvi told Sarah that as long as she associated with Lishansky, Sarah was unwelcome in his home. Zvi wasn't the only family member turning against Sarah. Her father, Ephraim, then nearly seventy years old, was just as fearful as Zvi and equally antagonistic to Yosef Lishansky.[3]

Sarah's strategy for dealing with the hostility of *yishuv* leaders was to give them gold, a tactic the British employed effectively elsewhere in the Middle East. In 1917 T. E. Lawrence had brought canvas bags filled with gold sovereigns bearing the stamp of the Bank of England to an enclave of Bedouin sheiks in Wejh in what is now Saudi Arabia. The gold (the sheiks had no use for paper money) helped secure the sheiks' allegiance to the British. Nearly fifty years later, Bedouin sheiks still remembered Lawrence as "the man with the gold."[4]

Sarah began negotiations with Meir Dizengoff, the head of a committee set up for the relief of the Jewish refugees. Dizengoff, the mayor of Tel Aviv, was not a Nili supporter, but the practical man recognized the expelled Jews desperately needed help. Sarah wrote to Aaron, "One day, D. came to Zichron to get the money and to talk, for we are Jews, talkers and businesspeople." The occasion may have been a rare instance of a Jewish man and a Jewish woman in Palestine negotiating an important transaction on something like equal terms. The gold, concealed in flour sacks inside wooden kegs labeled "salt herring," was delivered to Dizengoff by a wholesale grocer acting as a middleman.[5]

The gold did not fully appease the *yishuv* leaders, and they shifted their efforts to changing Nili's leadership. On July 4 a representative of the Nili opposition, Zichron resident Yitzhak Rosenberg, gave Sarah a letter that he wanted her to send to Aaron in Cairo. The letter was written on behalf of community councils in several settlements; prominent Jews, including Meir Dizengoff and Eliezer Hoofien, the manager of the Anglo-Palestine Bank; and, apparently, the self-defense organization Ha-Shomer. The letter proposed that Nili (although its name was not used) find a way for the Jewish leaders' representatives to travel to Egypt and discuss Nili's activities with Aaron.

While the letter was drafted to appear as though the Jewish leaders were seeking nothing more than a dialogue, Rosenberg added a condition in his conversation with Sarah when he delivered the letter for Aaron: Yosef Lishansky must accompany the emissaries to Cairo—and stay there. Rosenberg's argument was that Lishansky was too visible in Palestine to engage in espionage, as though Rosenberg was primarily concerned with Nili's effectiveness. Yosef's replacement, Rosenberg explained to Sarah, would be chosen by Ha-Shomer, which, as recounted, had a long-standing grievance against Lishansky over the shooting of an Arab in Menahamiya.[6]

Sarah wrote Aaron:

My opinion is that we shouldn't get scared by each rumor and story that passes around, today they say one thing, tomorrow it's another one. Our people here, and especially the family, Father, Hankin [Avshalom's uncle] and Zvi, they get immediately alarmed by every little thing and think, for example, that if some Jew says so and so, we have to immediately stop all the work and disappear completely and more nonsense of this kind. What I say to them is that they talk and they will talk, but the work will be done, so get used to the fact that this is how things are and keep quiet. So false alarms are giving us a lot of trouble. I do think that we should consider everything that happens, pay attention and understand what to do. But every leaf that falls from a tree frightens them and makes them want to stop. At home we often quarrel over these things and I am the one who all the complaints are addressed to.[7]

As to the demand that Lishansky leave Palestine, Sarah presented an extended defense of Yosef. She was apparently concerned that Aaron, who had been furious with Yosef while he was in Cairo, might be swayed by Rosenberg.

So why is it that Yosef is not to their liking? What I think is:

For them it would be obviously more convenient to have the work carried out by some Shomernik [a member of Ha-Shomer] so that they can control everything. Yosef is surely not the one to satisfy their objectives, this I can promise you. From all the reports and so on, you can see, Arale, that this man does nothing that doesn't come from you or before consulting you, and I am sure you understand that he is more loyal to you than some Shomernik would be. If so why would they be interested in keeping such a man? So what they are doing is trying to show us politically that Yosef is bad for us and must be sent away from Palestine. . . . So do we really need a new person? Someone who would not listen to me and would not listen to you?

Sarah explained that she had listened to the Jewish leaders' demand that she send Yosef to Egypt and only told them that she had to consult with Aaron. "What is your opinion of all my chattering, please let me know in your next letter." Sarah also described how Rosenberg and the other leaders had tried to intimidate her. "They think that they can scare us like they scare small children, 'the bogeyman is coming to get you' or 'there is a monster in the closet.' So they tell us that there is a new battalion here now, brought from Anatolia. All are 'pure' Turks, young and healthy as lions and equipped with good weapons etc. 'You won't be able to carry on your work for much longer as the plan is to send some of them to guard the coast at Atlit.'"

Sarah had investigated and found out that while a patrol of ten Turks had arrived in the area, their weapons and supplies had not. Furthermore, they were only relieving the existing patrol, and even the townspeople did not regard the men as formidable. "I doubt if these new patrols will disturb us too much." She advised Aaron that she and Yosef had decided to relocate their operations from Zichron to the research station in Atlit, which was more convenient since it was the location for the rendezvous with the *Managem*. Also, the new Turk patrol was possibly less of a hindrance to Nili's operations than the Zichron leaders were.

In a postscript Sarah added the "most important thing": her malaria, contracted during her stay on Cyprus, was gone.

My fever is completely over. I am cured. I guess that the journey and the delay had a negative effect on me as well as being without the work. If you saw me you would not realize how much anger and stress I endure, I work and toil and it makes me forget it all and I feel better than I felt when I was with you. (Although I am sorry to say so because like a good angel you were only concerned with my well-being when I was there.) But this is how it is, even if I have only a loaf of bread, I prefer to be here. Forgive me for telling the truth, but you know your sister, and that she says everything that she feels. So another good kiss to you, how are you? Are you still losing weight? And are you very, very busy?[8]

Sarah was not always consistent in describing herself. In her June 25 letter to Aaron, Sarah had called herself "as a tight-lipped person and therefore you have never heard me express my sorrows to you."

A few weeks later, the *Managem* delivered a letter from Aaron. He gave Sarah unequivocal support to keep Yosef Lishansky in Palestine—and active in Nili.

> The demand that Yosef leave is nonsense. . . . This is a man who has been through fire and water with us, he suffered until he got used to us, and we suffered until we got used to him. Now, after we have each learned to rely on the other, we are asked to send him away. For what? . . . Please calm Yosef on this matter, because he does not know me well enough. Is there one assistant of mine that ever complained that I deserted him in time of trouble?[9]

Privately Aaron was elated by the Jewish leaders' request to come to Cairo and meet with him. "Our Palestinian public," he wrote in his diary, "is already anxious to send me delegates. It is extremely important. Today I must say that the mission which I have undertaken has succeeded."[10]

The intelligence gathering went on despite the objections of the *yishuv* leaders. Sarah visited Dr. Neumann, who was now stationed with the Turkish army in Ramle on the coastal plain. Dr. Neumann provided Sarah with a detailed intelligence report covering the last several weeks, much of which concerned the movement of soldiers and equipment to the Gaza–Beersheba front. In a single day, Neumann reported, six railcars filled with munitions passed through Ramle on their way to Gaza, as well as a regiment of Austrian infantry, dispirited by the war. He said the health of the Turkish soldiers was generally good, other than the high proportion suffering from venereal disease. In a report that could have come from today's headlines, Dr. Neumann also described attacks by British airplanes at nearby towns, with one injuring sixty persons who had been attending a wedding.

Part of Dr. Neumann's report concerned Turkish air bases in the vicinity of Ramle. On July 25, 1917, the following entry was made in the "War Diary or Intelligence Summary" maintained by British intelligence: "3 aerodromes reported at RAMLEH about 23/6/17 (agent): (i) near cemetery outside town, 6 'good' aeroplanes, 9 others, (2) on Jerusalem road 1 mile from town near railway (3) on Jaffa road, exact place not given. Agent also told that 2 Albatrosses had arrived + 7 new machines were expected. On moonlit nights machines are removed from hangars + hidden in the yards. Germans estimate British aeroplanes in Palestine at 63, plus 24 recently arrived."[11]

That kind of detailed intelligence was Nili's stock in trade. It was also more than a month old, which the July 25 intelligence summary noted with the reference "reported . . . about 23/6/17 (agent)." On June 22 Sarah had gone to Ramle, picked up the report from Dr. Neumann, and then rushed back to Atlit, but she had missed a visit by the *Managem*. Military historian Yigal Sheffy argues that the "Achilles' heel of the [Nili] operation in fact was the slow communication process, causing most of the information to be outdated or already known by the time it reached Egypt." Sheffy also points out that the British received valuable, more up-to-date intelligence from the new technologies of airplane reconnaissance and wireless intercepts.[12]

The Nili spies would have agreed with him that the communication process was slow; indeed, it was a constant source of frustration for them. In June Aaron had proposed to a British expert in wireless technology that the British lay a telephone cable from the vicinity of the Atlit research station to a point at or near the shore, then lay a second cable from out in the sea to a point twenty meters from the shore, and connect the two cables by "some sort of wireless—transmissions through the ground—as it is practised in the case of electric bells." (Aaron was apparently talking about electromagnetic induction.) According to Aaron, "the expert opened his eyes wide—he had never heard of it, but would study the project." Ultimately, Aaron's proposal was not implemented for unknown reasons, but the complexity of the scheme and the relatively new state of wireless communications surely were factors.[13]

The British proposed using messenger or carrier pigeons. In fact, the British used one hundred thousand messenger pigeons on the western front with a success rate of 95 percent. A famous pigeon named Cher Ami (Dear Friend) would be credited in 1918 with saving the lives of two hundred men from the American 77th Infantry Division, the so-called Lost Battalion, which had become trapped behind enemy lines and was running short of food and ammunition. The pigeon, carrying a message about the battalion's plight, was shot down, but it managed to get back in the air and fly the twenty-five miles from the battalion to headquarters in barely over an hour. By the time Cher Ami arrived, she had been shot through the breast, had been blinded in one eye, had one of her legs hanging only by a tendon, and was covered in blood. (Cher Ami died of her wounds a year later.) The carnage among pigeons was not remotely close to the casualties among horses, however; eight million of them died in the war from causes ranging from gunshot to disease.[14]

The messenger pigeons apparently were not as effective in the Middle East as they were in Europe. The British had tried them in their campaign on Egypt's western frontier (now shared with Libya) against the Senussi, a puritanical Islamic sect that German and Turkish agents encouraged to launch a holy war against the British. The British eventually defeated the Senussi, but as a British officer told Aaron Aaronsohn, "Their experience with pigeons in the Senussi war was most discouraging." Nonetheless, the *Managem* took pigeons to the Jewish spies in Atlit.

Raphael Aboulafia, who, as mentioned, had fought on the British side at Gallipoli, was among the Nili spies who delivered the pigeons to Nili. The spies were landed by the *Managem* at the beach at Atlit, but they hadn't gotten far inland when the pigeons began cooing ("may their names be remembered for evil," Raphael later wrote). Someone suggested breaking the pigeons' necks, but shortly the pigeons quieted down and were allowed to live. Sarah waited at the entrance to the research station. Raphael noticed that Sarah showed no surprise or excitement as they approached her out of the dark. "All this seem[ed] quite a natural thing for her, as if this is the way life is always lived. . . . What amazed me more than anything. She even understood before-hand what I wanted to say. I don't know how. By my eyes? By the look on my face? There [was] no need to say anything. Before a woman like this, one must bow one's head."

In July, six pigeons were sent out from Atlit in a test run but with-out messages. One arrived in Egypt, and, given the experience in the Senussi campaign, that result was better than expected. Ultimately, the pigeons did not solve the communications problem, but they did manage to become part of Nili's lore.[15]

Stale or not, the British viewed Nili's intelligence as of sufficient value to risk a ship and crew month after month to obtain it. In fact, as Sheffy also notes, the British regarded the Nili ring as "the best human source extant in the country." At one point, British intelligence con-sidered closing down "some of our agencies along the coast" because, among other reasons, their information "is not of a very high order," but it ultimately recommended against doing this. "If anything hap-pened to our other and better sources ('The Very Reliable' [wireless intercepts] and 'Aaronsohn's organisation'), we should have nothing else to fall back on." Yigal Sheffy notes that "what particularly raised the ring's value in British eyes, however, was the reliability and pre-cision of its information, which became an authoritative means for verifying information from other human sources." As one example, Sheffy points out that other agents, as well as defectors, had reported on the arrival in Palestine of the 56th Infantry Division in April 1917. That information turned out to be untrue, and the British could have known because of the "omission of any mention of the existence of this division in Nili reports."

At the same time, Sheffy points out that one of Nili's most important intelligence reports, which concerned the advanced Turkish airplanes, was neither stale nor outdated. The British, alarmed by the report, rushed their own advanced planes to Palestine. Although it took some months, the planes arrived just in time, as will be seen, to restore air supremacy for one of the most important battles in the war in the Middle East.[16]

14

Everywhere I Turn I Feel His Absence

As the head of Nili, Sarah Aaronsohn's job was roughly comparable to a modern-day hands-on executive of a small business. She dealt directly with the group's sole customer, as well as managing personnel, travel, recruiting, accounting, payroll, and supply chain issues.

The sole customer, of course, was Aaron, whose demands for intelligence were precise, comprehensive, and unceasing. Where were the Turkish ammunition and provisions stored? In caves? Were Turkish units trained in the use of flamethrowers and poison gas? How accurate were the British aerial attacks? What was the weight of railway traffic passing from Afula to Ramle to Beersheba? Were north–south roads under construction? Were new bridges being built?[1]

Aaron needed more swimmers for the *Managem*'s landings. Sarah offered him a young man named Yitzhak Halperin, another Nili member from Zichron. His parents were one of the town's original founders, and Yitzhak had grown up next door to the Aaronsohns. Tall, courageous, and something of a thrill seeker, Yitzhak had volunteered for the Turkish army and, as mentioned, served in the Balkans, where he was his battalion's trumpeter. After his return to Palestine, Yitzhak worked at the research station and was recruited for the spy ring. Sarah described Yitzhak in a letter to Aaron as "a very good young man, sentimental and quite strong, doesn't fear fire or water and in fact is an excellent swimmer. He is modest as well and would carry out anything he is asked to do." She had a plan to bring him from Atlit to Zichron, "so the Zichronians can get used to the fact that he is our assistant and they can use his help for errands and different tasks. And then one day when he disappears for a few weeks it won't be too noticeable."[2]

The Turkish army transferred Dr. Neumann, Sarah's key agent, from Ramle to Petah Tikva to serve as a physician for the refugees from Jaffa–Tel Aviv. It was an important post for humanitarian reasons but had limited potential for gathering useful intelligence. As his replacement, Sarah selected the Nili member David Sokolovitz, who was married to one of her cousins. Sokolovitz, then in his midforties, was one of the older Nili members and spoke fluent Turkish, Arabic, and French. He had been serving in the Galilee area, where he reported on Turk army maneuvers, train movements, and economic conditions. Sarah sent Sokolovitz to Dr. Neumann's previous post, the railway junction at Afula, where the report on advanced Turkish airplanes had originated.

As his cover Sarah had Sokolovitz open a canteen at the Afula train station. Opening a canteen, however, took time because they required a permit and the wood to build the structure was scarce. She wrote Aaron, "You forget that we are not in Egypt where you go out and buy, even if sometimes at high prices. Here the prices are horribly high and some things are not to be found at all." Although the canteen did not give him the same access to Turkish soldiers that Dr. Neumann had as an officer in the Turkish army, Sokolovitz still managed to report on train and troop movements and provided details about the Turkish weaponry on the trains.[3]

But Sarah was not done with Dr. Neumann. After serving in Petah Tikva, Dr. Neumann left the army. He asked Sarah to help him leave Palestine; he wanted to go to Egypt and take his brother with him. Sarah wrote Aaron and asked whether Neumann could be of use in Egypt. ("Here he can no longer give us anything.") Aaron warned her that Dr. Neumann's sudden disappearance from Palestine might raise questions and therefore had to be avoided. Sarah agreed: "I intend to go to him and with some praise and a little money persuade him to stay where he is." In the end Dr. Neumann remained in Palestine.[4]

It was harder than ever to get *vasikas*, or travel permits, for her spies to move around Syria. "[For] two weeks we ran around Haifa to get a vasika for travel to Damascus, but it was impossible to get a vasika for a man, even if we covered the Turks in gold, and so we had to send a woman." Sarah sent Avshalom Feinberg's sister Shoshana, the wife of Nili spy Nahum Wilbushevitz, to Damascus with the *vasika*. She wrote Aaron, "To give you an example of how each one of our people is devoted to the work—Shoshana, who is no Sarah, is a fancy dresser and physically weak, went there [Damascus] and returned with reports. And if there is need to travel there once again believe me that I'll be the first one to go."

Sarah did not confine herself to Atlit. She traveled by the research station's horse-drawn carriage to meet her agents, give them instructions, and pick up their intelligence, but the carriage was constantly breaking down. On one occasion a wheel cracked, and Sarah and her driver had to tie it with rope. The dingy hotels at which she stayed had no restrooms. Just as she had on her prewar trip to Europe at Aaron's expense, Sarah complained about how much money she was spending on herself. At one hotel, she had to "drink barley water instead of tea, and all this at terrible prices."[5]

Another difficulty for Sarah was that the *Managem* was dropping off not just letters and gold from Aaron but also provisions that had to be carried stealthily from the beach to the research station.

Arale, thank you very much for the groceries you have sent us. I am sorry to complain about it because you sent it with the best intentions but the results were not good. In the package there were soap and chocolate and papers and bottles . . . and it arrived here all mixed up together, the chocolate turned into powder and was mixed with soap and pieces of broken glass. Isn't that a pity? And especially when getting it to the station is so hard because everything has to be carried on peoples' backs. Last time, for example, Menashe complained that he had hurt his back. If we can unload only what is most necessary for the work, it is enough. To be honest, we have no rice and it would be good to have some to hide in times of emergency. . . . If you could send us guns, now that would be worthwhile. . . . Guns are needed in Palestine as there are none, and who knows what's coming.[6]

Sarah also had to deal with the British intelligence equivalent of hypercritical and finicky bookkeepers. Captain Smith, who had refused to let Aaron take supplies for his agents on board the *Goeland*, reviewed the expense reports that Sarah sent back on the *Managem* and told Aaron that his field agents were spending too much money. Sarah responded with fury to Aaron's letter reporting Smith's criticism. After calling Smith a "swine," she wrote, "I would like to see him in our situation. He doesn't know how badly we feel when we haven't a lot of material ready in our hands. No matter how much information we get, we are not satisfied that it is enough." Sarah felt compelled to add, "I am not complaining that the work is hard on me, or asking for a raise in my salary. No. I just want the devil to appreciate our work."[7]

The workers at the Atlit research station, perhaps sensing that Sarah's mind was not on agriculture, had "allowed themselves to be negligent and pretty lazy." Sarah wrote Aaron that the one hundred Turkish liras a month he had promised would be enough to run the station and motivate the workers, "but where is the money for the station's expenses coming from?" Aaron responded that, until he came up with more money, Sarah would have to manage with the money that he had previously sent and any funds furnished by Alexander in the United States.[8]

Sarah's sister-in-law Miriam presented a special problem. Miriam was the wife of Sarah's brother Samuel, who had gone to the United States in 1915; from the outset, Samuel had opposed Nili's activities. Miriam had a four-year-old son, Yedidia, whom Miriam had struggled to raise on her own. "There is enclosed a letter from Miriam to you as well," Sarah wrote Aaron. "[Yedidia] became a better boy in the two months of my absence. He is more polite and understands that he should say hello etc. I spoke to her about going [to Egypt] and she said that under no circumstances will she do it, first of all because of Yedidia and second of all because she doesn't feel courageous enough to do it."[9]

Miriam soon became too afraid to stay. While she was not a Nili member, her last name was Aaronsohn; therefore, she would be among the first to be interrogated if the Turks discovered the espionage ring. Miriam began insisting that Sarah get her and Yedidia out of Palestine.

Sarah gave Miriam money, which appeared to calm her down for the time being, but before long she again demanded to leave with her son.

The dilemma Miriam presented was that if Sarah helped her own sister-in-law to safety, then the morale of the families of other Nili members might suffer. Her disappearance also could cause even more apprehension in the Jewish community and perhaps attract attention from the Turks. In a letter to Aaron, Sarah wrote that Miriam now "dreams of nothing" except leaving Palestine, but "her absence will cause us a lot of trouble and spoil our work." Sarah also wrote to Liova Schneersohn: "As to my sister-in-law, we still don't know whether to send her or not. If she disappears suddenly they'll start talking again." And in a subsequent letter to Aaron, Sarah was still torn. "Not to take her would be better for the sake of our work here. What's better, to risk [the] work or her?" In the end, Sarah decided that Miriam could leave, but delays in the *Managem*'s visits kept that from happening until September, by which time Yedidia had fallen ill and had become "scrawny, like a dog."[10]

Sarah also had to sort out misunderstandings over money. One involved Liova Schneersohn's brother, Mendel, who had also been born in Russia. He emigrated to Palestine in 1904 when he was fourteen years old and worked on the family farm in Hadera. After the war started, Mendel joined Nili along with Liova. Sarah gave him a monthly allowance, but Mendel claimed it was less than the amount his brother Liova had promised he would receive. Sarah complained to Aaron that Mendel was being greedy. "Sometimes we get complaints from those who think we are spending all the money on ourselves." Another money issue involved her father, Ephraim. Aaron had asked Sarah to give Ephraim money each month, but he refused to take it. She explained to Aaron that she would wait until Ephraim ran short of money. Then he would accept some of hers because he would have "no choice."[11]

From the Netherlands, Sarah's husband, Haim, sent a modest sum for refugee relief. Like a proud housewife who had started a profitable business on her own, Sarah wrote to Aaron, "What would you say about his kindness? This made me laugh so hard. If this poor man only knew how many thousands of pounds pass through my hands and how many thousands of francs I spend, what would he have said?"[12]

Not all problems could be solved with money. In January 1917 Sarah had written her sister, Rivka, about Avshalom's death. In the same letter, she mentioned happier news. "Tova [Gelberg] and Nissan Rotman plan to get married soon. May they have luck and happiness." Nissan, a friend of Avshalom Feinberg's, and Sarah's close friend Tova were both Nili members. Sarah once gave Tova documents to deliver in Damascus. Wearing a white dress and many bracelets—"like an Arab dancer," as Tova recalled later—she traveled alone by train to Damascus. "Throughout the journey I didn't say a word, for I didn't speak Turkish." Tova delivered the documents and returned safely.

Nissan and Tova had fallen in love, but in June 1917, before they could marry, the Hadera community council ordered Nissan to leave the settlement on suspicion of being a Nili spy. Sarah wrote Liova that Nissan and Tova "have to move from place to place." Although homeless, they evidently still worked for Nili.[13]

In August Sarah had to hide a deserter from the Turkish army. An Albanian divisional operations officer in the Turkish army named Baha al-Din had approached Nili operative Naaman Belkind, who was stationed in Rishon LeZion and whose field of operations was southern Palestine. Baha asked Belkind for assistance in going over to the British. Belkind went to Atlit and attempted to convince Sarah and Yosef to send Baha to Egypt on the *Managem*. Baha had intelligence value because he was based in Gaza, served as a secretary to a Turkish general, and had recently accompanied the general on a tour of the Gaza–Beersheba front.

Sarah had not tried to recruit deserters. She had enough to deal with without having to arrange to hide and feed them, and then get them aboard the *Managem*. Sarah was at best lukewarm to Belkind's proposal, but her hand was forced when Belkind revealed that he already had told Baha of the *Managem*'s regular visits, making it more dangerous to refuse to help him than to hide him. The plan was that Baha would take his scheduled four-day leave in late August and come to Atlit when the

Managem was expected to arrive. By the time his absence was noticed, he would be at sea.

The plan fell apart when the *Managem* failed to arrive on the anticipated day. Baha, still in Palestine, overstayed his leave. Sarah now had to deal with a deserter whom the Turks would be searching for. She hid Baha in Liova Schneersohn's home in Hadera and then moved him to Haifa. At one point, Sarah kept Baha in a room at the Atlit research station.

In addition to her other tasks, Sarah still found time to maintain Aaron's books and collections in his home in Zichron. "We have begun to rearrange the herbarium and the general library," she wrote him.[14]

Aaron again had been urging Sarah to leave Palestine and return to the safety of Cairo. "Soon I would like to see you here."

Sarah did not reject his request out of hand. But her two-month involuntary stay in Cairo had been something close to traumatic. She demanded that Aaron promise that she would be able to return to Palestine.

> As far as my leaving is concerned, I have consulted many people but mainly my own self. I don't know if I have the right to do it. I don't want to leave permanently because I should be where the danger is and I cannot leave the work and the people just when things are getting more difficult and when there is so much work to do. When we arrange the evacuation of our dear women, I shall be among them, but I will be the last one to leave. I will certainly come to meet [Alexander, then on his way to Egypt from the United States], this I want to do and with no excuses, but with one condition, my dear—that I will come back. We are not small children and I would like your word on that.[15]

Another consideration for Sarah was that without her, Nili would collapse, a point she stressed to Aaron more than once in her letters. In one she wrote, "If there are quarrels when I am here, what would happen if I left? Besides that Yosef wouldn't be able to work without my advice." In another letter Sarah explained that, "I would really be missed here, I help a lot and help in maintaining the relationships between everybody as well. What can I do? I am fortunate that they all believe in me very much. Maybe they are mistaken but that's how it is."[16]

Were these Sarah's only considerations in wanting to stay in Palestine? Sarah was spying because of the vulnerability of the *yishuv* to an Armenian-style massacre and to redeem the sacrifice of a man she held dear, but in various letters she revealed her feelings about espionage work and not always consistently. For example, in July she wrote Aaron that she had heard a false rumor that Germany was seeking peace terms but that the British had declared they were willing to fight for another three years. "It's terrible, if that's the case, isn't it? To live and work like this for three more years is impossible."[17]

But a few weeks later, contemplating the possibility that someday her espionage would be over, Sarah had a different perspective. Less than two years earlier, Sarah had been an unhappy housewife in Constantinople, where she had no outlet for her intellect and energy. Referring to the fables of seventeenth-century French poet Jean de la Fontaine, Sarah wrote that "If I ever have to leave I will suffer greatly. I don't know how I will get used to it, without the challenges here, and most of all the work. Do you remember Fontaine's fable of the dog who begged to have his collar put on again when they freed him? That's how I am."

She added that the work made her "feel good about myself. . . . without it, I shall suffer more. I do not say that I am always happy, there are unpleasant moments as well. Still, I love the work."[18]

Sarah's most difficult problem was Avshalom. His family, she wrote Aaron soon after returning from Egypt, "senses something, everyone wonders about his silence. How can he not write and not send anything?" She had "told them stories about Avshalom and they are beginning to accept that he is in London." Others were giving Sarah a hard time. "Father and Zvi are killing us: 'Where is Avshalom?' They scream that he is surely dead. The situation is already very bad and in addition to that we have to pretend and hide the truth. Everywhere I turn I feel his absence, especially here in Atlit where everything reminds me of Avshalom. My heart aches, but what can I do? Can he come back?"[19]

Sarah described her brother Zvi's increasing tantrums. "He is very angry that we haven't told him about Avshalom. He is screaming that he's certain the boy is not alive and why can't we just tell him?" Ten days later, she wrote that Zvi had vilified her in a letter and made a new allegation. "He claims that Yosef killed Avshalom in order to take over his position. Well, we have to bear this kind of thing until the 'end of the work.' And then we will consider ending our relationship [with Zvi]."

Aaron responded, "Regarding Zvi I am not surprised, just dreadfully sorry. I have always kept him away from the work because I couldn't trust him. But I could not anticipate that he would become so heartless and brainless as to make you suffer so much." Aaron promised to write a letter to their father, asking him to intervene with Zvi and "tell him to stop if he ever wants to talk to us again in peace."[20]

But the anxieties and suspicions of Avshalom's family and friends only worsened. Yosef Lishansky wrote a letter to Aaron explaining how difficult it had become to maintain the charade that Avshalom was alive. On behalf of himself and Sarah, Yosef asked whether "it might be a good idea for you to send a letter in Avshalom's name, to his mother and Sarah, from London, written in English." Yosef suggested that the forged letter describe the state of Avshalom's health and include requests about handling his personal affairs. "The handwriting should be more or less like Avshalom's, they will understand that because of the censorship, he had to write in English and [they] won't suspect anything. He will write as well that he will soon return to Egypt and go to the front line. He will write to Sarah that he is very sorry that he couldn't meet her in Egypt because exactly one week before her visit he was urgently called to the military school in England."[21]

Sarah had been deceiving everyone about Avshalom's death, from her brother Zvi to Avshalom's cousin Naaman Belkind to Avshalom's immediate family. Aaron had not objected and left it to Sarah to carry out the deception. Now, through Yosef, she asked Aaron for assistance in lying to their close friends. Aaron responded in a letter that, at first, did not address the request for a forged letter. He initially raised a painful topic, their failure to speak about Avshalom's death while Sarah was in Cairo.

Regarding your silence, do not think for a moment that I know or love you less because you didn't speak. On the contrary, I am proud of you because you possess this great power—to keep silent. Believe me, I read between the lines of the many painful and complicated things that you carried in your heart and dared not speak of. I heard you, and took part in your sorrow, but it wasn't the right time to talk and that is why I didn't implore you to talk. But you can be sure of one thing, Sarah, my dear. I understand you, I believe in you and give you every moral support a brother can give a sister.

Aaron then wrote meanderingly about other matters, as though he needed time to muster the courage to finally respond to Sarah's request for a forged letter. He inquired whether Sarah had heard from her husband, Haim ("Where is he? What is he doing?"), and reported on his ongoing feud with Captain Smith. ("I had a bitter argument with the devil.")

Finally pleading for Sarah's forgiveness and understanding, Aaron wrote that he would not forge a letter from Avshalom. "What you are asking is way beyond my powers. A letter in his handwriting, and his style, how would I know? It would be a sin. Please my Sarah, not this my dear. If there's no other option, then tell them, the whole bitter truth, but please do not ask me to do that. I cannot. I am sure you will understand and not be angry with me."

Aaron and Sarah had come full circle; their prewar relationship of the older and stronger brother and the younger and admiring sister had inverted, which Aaron now acknowledged. "In many respects I am a woman just like you, my dear, and you are in many ways a man, a strong man, whom one can only be extremely proud of."[22]

In her next letter to Aaron, Sarah apologized for her request. "As to not being able to create a letter from Avshalom, I agree with you. It is a sin on my part to make such a demand but do know that we shall not reveal our secret to his family." But Sarah nonetheless emphasized the need for the forged letter. If the Feinberg family and others, including Naaman Belkind—her best agent in southern Palestine—knew that Avshalom was dead, they "wouldn't take part in the work any longer. . . .

They are bitter because of his silence but in their hearts they probably don't suspect he is dead. It's only Naaman and Nissan [Rotman] who keep saying that even if he had lost his arms, Avshalom would be writing to his family with his feet." She added, "Everyone looks at Yosef with jealousy and thinks that he is Avshalom's angel of death, if not for him, [because] Avshalom would never have gone alone."[23]

As to Aaron's claim that he wouldn't know how to forge a letter in Avshalom's handwriting, Sarah pointed out that any number of samples of Avshalom's handwriting were available to guide him. "Regarding letters and writings from Avshalom, indeed, there are plenty. I don't know how valuable they are I just know that Nissan buried them in the ground. I asked him to dig them up so that I can send them to you."[24]

In hindsight, it is arguable whether the course of subsequent events might have turned out differently had Aaron forged the letter. Even had Aaron tried, the forged handwriting and the attempt to write in Avshalom's unique style might not have fooled anyone. But without tangible evidence of Avshalom's whereabouts, Sarah was unable to satisfy the spreading cry, "Where is Avshalom?"

In late August Naaman Belkind demanded that Sarah give him permission to go to Egypt on the *Managem* and find out for himself whether Avshalom was alive. If Sarah didn't permit him to leave for Egypt, Belkind threatened, he would go anyway across the Sinai Desert.

Sarah now had a more serious problem on her hands than the Feinberg family. Belkind was capable, like his cousin Avshalom, of dashing headlong into the Sinai Desert. He was a stalwart, physically strong young man and a resourceful agent with a dash of Avshalom's flamboyance. Belkind had been the source of potentially important intelligence about Turkish army deployments at the Gaza–Beersheba front, much of it gained from relationships he had formed with Turkish officers (some of whom, as recounted, Belkind met while working in the wineries in Rishon LeZion). He reported on the digging of trenches, the placement of artillery, and the rate of desertions at the front.[25]

At first Sarah thought that Belkind was just trying to scare her with his threat to search for Avshalom. She told Belkind to stop being so foolish, and, in any event, he had to wait until Aaron gave permission.

Belkind told her that unless he had immediate permission to go to Egypt on the *Managem*, "I will walk through the desert."

Yosef Lishansky then met with Belkind in Petah Tikva. The two reached an agreement, or so it seemed. Yosef promised to plead with Aaron that Naaman should be allowed to go to Egypt, and Naaman agreed to continue gathering intelligence. The two then discussed a plan for Nili spy Avshalom Fein to gain access to Turkish bases on the Gaza–Beersheba front. Yosef gave Belkind money to implement the plan and left. Later Naaman sent a short intelligence report to Atlit along with a letter stating that he was planning to travel to Hodj, an Arab village in the Negev Desert, to gather information. Naaman added that he expected this trip would take some time. No one in Atlit, including Sarah, could have known that Naaman Belkind had lied to them.[26]

On August 12 Aaron had a meeting with now captain Lawrence at the Savoy Hotel. Both men were at the top of their games. The British highly valued Nili's intelligence, Aaron himself was constantly sought out for military and political intelligence about Palestine, he dispensed (through Sarah) much-needed relief funds in Palestine, and *yishuv* leaders in Palestine recently had requested an opportunity to travel to Egypt and have an audience with him. The previous month Aaron had been granted a meeting with General Allenby, the new commander of British forces in Egypt, during which Aaron lectured Allenby on such topics as the quality of the Turkish army ("inferior on the whole but infinitely superior to what we had expected"), Djemal Pasha ("vain, superficial, very much inclined to plot and clever at it"), and general conditions in Palestine ("unbearable situation").[27]

Lawrence had recently won a military victory that would help make him a legend. Early in the war, Arab nationalists had begun organizing secret cells throughout Syria and what is now Iraq with the goal of achieving Arab independence. Sensing an opportunity, the British sought to persuade Emir Hussein, the religious leader of the Muslim holy cities of Mecca and Medina and the surrounding Arabian lands of the Hejaz, to lead an Arab revolt against the Ottoman Empire. The British vaguely promised Arab independence once the war was won (a promise not honored) while the emir kept his options open until he could gauge with whom—the British or the Ottomans—he could make the best deal.

In June 1915 Djemal Pasha had begun arresting Arab nationalists and putting them on trial. He instructed the judges to impose the death penalty on anyone found to be a member of a secret organization or to have conspired against the Ottoman Empire. The crackdown continued into 1916 with the arrests, trials, and hangings of more Arab nationalists. In early 1916, with fifty armed guards for protection, Sheikh Faisal ibn Hussein, the third of four sons of Emir Hussein, went to Damascus and held secret meetings with Arab nationalist leaders still at large.

Djemal Pasha, aware of Faisal's presence in Damascus (although evidently not the meetings with the nationalists), summoned Faisal to his office and complained about a letter the emir had sent to Enver Pasha. The emir's letter conditioned Arab allegiance to the Ottoman Empire on its formal recognition of the emir as the hereditary ruler of the Hejaz. Rather unpersuasively, Faisal—a mild-mannered man who was more of a dreamer than a warrior—explained the letter as a misunderstanding due to his father's poor grasp of the Turkish language.

Unconvinced that he was only dealing with a language barrier, Djemal told Faisal that emir was engaged in blackmail when the nation was in grave danger but not yet defeated. "If the war came to a victorious conclusion," Djemal menacingly warned Faisal, "who could prevent the Government from dealing with you with the greatest severity once it is over?"

In fact, Djemal had already taken such steps by dispatching 3,500 Turkish soldiers to Medina. Despite Djemal's assurances to the emir that the soldiers' destination was Yemen, that the force had been sent to arrest the emir was clear enough. Then, on May 6, 1916, twenty-one Arab nationalists were hanged in the central squares of Beirut and Damascus. The hangings, the threat from Djemal, and the soldiers making their way to Medina—all appeared to have made up the emir's mind to join the British side. On June 5 the Arab Revolt, under operational command of Faisal and his brother Abdullah, began.[28]

Initially, the Arab Revolt had a series of military setbacks. In early 1917 Faisal, who had met and been impressed by Lawrence several months earlier, asked the British to assign the young officer as his permanent liaison with their headquarters. Lawrence took it upon himself to disclose the Sykes-Picot Agreement to Faisal, arguably an act of insubordination (or worse). Then, in a second such act, Lawrence disregarded his chain of command ("I decided to go my own way with or without orders") and led an Arab attack on the strategically important port of Aqaba on the Red Sea's Gulf of Aqaba.

On May 9 Lawrence and Auda abu Tayi, a chief of the Howeitat tribe, led no more than forty-five Arabs out of Faisal's camp at Wejh. They crossed the Hejaz railway near Deraa and eleven days later began crossing the furnace known as El Houl (the Terror)—a scorching, black desert plain devoid of life, not even a blade of grass—while pummeled by desert winds. "By noon it blew a gale," Lawrence later wrote, "so dry that our shriveled lips cracked open, and the skin of our faces chapped, while our eyeballs, gone granular, seemed to creep back and lay bare our shrinking eyes."

In that crossing, memorably depicted in the 1962 film *Lawrence of Arabia*, an Arab named Gasim dozed off and fell from his saddle unnoticed until Lawrence spotted his riderless camel following behind their procession. Lawrence went back into the trackless waste; found Gasim, who was staggering around, almost blind, and going mad from thirst; and brought him back. Lawrence's feat did not impress Auda abu Tayi, a powerfully built man, around fifty years old, who claimed to have been married twenty-eight times and to have killed seventy-five men (not counting Turks) with his own hands. "For that thing," Auda said gesturing at Gasim after Lawrence brought him back, "not worth a camel's price." Lawrence, not one to be outdone in a verbal joust, quickly replied, "Not worth a half-crown, Auda."

The two recruited more Arab tribes over mammoth feasts (mutton and rice, drenched in fat and butter) with local tribal chiefs. On July 6, 1917, Lawrence led a raid that captured Aqaba, whose Turkish garrison never anticipated an attack by Arabs from the desert. He then crossed

160 miles of Sinai Desert in just over two days to reach the Suez Canal and bring word to British headquarters that Aqaba had been taken. He met with General Allenby to describe the victory and seek expanded British support for the Arab Revolt. Lawrence's uniform, stored in Cairo, had been eaten by moths. For the meeting with Allenby, Lawrence wore white silk Arab skirts, a head cloth, and a gold-bound head rope and carried a dagger.[29]

The meeting between the burly Aaron Aaronsohn and the diminutive T. E. Lawrence did not go well. The two did not get along personally, and their most cherished political objectives—Aaron was a Zionist and Lawrence was an advocate of Arab independence—appeared irreconcilable. By Lawrence's account, Aaron stated that "the Jews intended to acquire the land-rights of all Palestine from Gaza to Haifa, and have practical autonomy therein." Lawrence was so disturbed by the implications for the Arabs that he wrote to Mark Sykes. After recounting Aaron's statement, Lawrence asked, "Is this acquisition to be by fair purchase or by forced sale and appropriation? . . . Do the Jews propose the complete expulsion of the Arab peasantry, or their reduction to a day-laborer class?"[30]

Aaron's diary records a different meeting. "I had a chat with Captain Lawrence this morning. Our interview was devoid of amenity. He has been too successful at an early age—and is infatuated with himself." Aaron certainly missed the irony that this characterization might somewhat apply to him as well. Aaron nowhere mentions telling Lawrence that the Jews planned to acquire all land rights in Palestine. Rather, as Aaron recounted their talk, Lawrence gave "me a lesson on our colonies" and shared the "feelings (sentiments) of the Arabs, etc. etc." Listening to Lawrence, Aaron could "almost imagine that I was attending a conference by a scientific anti-Semitic Prussian speaking English. . . . I am afraid that the German spirit has taken deeper root in the minds of pastors and archeologists." Aaron concluded of Lawrence, "He is still at the age where people do not doubt themselves—happy young man! He is plainly hostile to us. He must be of missionary breed." Evidently their talk did not dwell on whether Arabs and Jews might find a way to coexist.[31]

Around this time, Aaron opened another battle front, in this case with the British Zionists, who were led in London by the forty-three-year-old Chaim Weizmann, president of the English Zionist Federation. Like Aaron, the Russian-born Weizmann was a world-renowned scientist but in the field of chemistry. He had recently earned the gratitude of the British government by developing a process for manufacturing synthetic acetone, which the British needed to make explosives.

Weizmann's and the English Zionists' long-cherished goal was in obtaining the official support of the British government for a Jewish homeland in Palestine. Anticipating considerable Arab resistance to that aspiration, British officials asked the Zionists to support the Arab Revolt and its goal of Arab independence from the Turks. In a speech to a Zionist gathering in England later that year, diplomat Mark Sykes reminded the audience that "today the Arabs were seven to eight millions [*sic*]. There was a combination of man-power, virgin soil, petroleum and brains. What was that going to produce in 1950? The Mesopotamian canal system would be reconstructed. Syria must become the granary of Europe. Baghdad, Damascus and Aleppo would be each as big as Manchester. Therefore, I warn Jews to look through Arab glasses."[32]

If for no other reason than political expediency, Chaim Weizmann and the English Zionists spoke in conciliatory, albeit nonspecific, terms about Arab independence: the Turk was a common enemy, and the Jews wanted only peaceful relations with Arabs and Christians. But conciliation was not one of Aaron Aaronsohn's strengths; neither was concealing his hostility to the Arabs. Aaron expressed his views in a paper, excerpts of which later appeared in the September 1917 issue of the *Arab Bulletin*, a secret, limited-circulation publication on Middle East politics started by the Arab Bureau in 1916. Its first editor was Lawrence. In his paper, Aaron called the fellahin "squalid, superstitious, ignorant." He acknowledged that at times the fellahin had been displaced by Jewish settlers and would be again, and from "national, cultural, educational, technical and mere hygienic points of view," the Jews had to live separately from the Arabs.[33]

The antagonism between Aaron and Chaim Weizmann and Weizmann's colleague Nahum Sokolow had less to do with specific policies and everything to do with ruffled feathers—namely, Aaron's. He felt that Weizmann and the Zionists in England had treated him disrespectfully and reciprocated in his communications with them. "Received a telegram from Sokolow [and] Weizmann. They are maintaining their former attitude—and are indulging in demagogical phraseology. I replied to them frankly and crudely."[34]

Aaron was so angry that he told Reginald Wingate, the British high commissioner to Egypt, that he would disband Nili unless the British supported his demand for recognition and respect from the London Zionists. While Aaron had made such threats before, and never followed through, Wingate was alarmed enough to write the British foreign secretary and ask him to support Aaron in his feud with the English Zionist Federation. "An additional reason for not alienating him, and one which may perhaps appeal to you, is that the military authorities attach importance to retaining the use of the organization which he has created in Palestine." Aaronsohn, Wingate emphasized, was "in a position to destroy the organization," and in his current state of mind, "he will be tempted to do so unless some concession is made to his views." Wingate added, "How far his difference with the Zionists in England is due to questions of principles and how far to wounded susceptibilities I am unable to tell."[35]

On August 20 while riding his bicycle through the moonlit streets of Cairo, Aaron decided that exchanging telegrams with the London Zionists was getting him nowhere. "Our dispute with Sokolow [and] Weizmann cannot be settled. An interview is necessary. . . . Why should I not go to London?" The British intelligence officers, perhaps relieved to hand Aaron over to someone else, agreed to his proposal. Aaron's plan was that his brother Alexander would return from the United States and assume his role in Cairo as the liaison between British intelligence and Nili. In the meanwhile, the Nili spies in Atlit waited for the *Managem*'s next visit—and waited and waited.[36]

To Sarah and her spies the *Managem*'s landings represented more than an opportunity to deliver their intelligence reports to Aaron and the British in Egypt. The appearance of the surfboat at the beach, the hurried exchanges of whispered but friendly greetings, the letters from Aaron—all were crucial to their morale. The *Managem*'s last visit had been on August 14. Through the rest of August and into September, Nili spies had gone down to the beach night after night and endured, as Yosef Lishansky put it, "kisses from hundreds of mosquitoes, and aching sides from the rocks we lay on," but the ship never appeared.[37]

The *Managem* had tried again on August 23, but the weather prevented a landing. Sometime after that, Yosef wrote a letter to Aaron, not knowing when or even whether it would actually be picked up. "Now, listen. Tens of people are risking their lives, working, and hurrying here and there, to get their material, and return to the Station with it, so that, Heaven forbid, they should not be late for the ship and displease our partners; so that our partners won't say we are lazy (again Heaven forbid!). But from your side, what?"[38]

Apparently in the hope that the *Managem* would appear on September 12, Sarah wrote dispirited letters to Liova and to Aaron. In both letters Sarah insisted she would not return to Egypt. And, once again, she told Liova that he had to stay in Egypt. "Liova, Shalom. This time we shall not see each other. Even if you wish to come to me you won't be allowed and rightly so because this time they are guarding the coast more closely. So why walk around too much when there are guards wandering about? As you can see, I am not accompanying you after all [back to Egypt], and even if Aaron demanded it, I couldn't."

Sarah did not expressly say that she was tired; nonetheless, that was the implication. "When will it be finished?" she asked in her letter. "All eyes are looking at us now. Maybe it will pass, like most things that begin at a high heat and then cool off." In an implied reproach of the British, Sarah observed that the *Managem*'s failure to land for many weeks meant that much of their intelligence was outdated. "It's a real shame you didn't come during August. We had news back then, but today it is surely old. We still have a bit more material that we have gathered up until today."[39]

Sarah's letter to Aaron had little to say about her espionage. "I really don't know what to write to you." So she wrote about her foot, which was giving her trouble. Evidently she suffered from a painful condition known as *mal blanc* (bad white, or paronychia), in which the toes develop abscesses from a bacterial infection. She mentioned that their father was alone and unhappy, and for the past two months he had been without household help. "The house is deserted and he suffers a lot from that." Sarah expressed doubts about the value of her work while making clear at the same time that she would not be returning to Cairo.

Believe me Aaron, I am sick of working in this way. I tell you the truth, being here is sometimes necessary, but there are times when I think, what am I accomplishing? Maybe I should leave Yosef alone to do what he pleases, one way or the other he does not like taking advice and does things in his own way. So, why should I sit here? Had I liked living in Cairo, I would have left long ago. But I am not comfortable saving my soul before saving others, and as well, I am curious to see the outcome of the war in our country.

She wrote a series of discordant notes.

What about the British? It's a disgrace to fight against such a lazy and exhausted people like the Turks and not win. . . . Where is Alexander? What news does he have? . . . I am not in the mood to write . . . it is very hot and we bathe in the sea . . . we are waiting for you [the *Managem*] today, but who knows? . . . Father is healthy and sends his love. He wishes for the world to calm down . . . . Zvi is very angry with me, I seldom speak with him.

Toward the end of her letter, Sarah wrote about Avshalom. She dreaded the day when the Feinberg family finally learned what had actually happened to him. "All their hatred and agony will be directed at me." She even imagined her conversation with Avshalom's family. "Yes, the disaster is big and terrible, there's nothing to say. Had he still been alive, so be it, everything would have been different, wouldn't it?" Sarah added that she preferred to forgo that ordeal. "And I am terrified by this prospect. I'd rather escape to the end of the earth. I don't have enough courage for that."

She ended the letter, "Be well, Arale, good luck in your work, and please try to put an end to this as fast as you can."[40]

Tension was building in other ways. Yosef Lishansky's wife, Rivka, had reached her breaking point. As mentioned, Yosef had moved his family to Zichron to end their somewhat nomadic existence. Rivka and the two children lived in a rented room, but it's unclear how much time, if any, Yosef spent with them. "It was the first time that our life was a bit more organized," she recalled later, "despite the fact that we still didn't have proper food, like everyone else and so we had to settle for anything we could get." Rivka did receive some sugar from Egypt, probably delivered by the *Managem* as a secret reward for the family members of Nili spies. "I had to sneak a piece of sugar for the children every day, and be cautious that no one knew. I lived in constant stress."

Rumors about Turkish informants in Zichron reached Rivka. She decided to warn her husband and enlisted Menashe Brunstein, a Nili spy she trusted, to take her in a wagon to Atlit, where Yosef then was staying. The two arrived at night. Rivka went to Yosef's room to tell him that he was in danger.

"I found him in bed," she recalled later. "Sarah's clothes were also in the room."

Rivka already suspected that Sarah and Yosef had a relationship, but the discovery wounded her nonetheless. Her daughter, Ivria, later recalled that Yosef's relationship with Sarah "hurt [my] mother very much."[41]

On September 13, 1917, Aaron sailed for London.

That same day Turks in southern Palestine caught Naaman Belkind, who had been trying to cross the Sinai Desert into Egypt, where he hoped to find his cousin Avshalom Feinberg.[42]

15

The Situation Is Getting Worse

It's unclear exactly what led the Turks to Nili. One reason is that as various messengers came and went from Atlit with alarming reports, facts and rumors then were difficult to separate, and they have been ever since.

Part of Nili's lore is that the pigeons sent by the British were to blame for the Turks' discovery. On August 30 evidently out of frustration over the *Managem*'s failure to land a surfboat or a swimmer at Atlit for several weeks, Sarah sent off several pigeons with messages, despite their poor track record from the test flights in July when only one of six pigeons had reached its destination. Tied to the legs of Sarah's pigeons were tiny metal capsules containing her coded messages. A few days later, Sarah went down to the beach for a swim. One of the pigeons she had sent aloft was perched on a water tank near the beach.

Then reports reached Sarah that another of her pigeons had somehow managed to land amid a flock of pigeons kept by a Turkish official. The official had gone out one morning to feed his pigeons and found the unfamiliar pigeon with a capsule tied to its leg; the capsule contained an indecipherable coded message. After learning that the pigeon was in Turkish hands, Sarah wrote Aaron on September 10 when she anticipated the *Managem*'s imminent visit (it would not appear for nearly another two weeks). Sarah whimsically reported that the pigeon was now on its way to an audience with Djemal Pasha. A Turkish commander, she wrote, had joked that the pigeon speaks "Jargon [Yiddish], English and French, and then added that it knows Arabic as well, so it appears less obvious that we, the Jews, are the main suspects."

Nonetheless, the rumors left Sarah uneasy. "I say, as far my limited comprehension is capable of, that I do not like this. Had they searched us, I would have been more comfortable since they wouldn't have found anything and would have stopped suspecting us. This way I don't know if they are planning to arrest us at work. Don't you think they have an eye on us without our knowing it?" As a precaution Sarah ordered the remaining pigeons to be destroyed and buried, but the discovery of the errant pigeon likely alerted the Turks to the existence of a spy ring in Palestine.[1]

That same month Sarah and Yosef learned that the Turks had arrested two young Arabs from Nazareth as British spies. In a letter to Aaron, Sarah reported that the two Arabs had confessed that a ship had recently dropped them on the coast near Mount Carmel and that they had expected a French ship would pick them up in October. "We still don't know how the government found out about their coming ashore. But we know that when the fools were caught they admitted everything." Sarah added that "more police forces were deployed to guard the coast."[2]

This story appears to be corroborated by the postwar account of a Turkish intelligence chief. In his telling, the Turks were alerted to the presence of a British spy ring in the country by the discovery of English coins minted in 1916. In turn, they led to a priest with a connection to the coins. The priest told the Turks about two Arab agents from Nazareth who had been dropped by a British spy ship on the Palestinian coast. The Turks arrested the two Arabs, who disclosed that the British ship, before dropping them on the coast, had landed Jewish spies in the vicinity of Atlit. The postwar account apparently described the same event that Sarah and Yosef reported even though important details, such as the nationality of the spy ship, differed.[3]

As far as Sarah was concerned, the most alarming event had to be the report of Naaman Belkind's capture. The pigeon and, almost certainly, the two Arabs did not know the names of any Nili spies. Naaman, however, knew many of their names. Unlike many espionage rings, Nili was not organized around clandestine cells, where the members of one cell are ignorant of the other cells or the identities of the senior leaders. In the case of Nili, where Avshalom and Sarah had recruited from a network of family members and friends, a cell structure was impractical, especially when Nili's effectiveness depended on Sarah's leadership and personal relationships with her spies.

On September 21, 1917, apparently unaware that Aaron had left Egypt, Sarah wrote him another letter to be picked up by the *Managem*. The letter concerned Naaman Belkind, but as in other letters, Sarah first dwelled on other matters before getting to the most difficult topic. The *Managem* had passed by Atlit, she wrote, but had not sent the surfboat to the shore because the sea was rough. Today the sea was calmer, so she had permitted herself to hope that the British would finally land a boat. If once again her people at the beach came back "empty handed, I am sure they will not have any desire to go next time. Do not forget, dear, that it's been a month and a half that you've left us without any information, and our material is already out of date and it's worth nothing."

Then Sarah got to the real, and unnerving, point of her letter: despite her best efforts, she had been unable to keep Naaman Belkind from trying to get to Egypt. "He said that if we didn't allow him to leave [on the *Managem*]," Sarah wrote, "he would walk through the desert. We knew he had courage but never thought he would dare, that he simply wanted to scare us." Left unmentioned was Aaron's refusal to forge a letter in Avshalom's handwriting to reassure the Nili spies, including Naaman Belkind, that Avshalom was alive.

> On Sunday, the 17th [of September] a messenger came to Zichron and gave us this message: Naaman Belkind was captured in Ruchema [in the Negev Desert] as a spy. The Bedouins turned him in to authorities in Beersheba. Yosef was asked to come urgently and bring 400 Liras. . . . I immediately sent for Yosef in Atlit and he came to Zichron, where he met Nissan [Rotman] and they left together. I went to Atlit. . . . Today the messenger came again with the following message: Immediately after Naaman was arrested, [German general Friedrich Kress] von Kressenstein was informed about it and gave the order to hang Naaman with no excuses, but to torture him before the execution to find out who else is working with him because he knows that there is a whole group of spies. . . .
>
> The boy was badly tortured, for three days he was deprived of food and kept in heavy chains, it didn't go as far as falaka. He kept his mouth shut, and didn't say a word. . . . Even if they don't hang

him, you can imagine how we will be looked at. And if they do then it would be really the end of the world. [The *yishuv*] will refuse to talk to us and keep kilometers away from us. . . . They would say that we are not cautious . . . and a thousand more claims like that and not without reason. And if they hang Naaman is it good for us the Jews? It would be charming, don't you think?[4]

Notwithstanding the assurances he had given Yosef Lishansky in Petah Tikva, Naaman Belkind had planned all along to cross the Sinai and find Avshalom Feinberg. With the assistance of his brother-in-law, Naaman had hired a Bedouin guide. He ignored the pleas of his brother, Eitan, also a Nili spy, and went into the desert. Naaman apparently had not gotten far before the Turks caught him.

How Naaman was caught and what happened afterward are uncertain. By the account a second messenger brought to Sarah, Naaman had fallen sick in the desert and rested in a Bedouin tent. Sensing an opportunity to obtain a reward from the Turks, the local Bedouins seized both Naaman and his guide, who managed to escape. They turned Naaman over to Turkish authorities in Beersheba, where General von Kressenstein happened to be at the time. Upon learning of Belkind's arrest, von Kressenstein ordered him to be tortured and, once Naaman revealed his secrets, hanged. It didn't help that Naaman, for inexplicable reasons, had been carrying documents sewn into his clothes that may have been incriminating.[5]

The accounts of the ensuing efforts to free Naaman Belkind lack coherence, possibly because the rescue efforts themselves did not make sense. In her letter to Aaron reporting on Belkind's arrest, Sarah mentioned a man named Mizrahi, the Turkish government's demand that two members of Naaman's family had to come to Beersheba, and the family's decision to send Naaman's wife and sister. "The Government demands two people from his family. I don't know why it is that his wife and Sonia were chosen to be the ones to go, probably because they can beg for him. Today I sent our wagon to Haifa to get Sonia and take her there. You do understand [the] complex situation we are in at this moment. There is no money in the box." The wagon driver was Yanko

Epstein, an occasional Nili helper from Zichron. (Why Naaman's wife did not join Sonia is unclear.)

Eliahu Mizrahi was a Jewish agronomist who worked for the Turkish government in the Beersheba region. His role in the affair had to do with the documents that Naaman had been carrying at the time of his arrest. The documents had been confiscated by Atif Effendi, an opportunistic secretary to a Turkish commander in the area, Bhagat Bey. In a subplot to the drama of Belkind's capture, Atif apparently saw a moneymaking prospect in the documents and contacted Mizrahi, telling him that for five hundred liras he would return the documents to Belkind's family. Mizrahi contacted Belkind's family, who in turn contacted Sarah and Yosef.

Yosef Lishansky and Eitan Belkind managed to come up with the money. Yosef found three hundred liras somewhere, and Eitan borrowed the rest from family friends. Eitan then went to Rehovot, about twelve miles south of Jaffa–Tel Aviv; met with Mizrahi; gave him the money; and implored him to go immediately to Beersheba and get the documents back. Mizrahi returned to Rehovot and informed Eitan that he had completed his mission and successfully recovered all the documents. Eitan demanded that Mizrahi hand over the documents.

"Are you out of your mind?" Mizrahi yelled. "Do you really think I'd take a risk carrying such materials in my bag! I burned them immediately after I received them!"

No one knows whether Mizrahi was telling the truth, whether it was a ruse by Atif Effendi or even by Mizrahi, or whether Belkind was even carrying documents in the first place. The only things Nili had accomplished were spending more of whatever dwindling funds were still available and delaying the implementation of Yosef's desperate plan for freeing Naaman Belkind.

That plan was conceived at a meeting in Gedera (not to be confused with Hadera), a settlement about forty miles north of Beersheba. The meeting was attended by, among others, Yosef Lishansky and Nili spy Avshalom Fein, who had gone weak at the knees when he first met Sarah. The idea was that a group would dress up as Turkish policemen, charge the prison on horseback, subdue the guards, and free Naaman Belkind.[6]

The plan resembled a suicide mission more than a rescue. Given Belkind's importance, the Turks undoubtedly had a heavy guard at his prison. Yosef Lishansky was capable of leading such a mission, suicidal or not, but the plan was never implemented. This may have been due to the group's inevitable demoralization over the Mizrahi fiasco, to their sense that Belkind was beyond help because the matter was too big to be resolved by either bribes or force, and, perhaps most decisively, to Yosef Lishansky's sudden illness from malaria. Nissan Rotman, a Nili member who was also in Gedera but who may not have attended the meeting, took Lishansky back to Atlit in a carriage.

What occurred next was luck. Sonia Belkind's carriage was headed south on the same road that Nissan Rotman traveled north to take the malarial Yosef Lishansky back to Atlit. Sonia's driver, Yanko Epstein, stopped to rest and feed his mule at a khan (rest stop). As Yanko was getting coffee, Nissan Rotman's carriage pulled up with Lishansky. The passengers in each carriage began arguing with each other.

The ill Yosef Lishansky from the northbound carriage cautioned, "Don't do it. You're heading straight into the fire! Straight into the fire!"

The argument ended with Lishansky getting out of Rotman's carriage and climbing into Yanko Epstein's carriage. "Turn around and head back, Yanko," Lishansky told him. Yanko turned the carriage around and went to Zichron. The passengers were silent most of the time, except for Sonia, who was a doctor in Haifa. "Here, take this pill," she said to Lishansky. "You'll feel better." That was the only time that Sonia, who wore a veil throughout the trip, spoke.

They reached Zichron just before dawn. Lishansky demanded that Yanko Epstein take him to Atlit. "I have to see Sarah right away. If you don't drive me, I'll walk." Yanko's mule was tired, but Yanko couldn't let Lishansky walk, so they kept going. Finally Yanko had to stop for the sake of his mule. Lishansky got out and started walking after Yanko and Sonia fell asleep. The two awoke at midday and hurried to catch up with Lishansky. By the time they reached him, Lishansky was nearly at Atlit, about twelve miles away. "He had walked the whole distance in three hours," recalled Yanko Epstein decades later in a conversation with Israeli writer Hillel Halkin, "and with a fever."

At the research station, Lishansky went inside to speak to Sarah. She came out and asked Yanko to take Sonia to Haifa.

"Miss Sarah," said Yanko, "this is as far as I go. My mule is half dead and the other half has to work tomorrow." It was the only time that Yanko said no to Sarah because "she could make you feel small for doing that."

"Well, at least come in and have a cold drink."

Yanko declined. He was uncomfortable because he knew that Sarah shared a room with Lishansky. Further, Yanko himself may have been in love with Sarah and didn't consider Lishansky to be in Sarah's league. "I grant you," Yanko Epstein told Halkin, "a woman who stoops to spying doesn't stop there. What is it to surrender your body when you've already surrendered all else? He had a family. She wouldn't have done it if she had thought there was a way back. But she didn't love him."[7]

Naaman Belkind was still in Turkish hands. According to one account, before torturing Naaman, the Turks had pretended that he was going to be freed and that they were all good friends. Turk officer Ali Faud Bey supposedly entertained Naaman with a jovial banquet, where he was plied with wine and hashish. Under the influence of both, Belkind boasted of his exploits as a spy. Then the Turks tortured him to extract whatever other information he might possess.[8]

On September 20 shortly after a messenger had brought the initial news of Belkind's capture, Sarah was summoned by the Zichron community council, the stern and dour elders of the community. The middle-age or older men, to emphasize their dignity and authority, might have dressed in their prewar European finery: three-piece suits, white shirts, upright collars, and, whether needed or not, walking canes. Facing them was a young woman they had known since she was a child but whom they now regarded as a threat to their lives and homes. The occasion was not one for small talk about this year's harvest, and they were uninterested in gold, even if Sarah had any to give them. They were deeply angry at Sarah.[9]

The scene had been recurrent in Jewish history. The Zichron leaders were acutely conscious of the *yishuv*'s vulnerable, minority status in the Ottoman Empire. Like their forebears in Europe and Russia, they believed in an ancient, time-tested wisdom that had well served the Jewish people through centuries of oppression, brutality, and pogroms: in times like this, Jews must keep their heads down and ride out the storm. It will inevitably subside. In this fashion Jews had kept their communities and their traditions intact for two millennia. Rebels such as Sarah only brought ruin.

The leaders began by denouncing Sarah and her spy ring. "We have to inform you that you are engaged at terefah work." The term "terefah" is used to describe food that is not ritually clean or prepared in accordance with Jewish law and is therefore unfit for Jewish use. The Jewish leaders evidently intended to convey to Sarah that her espionage violated the rules that Zichron Ya'akov lived by, including obedience to the Jewish elders and conducting oneself so as not to jeopardize the health and safety of the community. That Sarah was a married woman who spent time in the company of Yosef Lishansky, a married man who was himself something of an outcast in the *yishuv*, could have further provoked the Zichron leaders.

"You are the sister of the one leading all this work. You are a daughter of this village. Your family is at the highest risk."

The leaders explained that they hadn't approached Yosef Lishansky because "he is one day here and one day there." As to Sarah, "this is the third time we turn to you. All you have given us is excuses and explanations. Today we don't want to hear any more explanations, only a proper answer, that you will cease this work."

Unlike her past confrontations with the Zichron leadership, Sarah was largely silent. "What do you mean by stop this work?" she asked at one point. "What sign do you want?"

"The sign will be that none of you will remain in Zichron, Atlit or Hadera." Even so, apparently uncertain as to whether Sarah's espionage might actually help the British drive the Turks out of Palestine, the Zichron leaders gave themselves a small out. They suggested that an imminent British victory might change their minds. "Perhaps you will send us such good news that everything will change." One leader scornfully added, however, "But it is difficult to rely on your cold

Englishmen. How long will this continue? Even the little children are mocking the English. 'Why don't they come to take the country? Who is stopping them?'"

The Zichron leaders bluntly told Sarah that Zichron's Jews did not support what she was doing. "We don't want to risk an entire community. We don't want this imaginary treasure that you are getting for us. We don't want the Turks to slaughter us . . . we don't want to be hanged because of a few people whose work puts them in danger."

The leaders gave Sarah an ultimatum: stop the work and the activities at Atlit, and if she wanted to continue spying, then she had to go somewhere else not in Palestine. Otherwise, they warned Sarah, "we will have no choice but to sabotage it in all possible ways, it will simply become a war between Jews and Jews, and even if we don't intend it, simply because of all the disputes and the quarrels, it will eventually reach the Government."

Sarah told the leaders that she had to consult with others. She would give them an answer at the end of September.[10]

In her letter to Aaron describing the meeting, Sarah wrote, "I am not afraid of barking people." Even so Sarah appears to have been more shaken by this meeting, coming so soon after news of Naaman Belkind's capture, than those of her past confrontations with Zichron's leaders. She suggested to Aaron that Nili temporarily suspend its activities. "Now, what can we do? I think, Arale, to cease for a while." If they did stop their work, Sarah pointed out, they would have to find money to pay the Nili spies because "wherever they turn, they will not get work."

Sarah complained that it had been too long since the last visit by the *Managem*. "Don't forget, my dear, that we have already gone a month and half without hearing from you. Our situation is very complicated now, and we need you. And there is not even any money in hand. And what do we do if they [the British on the *Managem*] don't come? Who would help us?"

But above all, Sarah was afraid that Naaman Belkind would break down under torture and reveal the identities of the Nili spies.

To tell you the truth, if I knew that Naaman is the only victim then it's a pity but there's nothing we can do. But if finally he is forced to talk and reveals our secret? Then what? The man had already grown sick and weak while being in prison and if they give him a good falaka who knows if he won't talk? And if they [the Turks] have suspects, who knows if we are not among them? And especially now, after the story with the pigeon when we are being watched by everyone, both the Jews and the Government.[11]

Despite the *Managem*'s failure to appear, the *yishuv*'s opposition, and Sarah's anxiety over Naaman Belkind's fate, the espionage continued. Avshalom Fein worked for a German businessman who had a contract to deliver supplies to the Turkish army along the Gaza–Beersheba front. With a wagon drawn by two horses, Fein had considerable access to the Turkish camps and fortifications. He carried with him a bottle of wine or cognac to create a convivial atmosphere with the Turkish officers he encountered, some of whom invited Fein into their tents. One officer, who happened to be Jewish, told Fein that the talk in the Turkish army was that "the British would never break through at Gaza unless they first captured Beersheba."

Fein delivered a report to Sarah on the conversation with the Jewish officer and a detailed report on machine gun positions along the Gaza–Beersheba front.

"Avshalom, you're doing good work, and you're very quick. Continue in that spirit. Our days may be numbered. Every moment that we're not active is wasted."[12]

The *Managem* had left Egypt on September 11, with Liova Schneersohn on board. Before his departure, Liova promised Aaron, who was about to leave for England, that "everything shall be done just as it should be." But nothing went as anyone had hoped.

The next day Liova sighted the white houses and red roofs of Hadera, his hometown; gazed at the Roman ruins at Caesarea, "now empty like a ghost town"; and came in view of Zichron. Using binoculars, Liova saw "the trees of the park, the administration building, the winery and the ordinary homes . . . what a lovely view this is; my heart is opening and my spirit is rising." Liova wanted to leap from the ship, swim to the shore, and kiss the land. The *Managem* went on to Atlit, where the wind picked up. Captain Weldon refused to let Liova off the ship. "Going to the shore is absolutely impossible," another British officer told Liova, who responded that he had to go ashore no matter what.

The following day was even worse, with a strong wind from the west. As the *Managem* approached Atlit at night, Liova begged for the surfboat to take him to the beach. It was impossible, the officers told him, given the conditions. "They say we shall return again tomorrow. God bless the believer!" Liova wrote in his diary. Weldon was overheard saying to a crewman, "What will I do if he really jumps in the water? He doesn't care about any danger."

The winds and waves worsened that night. The *Managem* sailed to Cyprus, where it waited for several days for the weather to improve. Liova prayed at a temple in Nicosia on Rosh Hashanah and dreamily watched a dust whirlwind rise from the ground, "spinning round and round trying to reach the sky, in its secret prayer to God."

On September 21 the *Managem* sailed back to Atlit. The sea was calmer, and by ten o'clock that night, the surfboat was in the water with Liova on board. He made it all the way to the beach. While the *Managem* had brought gold for the refugees and Nili, Liova had left the gold on the ship because he wanted first to find out what was happening at the research station.

On shore Liova was enveloped in darkness and silence, broken only by the chirp of a bird. He cautiously crossed the small stream and went into the field to the stone heaps where the Nili beach watchers sometimes waited. No one was there. Liova was about to turn back when he heard, "Nili!" It was Menashe Brunstein and two other Nili spies.

"How are you? Where is Yosef? Where is Sarah?"

"Yosef is not here, he went south. Sarah is alone in the station. A disaster happened. Naaman Belkind was captured and sentenced to death. He is expected to be hanged any day."

And that was how Liova found out that Nili was in peril. He returned to the surfboat, went back to the ship to pick up the gold and his own belongings, and took the surfboat again to the beach. Brunstein and the others escorted Liova to the research station. They paused at the Haifa road and listened for sounds because the Turkish patrols had become more vigilant. After a few minutes, someone coughed—the signal that it was safe to proceed.

At the station Sarah was happy to see Liova but upset about the *Managem*'s delayed arrival. "They suffer so much because we are not punctual and don't appear at the appointed times," Liova wrote in his diary entry for that day. "But what can we do? We depend on the sea. The rulers of the sea are not at our command." He added, "The story with Naaman Belkind is a disaster."

Liova told Sarah that Aaron had left Egypt and was on his way to London. Her brother Alexander had arrived from the United States and had taken Aaron's position as the liaison between Nili and British intelligence. The availability of gold should have heartened Sarah because it meant that a bribery-rescue plan might be implemented after all. Then the one man best able to execute such a plan, Yosef Lishansky, arrived at the research station sick with malaria.[13]

Liova spent the next two days going over intelligence reports with Sarah and sitting by Yosef's bedside. "Yosef's fever rises," Liova wrote in his diary, "and it becomes impossible to talk with him." In Yosef's lucid moments, the two spoke together in low voices about Naaman Belkind, rescue plans, and an evacuation of Nili. They realized the *Managem* could not just take the Nili spies, however; their families would have to be evacuated, too. The problem, both agreed, was that a mass exodus by Nili might cause the Turks, frustrated that the Jewish spies had slipped away, to punish Zichron and other communities for harboring an espionage ring. Both were aware that in Tyre, in what is now Lebanon, an agent and his family had been picked up by a British ship. As a result, the Turks had considered all the citizens of Tyre to be traitors and arrested the town's sailors and fishermen. Reportedly, the leaders of Tyre were also arrested and sentenced to death.[14]

The Atlit research station hadn't changed since Liova had last been there in April, when he boarded the *Managem* and escorted Sarah to Cairo. The fields were plowed; a horse walked in the yard, its chain jangling; a carpenter worked under a sunshade; and another worker passed by with a shovel on his shoulder. But his Nili comrades had changed. "Their personal life is of no account to them," Liova wrote. "They have ceased to exist as people. They are carrying out an historic task. They are only clay in the hands of the potter."[15]

The *Managem* returned on the twenty-third. The day was calm; the sky and water were the same shade of blue. The ship picked up Liova; Nili's intelligence, including Avshalom Fein's report; and Baha al-Din, the Albanian defector whom Nili had kept hidden for weeks. Before returning to the ship, Liova promised Sarah that the *Managem* would return in two days' time although he had no way of knowing if Captain Weldon would comply with his promise.

Once on board Liova explained the plight of his friends to Captain Weldon. "I listened to his news, which was not altogether good," recalled Weldon, who came away with the misimpression that all Zichron's residents, and not just the members of Nili, wanted to escape from Palestine. "It appeared that the Jewish colony were [*sic*] becoming nervous and that they wish us to take them out of the country." Instead of returning to Egypt, the *Managem* sailed to Cyprus so Weldon could drop off Baha al-Din and report to his superiors on Nili's plight. Baha, a tall, handsome young man, spoke excellent French. On the way to Cyprus, Liova talked with Baha, who sat in an easy chair on the deck, about new borders for Turkey, independence for the minorities under Turkish rule, and the future of Palestine and the Jews. Baha grimaced, leaving Liova with the impression "that in the future he might laugh at us." Liova found a gray civilian suit for Baha "because he couldn't go on wearing his Turkish uniform on an English ship."[16]

While the *Managem* was at Cyprus, a wireless message came in from Cairo with an ominous report. Naaman Belkind's brother-in-law, who had supplied Naaman with his guide and horse, had been arrested by the Turks.[17]

Naaman Belkind had finally broken down. In return for a promise that he would be freed, Naaman told the Turks enough to implicate his brother-in-law and disclosed information about the location and leaders of Nili. Belkind was then sent to Damascus, where he appeared before a court.

"I've kept my word to you. I've told you all I know. Now you must keep your word and release me."

"Yes, yes, my son," the Turkish judge told him. "You will be released. But I'm sure there is just a little bit more you can tell us first."[18]

From Cyprus Captain Weldon sent a report to British headquarters in Egypt about Nili's predicament and requested the assistance of the *Veresis*, a trawler recently assigned to intelligence work. "With her help I knew that, if all went well, we could 'evacuate' the whole Jewish colony." British headquarters ordered the *Veresis* to sail with the *Managem* to Atlit even though, when they arrived on September 25, there would be enough of a moon that a Turkish patrol might spot the ships from shore.

The *Managem* and the *Veresis* reached Atlit early in the morning of September 25. White seagulls flew over the ship and sometimes alighted on the sails to rest. Liova regarded the seagulls' decision to perch on the sails as a favorable sign. That night a surfboat from the *Managem* landed on the beach. At the stone heaps, Liova was met by Yitzhak Halperin and Menashe Brunstein.

"How are you?" Liova asked. "Are we taking people on the ships?"

"No, there is no need to take people. We evacuate only Miriam, the wife of Samuel Aaronsohn, and the child, Yedidia."

The two Nili beach watchers gave Liova a letter from Sarah. "We are not sending a report on Naaman's situation this time," she wrote, "first of all because Yosef is sick and though he feels better today, he still cannot write, and besides that, if we are lucky and manage to do it, we will travel there [Beersheba] soon and then write a detailed report." She then described a plan to delay Nili's evacuation for two days, evidently to arrange for a small contingent of spies to stay in place.

And now to our situation. The situation here is getting worse from moment to moment. Nevertheless, we cannot run away at this moment because a sudden departure will harm the whole Yishuv and, in particular, those close to us. We've decided to organize our affairs so as not to cut off the connection between us and Palestine so that we can steal back here one of these days and see what is going on with those we left behind. Very likely this is a mistake on our part, and we will be too late to escape, but we are endangering ourselves to the last minute, and are keeping our people with us so that if we can't get to the shore by stealth, we'll get to it by force of arms, come what may. . . .

You must understand that we cannot remain much longer, because our hours are numbered. So, without any excuses, on the 27th of the month, immediately after the moon sets, you must be by the coast, and we will be waiting for you. Possibly with the families, or without them. We don't want to take off too many people at one time so that no great suspicion should fall on the Yishuv. If you have time to come to us for half an hour it would be good. If not, may God be with you. And if, with God's help, we are not caught by then, we shall see each other on the day after tomorrow, at midnight.[19]

Sarah, under stress, evidently did not appreciate that in two days the moon would be full and the night sky too bright for the *Managem* to return. The earliest the ship could return to Atlit would be mid-October. After reading Sarah's letter, Liova said to Menashe Brunstein, "Tell them, Menashe, that we will come on October 12, and maybe with Alex, too, and shall do everything we can to rescue them." Liova later wrote in his diary, "Sarah insists that we come back in two days from now. But how can we? It means coming on the night of a full moon!"[20]

Miriam and her four-year-old son, Yedidia, had been brought from Zichron to Atlit. In a separate note, Sarah had written Liova, "I am sending you my sister-in-law and all of her property, that is, her son Yedidia. Watch over this property of hers and settle her and the child as well as you can. . . . Try without fail to come on the 27th, for who knows if you will find us after that."[21]

It was now one o'clock in the morning. After they had arrived in Atlit, Miriam told Yedidia not to make a sound. So far even in the pitch-dark crossing to the beach, the little boy had managed to remain silent despite the tension of the adults around him. Captain Weldon was in the surfboat when mother and child climbed in. The boat rowed away from the shore, and Yedidia, wrapped in a black scarf, still remained quiet. When the boat was well clear of the shore, the boy turned to his mother and said something. Captain Weldon asked Miriam what her child had said and why he was now sobbing. Miriam explained that he had asked her, "Mummy, may I cry now?" and that she had told him, yes, he could.[22]

The *Managem* put in at Port Said on the evening of September 26. The next day Liova reached Cairo, where he was met by Alexander Aaronsohn and Aaron's friend Peretz Pascal. They conferred and agreed that, even apart from the full moon, an evacuation of the Nili spies would put the Jews in Zichron and elsewhere in danger, as Sarah had warned in her letter to Liova.[23]

Even if the *Managem* had returned on September 27, Sarah likely wouldn't have boarded it. "Sarah, get out while you can," a Nili spy had warned her at one point. "They'll start with you first." She declined. "I want to be the last, not the first to leave." Sarah may have written the note to Liova—"try without fail to come on the 27th"—in a panicky moment, but in any event the *Managem* did not return on the twenty-seventh.

That night Sarah and Mendel Schneersohn, Liova's brother, were at the research station. As the night wore on, it became increasingly clear that the *Managem* was not coming. Sarah was casually holding a small revolver.

"Where is the safest and surest place to fire to be killed instantly, should one decide to commit suicide?" Sarah asked.

"Just put the barrel in the mouth, pull the trigger gently, and all is over in a flash," he replied.[24]

Even though the *Managem* had delivered gold on its September 21 visit, Nili did not use it to bribe Naaman Belkind's guards. No rescue of any kind was mounted in Beersheba to free Naaman. Perhaps they all sensed that by now he had been in Turkish hands too long not to have talked, and, in fact, he had.

In a letter to Aaron, Sarah had asked, "I tell you the truth, being here is sometimes necessary, but there are times when I think, what am I accomplishing?" Since returning to Palestine in mid-June, Sarah had no way of knowing whether her espionage was having any appreciable impact. Indeed, despite running an intelligence network, she did not even know how the war was going in Palestine.

While in Egypt Sarah had learned of the British defeats in the First and Second Battles of Gaza. Since then the British advance appeared stalled, despite false rumors that the British had captured Beersheba. Sarah repeated one such rumor in another letter to Aaron. "What's new overseas? Any news? Here in the south the Turks were badly defeated, but how badly is unclear to us. Please send us some news for we feel as isolated as if we live in a desert." Her next letter to Aaron disclosed that she now knew that the rumor was untrue. "I wrote that the British had conquered [Beersheba]. It was not correct. The British have yet to enter Beersheba and I am sure you know better the reason why."[25]

In late September, as Nili's dire hour approached, Sarah's question of "what am I accomplishing?" was indirectly answered by General von Kressenstein, who had ordered Naaman Belkind to be hanged. Nili's intelligence on advanced Turkish airplanes, based on Dr. Neumann's reports in March 1917 that Sarah then sent to Aaron in Cairo, had caused the Egyptian Expeditionary Force to urge the British War Office to rush more capable planes to the front in Palestine. The British began sending better airplanes to the Middle East that would prove indispensable to Gen. Edmund Allenby's strategy.

General Allenby was not about to mount a direct assault on Gaza for a third time when the first two attacks had been disastrous for both the Egyptian Expeditionary Force and his predecessor. Through a series of deceptions, including a naval bombardment of Gaza from British ships in the Mediterranean and the positioning of troops, Allenby's strategy was to convince the Turks that the coming British attack would again focus on Gaza. In fact, Allenby planned first to assault Beersheba, take the town, and then roll up the Turkish defensive line to Gaza from the east. But as Matthew Hughes wrote in *Allenby and British Strategy in the Middle East, 1917–1919,* "Control of the air was essential if Allenby's preparations for the Third Battle of Gaza were to be kept secret."[26]

Developing and refining the strategy to attack Beersheba required daily air reconnaissance and aerial photography patrols by British airplanes, which operated from airfields behind Allied lines. The Australians recruited many pilots from the horse cavalry brigades on the theory that the skilled horseman has the necessary qualities to be a capable pilot. They were trained in England and then sent to the Sinai to join the Australian Flying Corps (AFC). The AFC's No. 1 Squadron took aerial photographs, which were used to create maps of the Gaza–Beersheba front. But according to an official history of the AFC, "for a long time the technical superiority of the enemy's aircraft made this photography trying and dangerous." For example, on July 8, two single-seater AFC planes from the No. 1 Squadron escorted a double-seater plane on a photographic reconnaissance mission. Two German planes attacked and shot down one of the AFC escorts, killing the pilot. They forced the other AFC single-seater plane to land, but the two-seater reconnaissance plane escaped. A German plane landed by the downed AFC plane, captured the Australian pilot, and flew him to a German airfield behind the Gaza-Beersheba front. That morning the Australian pilot could not have dreamed that he would take off from an Australian airfield in a British airplane and land in a German airplane at a German airfield.

Despite the brutal carnage on the western front, chivalry still existed in some places. Two days later, a German plane dropped a message from a German aviator on the AFC airfield where the downed planes had been based. It said one of the Australian pilots was dead and had been buried by the German aviators with full military honors. The other pilot was unharmed—a photograph of the pilot with a German officer was included in the message bag—but unfortunately he was short on clothes. Shortly afterward an AFC pilot flew across the lines to the German airfield and dropped a parcel of clothes and letters for the captured Australian pilot, returned the waves from the German airmen with his own, and flew off. A later message in poorly written English reported that the German aviators were enjoying the captured Australian pilot's company. "He is such a well-educated and genteel boy, that we do with pleasure all, what is pleasant for him. . . . Perhaps I can see the sun later in Australia."

By the end of the summer of 1917, as a result of Sarah's intelligence, air superiority belonged to the British. A German report dated September 29, 1917, apparently written by General von Kressenstein, observed that "the mastery of the air has unfortunately for some weeks completely passed over to the British." The report attributed the British air superiority to the sheer numbers of British planes and to "the appearance of a new type of machine which is superior to our single seater."[27]

British air superiority meant that not only could Allenby conduct the air reconnaissance necessary to his strategy but also, as historian Anthony Bruce noted in *The Last Crusade: The Palestine Campaign in the First World War*, given the Turks' "much more limited opportunities for regular surveillance, British preparations on the ground escaped the enemy's attention." Air superiority thus mattered greatly to the deception so essential to the British victory in the Third Battle of Gaza, which would be fought from late October to early November 1917.[28]

Sarah would never know that.

In early October word of Belkind's plight and the dire implications for Nili reached Aaron in London. He persuaded the British to pay four thousand pounds, a considerable sum, "to buy off Turkish torturers." But Aaron could not come up with a means to hand over the money.[29]

The *Managem* returned to Atlit on October 12. Alexander Aaronsohn, who had now taken Aaron's place at British headquarters, and Liova were on board. So were other Nili agents based in Egypt. In light of Nili's uncertain fate, two British warships accompanied the *Managem* although they remained at a much greater distance from Atlit. The *Managem* carried Very lights, which are powerful flare guns that had been known to bring down airplanes, to signal the warships to come to its assistance if necessary.

In the daytime no one was visible on the balcony of the research station, although Liova thought he saw something white stretched out there. "Is this a good sign? We wait impatiently for the night to come." At 8:30 p.m. the *Managem* dropped two surfboats in the water. Alexander and Liova were in one boat. It was a calm night, and they reached the shore without the need for a swimmer to ferry them to the beach.

There were no beach watchers to greet them. The little band of tense British sailors and Jews cautiously left the beach and crept toward the station, halting at the stone heaps. They listened but did not hear the whispered password, "Nili, Nili." A bird flew overhead, frogs croaked as always in the swamps, and mosquitoes buzzed around the increasingly nervous men. Then they heard the sound of a shot.

"They're shooting in our direction!" Alexander was new to the landings and perhaps was more startled than the others were.

"Yes, they are shooting," Liova said.

They heard no more shots. They waited in the blackness and the stillness, but they saw and heard nothing. Finally they returned to the beach. They gave the signal for the surfboats to take them back to the *Managem*.

"Inside we are devastated," Liova wrote in his diary. "All night—a dreadful sleepless night—we are on our way to Port Said."

Alexander had brought with him a message for the Nili spies from Zionist leader Chaim Weizmann that had been dispatched to British headquarters in Cairo shortly after Aaron's arrival in London. Weizmann's message was, "We dedicate all our efforts to securing a Jewish Palestine under the auspices of Great Britain. Your heroic suffering is the greatest encouragement for our difficult task. Our aspirations are great. Be strong and of good courage until the redemption of Israel."

But no one was at the research station to receive Weizmann's message.[30]

16

She Is Worth a Hundred Men

The days following the *Managem*'s departure, with Miriam and her young son aboard, coincided with two of the most important holidays on the Jewish calendar. That year Yom Kippur, the Day of Atonement, fell on September 26, and Sukkot—the weeklong commemoration of the forty years that the Jews had wandered in the desert, living only in temporary shelters—was on October 1.

In Atlit Sarah presumably fasted and prayed on Yom Kippur, just as Jews around the world did. The next day, when Sarah had asked the *Managem* to return, the Nili beach watchers waited in vain for the ship to appear.

Sarah wanted to be with her father for Sukkot. On September 30 she and Yosef Lishansky, who was now able to travel, left Atlit and went to Zichron. In the town Jews had set up small booths outside their homes—a symbolic re-creation of their ancestors' abodes in the desert—in which to eat their meals.

On the night of October 1, a wedding took place at the Schechter home. Afterward people went out into the streets, standing and talking. Word reached the revelers that Turkish soldiers had surrounded Zichron. No one knew what it meant, but the Turks had conducted searches for deserters before. The partying ended.

Yanko Epstein, knowing of Naaman Belkind's arrest, went home to get his *vasika*. His father sat on the bench in their front yard, smoking a cigarette. Sarah passed by, returning from a visit to the home of Tova Gelberg's family. She crossed to the Epstein side of the street.

"Do you think it's routine?" Sarah asked Yanko's father.

"Miss Sarah, you know better than that. It's not for deserters this time. It's for you."

"Really? Do you think so?"[1]

Sarah did know better. Several hours earlier, Re'nam Nazzer, the Maronite-Christian wagon driver at the Atlit research station, had gotten word to Sarah and several Nili spies that Turkish soldiers were on their way to Zichron. Sarah had met with Nili spies Yosef Lishansky, Reuven Schwartz, Menashe Brunstein, and Yitzhak Halperin in Aaron's house and told them to get away before the Turks arrived. She asked Halperin to find a safe place for Lishansky to hide outside Zichron. Sarah told all the men that if they were caught by the Turks, they must put the blame on her. Lishansky and Halperin left through a secret escape tunnel that had been dug below the house in anticipation of the present circumstances. Halperin disobeyed Sarah and remained in Zichron. Meanwhile, Lishansky and the other two spies hid in the hills outside the town. Sarah left Aaron's house and went inside her father's home.

The sounds of galloping Turkish cavalry and speeding military vehicles were soon heard in the streets of Zichron. A battalion of Turkish soldiers under the command of the *kaymakam* (governor) of Haifa surrounded the town. The Turks posted guards at every road leading into Zichron and set up two perimeter rings around the town. The remaining Zichron residents still on the streets fled to their homes and locked themselves inside.

The Turks evidently had a list of suspects. They went straight to the Aaronsohn compound, stormed into Ephraim's home, and arrested Sarah; her father, Ephraim; and her brother Zvi. The three were beaten and then taken to the Langa family's now empty home, which the Turks had commandeered as a headquarters. The Turks also arrested Yosef Lishansky's wife, Rivka, and took her and her two children to the Langa home. Before leaving, the Turks looted the Lishanskys' home.[2]

The interrogations commenced that night. As a start, the Turks, for whom torture was a standard police practice, used the *falaka*, which they had administered to Alexander Aaronsohn in 1915. The prisoner is tied down in some manner, his or her legs are extended or elevated, and the soles of the prisoner's bare feet are beaten with a stick or other blunt object. The method is still in use today, not only in the Middle

East, where it originated, but also in India, Uganda, Chile, Peru, Bangladesh, and Azerbaijan.[3]

"I had never experienced anything like it," recalled an Iranian women whose feet had been beaten after the Iranian Revolution. "I couldn't even have imagined it. It exploded inside me like a bolt of lightning. . . . How could anything hurt so much? . . . My breath stopped in my throat. I tried to think of a way to help myself bear it. I couldn't scream, because there wasn't enough air left in my lungs."[4]

The Turks didn't apply the *falaka* to Sarah, at first. The Turks beat the feet of her father and Zvi, evidently in the belief that even if they didn't talk, Sarah, unable to bear their suffering, would disclose the names and whereabouts of the Nili spies to stop it. The cries of Ephraim and Zvi were heard throughout Zichron, but neither they nor Sarah gave the Turks any information. During his beating, Ephraim cried, "Shema Israel" (Hear, O Israel).

Sarah insisted to the Turks that her father was innocent. Far from trying to stop her father's torment, Sarah instead encouraged him to resist. "Be strong, Father, and do not let your spirit fail. . . . Be proud. . . . They did the same to your sacred late fathers. . . . Stand the trial, Father. . . . Remember, you are one of the descendants of the Maccabees."[5]

"Girl, do you warn me?" Ephraim said angrily to Sarah.

At dawn, now Tuesday, October 2, the prisoners were allowed to return home under guard. A donkey had to carry Ephraim because he could not walk on his swollen, bleeding feet. In the morning, the Turks came to Ephraim's home in the Aaronsohn compound and continued torturing Ephraim and Zvi there. None of the Aaronsohns provided any information, so the Turks began beating and whipping Sarah.

"Tell us where Yosef Lishansky, Reuven Schwartz, and the other spies are or else we will keep beating you to death."

Sarah still refused to talk. Frustrated, the Turks arrested Albert Alter, the head of the Zichron community council. The Turks had learned, probably from Naaman Belkind, that Alter was the father-in-law of Nili spy Reuven Schwartz, who was now hiding outside Zichron. The Turks alternately beat Alter and forced him to watch the beatings of the prisoners in the Aaronsohn family home. Then Alter was marched through the empty main street of Zichron, crying, "Reuven, Reuven, where are you?"

Alter as well as Reuven's father, R. Chaim Bar Schwartz, were beaten badly in the main street. A few hours later, Reuven went into the town and surrendered to the Turks.[6]

That day the Turks brought Dr. Hillel Yaffe, the Zichron physician, to the Aaronsohn family home and allowed him to examine Sarah and her father. The Turks may have wanted his medical assistance in keeping the prisoners both alive and conscious as long as possible so their torture could break their wills. Dr. Yaffe found that Ephraim Aaronsohn "had been beaten mercilessly. His legs were swollen and blue, he breathed with difficulty, but he was holding out bravely." Sarah had marks on her legs and waist from whippings. Dr. Yaffe complained to the *kaymakam*.

The *kaymakam* apologized and promised to discipline the responsible officer. "Under no circumstances do Turks beat women." But he threatened to keep lashing Ephraim if Sarah refused to reveal Yosef Lishansky's hiding place. The *kaymakam*'s assurance lasted no more than a few hours, and the Turks began beating Sarah again.[7]

The Turks moved Sarah, her father, and her brother to the Hershkowitz house and then to the Rivniker house, where Osman Bey, a Turkish officer, had set up a makeshift torture chamber and, bizarrely, what amounted to a child care facility. Rivka Lishansky and her two children, Ivria and Tuvia, were also brought there. So was Zvi's young son, Avner. Other prisoners, such as Reuven Schwartz and his father-in-law, were shuttled through the Rivniker home as well. The captive children were allowed to wander from room to room and witness the torture. Ivria and Tuvia Lishansky retained clear memories of what happened in the Rivniker home.

Sarah, Rivka Lishansky, and Rivka's children were put in a room without furniture, so they sat on the bare floor. Speaking in Yiddish, Sarah told Rivka that she would take all the blame and insist to Osman Bey that Rivka knew nothing. To make Sarah's explanation convincing, Sarah and Rivka pretended to be bitter enemies (given Rivka's discovery of Yosef's affair with Sarah, this may not have been difficult for her).

They turned their backs on one another, acting out what Ivria Lishansky later called a "game of anger." The Turks must have found the mock anger between the two women convincing because Rivka Lishansky was only interrogated and not beaten.

Sarah was tortured in an adjacent room. Osman Bey demanded that Sarah reveal Yosef Lishansky's hiding place. He again applied the whip to Sarah, but when that proved unsuccessful, Osman Bey moved on to other methods.

Ivria Lishansky watched through the doorway. "I shall never forget the sight of this remarkable woman," she recalled years afterward, "how she stood there with her head held high, never leaned against the wall, and stretched both hands forward while a Turkish soldier whipped them hard."[8]

Sarah managed her pain by constantly mumbling in French. "Torture me, beat me, as much as you please. It will be in vain. You will get nothing from my mouth. Your last day has arrived. You think that since I am a woman, I will be weak. . . . I laugh at you. I despise you. I did not have any partners in my actions. I alone did the work and dug your grave. . . . And why did I do that? For I have seen with my own eyes how you shed the blood of the Armenians."

One of the Turkish officers, who spoke French, was enraged by what she said and ordered even more vicious whipping. Between beatings and whippings, Sarah was tied to a door handle so that she could not sit or lie down. Thirsty, she demanded, as though she were in charge, that an officer bring her a glass of water. Torturing a woman appeared to be acceptable, but apparently it was against Turkish etiquette to refuse her demand for a glass of water. Since her hands were tied, Sarah insisted that Tuvia Lishansky, and not a Turk, hold the glass to her lips. She sipped a little and then continued her mumbling when the whipping resumed.[9]

"You—go and tell your Turkish dictator that you can crush my body, but you can never rule my soul. . . . You Turks, your time is up. This country is our homeland and it shall be ours."

The Turks began to prepare Sarah for the *falaka*. She refused to allow her legs to be tied together so, as Ivria recalled, "the officer ordered one of the soldiers to hold them together, but she did not agree to this either, saying that she wouldn't permit an ordinary soldier to touch her legs. The officer decided to call over another officer. Sarah instructed him how to tuck in the edges of her dress so her thighs won't be exposed while he was holding her legs together." Sarah was beaten on the soles of her feet.[10]

"You, Osman, the master of the inquisitors, this time I overpowered you. I do not fear you, you cannot harm me, you coward, a 'hero' to fight women."

At some point during the days of Sarah's torture in the Rivniker house, Ivria fainted. It may have been when the Turks began mangling Sarah's skin with tongs, pulling out her hair, and crushing her fingers. Or it may have been when Sarah cried out, "Mother . . . Mother . . . I can't stand any more!"[11]

By fainting Ivria afforded Sarah temporary relief, because the Turks suspended the torture for the rest of the day. Sarah's torture resumed the next day, but she still refused to give the Turks any information about the Nili spy ring, its members, or its activities. The Turks had apparently assumed that a woman would be unable to resist their well-proven methods. Watching Sarah, an impressed Turkish officer said, "She is worth a hundred men."[12]

On October 4 the frustrated *kaymakam* assembled the Zichron community council and other prominent townspeople and addressed them in French. For those who did not speak French, the *kaymakam*'s words were translated into Yiddish. He explained that Yosef Lishansky, the spy leader, must be found. The concept that a spy ring might be led by a woman was still beyond the Turks' thinking.

"When the Fatherland is in danger," the *kaymakam* told the crowd, "I am prepared to punish a hundred innocents in order to find the one guilty man." For the benefit of his audience, the *kaymakam* listed his feats during the Armenian genocide, including killing Armenians with his bare hands. He gave Zichron twenty-four hours to produce Lishansky, or he would destroy the town. The Zichron leaders met alone, and each swore on the Torah to find Lishansky and give him to the Turks. Their plan was to send delegations south and north to look for Lishansky while those remaining in Zichron would plead with the *kaymakam* for an extension of the deadline.[13]

By now the Zichron residents, cowering in their homes and listening to the screams and cries in the Rivniker house, were in a state of near hysteria. Some women from the town cooperated with the Turks. They pointed out the homes of the Nili spies and urged the Turks to search them again. During Sarah's torture, the Turk soldiers, not realizing that she understood Turkish, mentioned the names of several of the women.[14]

Meanwhile, the Turks told Sarah and Rivka Lishansky that they would be taken the next morning to Nazareth for further interrogation. This meant Sarah would have to endure more torture before being taken to Damascus for a trial and hanging. Rivka asked and was given permission to take her children home in Zichron and give them baths and fresh clothing. Sarah would be allowed to go home and change her clothing at the same time.[15]

On her final night in the Rivniker house, Sarah managed to find a piece of paper and something to write with. Writing in dim light, in a room that the Turks had vacated, Sarah began her note by giving instructions for the disbursement of funds to the families of Nili spies and the Atlit agricultural workers. "After our departure please give the Zeldin family 105 francs, the Schwartz family 105 francs, and to Menashe Brunstein 102 francs." She did not know whether the Turks had arrested the workers at the Atlit station. If they had, then when the workers were released, they should receive "30 francs a month" and live on the "wheat and barley at the station."

Sarah settled other accounts as well. She wrote of overhearing a Turkish officer discuss Zichron residents with a superior: "Applebaum, Feitelson, and Madorsky of Hadera. It seems to me that these have given our work away; they have simply betrayed us."

> Our situation is very bad, mine most of all because the whole blame falls on me. I was beaten murderously, and they bound me with ropes. Do remember to describe all our suffering to those who shall come after we have passed away. I do not believe that we shall survive after having been betrayed, and the whole truth about us probably exposed.

Sarah asked that whoever read her note to tell her brothers—likely meaning Aaron and Alexander—"about our martyrdom, and let them know that Sarah has asked that each drop of her blood be avenged measure for measure; vengeance both upon our Jews and, especially upon the rulers under whom we are living; that no mercy shall be shown, just as they have shown no mercy to us."

Believe me, I have no more strength left to endure, and I prefer to kill myself than to be tortured anymore at their bloodstained hands. They say they will send us away to Damascus; there they will surely hang me. I shall try to get hold of some small firearm or poison. I do not want them to abuse my body. My sorrow is the greater for seeing my father suffering in innocence.

Sarah reached a central point, her concept of her legacy, near the end of her note. Sarah wanted to be remembered as a soldier willing to fight to the death to protect her coreligionists. It made no difference that those for whom she had fought had disavowed her or, indeed, even had betrayed her. In fact, despite what she had endured, Sarah seemed to relent in her demand for retribution.

But there will come a day of reckoning; we have died as warriors who have not yielded. Tell the Committee of Zichron that on the judgment day they will be judged. Let it be so, we have striven to pave the road of great happiness for the nation so let wicked Pearl and Adele enjoy it. I am not even judging or condemning, I just say let them enjoy it. I am not keeping score with bastards. I have striven for the good of my people and if my people are despicable, so be it.

Sarah left instructions for Yitzhak Halperin to find Yosef Lishansky and tell him "he must never give in, far better that he should kill himself." Sarah heard the sound of footsteps of a Turkish soldier. "They have come and I can write no longer."

Sarah threw the paper out a window and told her nephew Avner Aaronsohn, who also had been allowed to wander through the chamber of horrors in the Rivniker house, where to find it. After Avner found the note, he gave it to David Sternberg, an Aaronsohn relative, who hid it in the empty container of an old oil lantern. When the note was later retrieved, it had been damaged by insects but was largely intact.[16]

The next morning, Friday, October 5, a procession of Turkish soldiers and prisoners left the Rivniker home and made their way along the main street of Zichron, where Sarah had played as a child and later, as a grownup, had strolled in the afternoons with her sister, Rivka. Sarah wore a green dress, a green headscarf, and a rope tied around her hands, which were in front of her. A Turkish soldier led her with the rope. Several more soldiers marched on both sides of Sarah with fixed bayonets. Sarah had difficulty walking because her feet were badly swollen.

The procession included Rivka Lishansky and her two children. The street was largely empty, and Zichron residents peered out from their windows. Ivria recalled that some residents came out of their homes. "The women of the settlement stood on both sides of the street, yelled strange things to us, and threw stones at us," was how she recalled the scene. Ivria believed that if her father had been there, no one would have dared treat them this way.[17]

The group of Turkish soldiers, the badly beaten and tortured young woman, and the mother with two small children reached the Aaronsohn compound. Sarah paused, the procession halted, and the rope was untied. She gazed around and then went alone into Aaron's home. The soldiers took up positions outside Aaron's home at each door. Even had she tried to get away through the underground escape tunnel, too many Turks were around the house and in and around Zichron for her to escape.

Inside the house Sarah pressed a recessed button in a double wall near an entranceway. A panel swung out, revealing a compartment. Sarah reached into the compartment and pulled out the small pistol that Aaron had earlier sent on the *Managem* for her own protection. She took the pistol into Aaron's bathroom at the rear of the house.

The shot was heard by the Turkish guards standing outside the house. They charged inside and opened the bathroom door. One ran into the street, shouting for a doctor. A Turkish official summoned Dr. Yaffe:

"Sarah has committed suicide, hurry, save her." Dr. Yaffe took his medical bag, went to the Aaronsohn home, and found Sarah lying on the floor of the bathroom, unconscious. Blood gushed from her mouth; a pistol lay next to her on the floor. He gave her an injection of caffeine. Sarah regained consciousness and recognized Dr. Yaffe.

"I beg you, kill me. I cannot live and suffer. I cannot."

Dr. Yaffe managed to lift her onto a bed in another room. After an examination, he concluded that Sarah had shot herself in the mouth and that the bullet had lodged in her spine, paralyzing her arms and legs. Sarah pleaded to be given poison and cursed the Turks, especially Osman Bey. She wouldn't allow Dr. Yaffe to rinse her mouth.

Dr. Yaffe informed the *kaymakam* that he would not give Sarah medical care unless the Turks agreed not to torture Sarah if she recovered. The *kaymakam* told him, "In the presence of the government officials who are here, I give you the word of a soldier that she will not be touched if she gets better." Evidently Dr. Yaffe was persuaded that this time the *kaymakam* was sincere, although he could not do much for Sarah except try to ease her suffering.

Sarah lived for another four days. In excruciating pain, she lapsed in and out of consciousness, sometimes mumbling in delirium. On Sunday, October 7, Dr. Yaffe wrote in his diary that "Sarah's temperature has gone up, but her pains are slightly weaker. She is lucid. . . . [She] keeps asking for poison, to end her suffering. She demands morphine. In the evening I gave her a morphine injection. . . . In the settlement, complete panic. The period for handing over Lishansky has expired."

Sarah was attended to by Zvi's wife and his eight-year-old daughter, Yardena, as well as other relatives and friends. Once, when she regained consciousness, she noticed that Yardena's eyes were red and swollen. "There is nothing to cry about," Sarah managed to say to her niece. "It will be all right." On Monday Dr. Yaffe wrote that "Sarah's condition [is] worse. . . . I came to examine her 3 times during the night. She often asks for death. Her consciousness is limited. . . . At 3 a.m. she screams, afraid that she will lose her mind."

On Tuesday, October 9, he noted, "All her relatives came to say goodbye. She asked everybody to protect her father and set him free.

She pulled herself up for a short moment and then fell back on the bed and lay motionless. . . . At 8 a.m. she passed away." She hadn't told the Turks anything. Sarah Aaronsohn was twenty-seven years old.

Dr. Yaffe signed two documents. One was a death certificate. He also signed, with two witnesses, a declaration affirming Sarah's final request that the Turks free her father. In fact, Ephraim continued to be tortured, but when the Turks became convinced that he was dying, they moved him to a hospital. He eventually recovered and returned to Zichron.[18]

Sarah Aaronsohn, in keeping with Jewish custom, was buried that day next to her mother, Malka, in the Zichron cemetery. Her body had been swathed in mosquito netting for lack of any other material for a shroud. The fear and panic that had enveloped Zichron abated with Sarah's death. Some Zichron residents, with the permission of a Turkish commander, joined the funeral procession. Several at the gravesite later recalled that, under the mosquito netting, Sarah's face was beautiful.

The ground in the cemetery was rocky, and it took two hours to dig Sarah's grave. As her coffin was lowered into the open grave, the sky grew overcast. In the distance, a mist floated in from the sea, and it began to rain.[19]

17

The Boys Will Turn into Green
Crowned Date Palms

The Turks rolled up the Nili spy ring. Among others, the Turks arrested Nissan Rotman, Tova Gelberg, and Mendel Schneersohn, Liova's brother. Dr. Neumann, still in the Turkish army, was arrested and sent to Damascus for a court-martial.[1]

Several spies turned themselves in, including Menashe Brunstein (who had gone into Zichron during Sarah's torture) and Yitzhak Halperin. Some got away. David Sokolovitz left the Afula railway junction as soon as he heard of the arrests and, with the aid of a Bulgarian passport procured by a friend, remained at large in Palestine. Rivka Lishansky and her two small children were sent to Nazareth in a wagon transporting the captured Nili spies. The Turks allowed her to feed and give water to the handcuffed Nili prisoners, who were in terrible pain from beatings and torture. In Nazareth the captured Nili spies were held in an abandoned monastery and tortured further. One morning Reuven Schwartz's body was found hanging above a window. The Turks unconvincingly claimed that it was a suicide. Eventually, the Nili spies were sent to Damascus for trial.

Rivka and her two children were permitted to stay in a hotel in Nazareth and, after a few days, released. She had difficulty finding a home for herself and her children because no Jewish settler wanted to take them in. A friend finally allowed her to live in a corner of his dairy barn. The neighbors threatened to expel Rivka's benefactor from the settlement if Rivka continued to live there, but he defied them and let the family stay. Rivka eventually moved back to her parents' house.[2]

For a few weeks, Yosef Lishansky stayed ahead of the Turks. After fleeing Zichron he hid in a cave, but he had no food and left after three days. Wearing Arab clothing, he tried to make his way north, where his Druze friends might help him get to Lebanon. During his furtive movements around Palestine, Lishansky fell into the hands of Ha-Shomer, whose members for a time couldn't decide whether to help him escape north or to kill him.

Emissaries from Zichron heard that Ha-Shomer was holding Lishansky in the Galilee region. They went to the Ha-Shomer leader, Yosef Nahmani, in the Galilee region and demanded that he turn Lishansky over so that Zichron could get the credit for delivering him to the Turks. Nahmani decided not to give Lishansky to the Zichron emissaries; instead, he sent a Ha-Shomer member to shoot Lishansky. Nahmani also made a deal with the Arab police chief Fuad Nashashibi in Tiberias. The deal was that Fuad would turn the body over to the Turks and claim the reward that the Turks had offered while crediting Jewish Ottoman patriots for capturing Lishansky.

The plan might have worked except that the designated Ha-Shomer executioner failed to kill Lishansky and only wounded him in the left shoulder. Lishansky, despite the gunshot wound, managed to get away. He headed south in the hopes of staying ahead of both the Turks and the Jews until the British forces arrived. Lishansky's luck ran out at Nebi Rubin near Rehovot. Disguised as a Bedouin, he tried to mount an unattended camel when children playing nearby noticed him. They ran to report the presence of the suspicious man to adults. The adults came, realized who Lishansky was, detained him, and turned him over to the Turks. He probably was the last of the Nili spies to be caught. Lishansky was sent to the prison in Damascus. His jail mates included the Nili spies tortured in Nazareth: among them, Yitzhak Halperin, Zvi Aaronsohn (whose torture left him an invalid for the rest of his life), Menashe Brunstein, Nissan Rotman, Dr. Neumann, and others.

The Nili prisoners found ways to communicate from their cells by pretending to recite the Psalms in a singsong manner but using disguised phrases. Sometimes the prisoners were briefly together in the lavatory, where they could talk to one another in low voices. During the day, Lishansky seemed buoyant and cheerful, but at night Dr. Neumann and others heard him sobbing in his cell. "From my conversations with

Yosef in the prison," Dr. Neumann later wrote, "it became clear to me that he knew he was going to die."

Yitzhak Halperin asked Yosef Lishansky about the rumors that he had killed Avshalom Feinberg in the desert. "I swear with my life, that this never happened," Lishansky replied, very upset. "Believe me that what had happened to Avshalom is what I've told. He fought the Bedouins who attacked us to the last bullet. He was covering me and implored me to run away, hoping that I would be able to reach the British lines."[3]

The Nili spies were tried in Damascus in groups of four or five. Most were given relatively lenient prison terms, such as Dr. Neumann's sentence of a year in prison. The Germans, fearing a propaganda debacle like the Jaffa–Tel Aviv expulsions, also had been pressuring the Ottoman government to avoid acts of retaliation against the *yishuv* because of Nili's work. While the German government did not take a position on the trials of the Nili spies, its overall stance might have avoided more severe punishment. The Nili spies were freed in 1918 when the British captured Damascus.[4]

In the end the only Nili spies whom the Turks hanged were Yosef Lishansky and, due to some unfathomably cruel whim, Naaman Belkind, who had made it possible for the Turks to destroy Nili. The Turks deliberately starved Lishansky and Belkind in prison until they were emaciated shadows of their former selves. On the morning of December 16, they took the two from their cells to the central square of Damascus, where workmen were still assembling the gallows. "You are even incapable of putting up gallows in time," Yosef called out.

The chief rabbi of Damascus attended the hanging. He later wrote down Yosef's last words.

We are not traitors, for treason must be preceded by love. Only a lover can betray his beloved. But we never loved the homeland of the falaka and the baksheesh, the homeland of the hangman of the Armenian people. . . . We, members of Nili, headed by the great Jew Aaron Aaronsohn, have dug you a big grave, contemptible Ottomania. We made contact with the English army which has come to liberate our country and to hand it over to us. And while you are preparing to hang us, Great Britain's army is entering our Holy City Jerusalem—and your armies are fleeing the city without resistance.

As Lishansky spoke, his words were translated into Turkish. The Turk officers had heard enough and ordered a trumpeter to drown out Lishansky. The bodies of Belkind and Lishansky were left hanging on the gallows for the rest of the day.[5]

On October 31, 1917, after a diversionary infantry deployment and artillery bombardment of Gaza, the British began their attempt to break through the Gaza–Beersheba line. The British feints and intelligence disinformation had convinced the Turks to mass their defensive forces at Gaza, leaving a relatively weaker force at Beersheba to face the main British assault. The ultimate British victory at the Third Battle of Gaza was due to a number of factors, including a glamorous cavalry charge by the Australian Fourth Light Horse Brigade that succeeded in capturing most of the Beersheba wells before the Turks could blow them up; without the wells, the British army could not have held Beersheba or attacked into Palestine. But the victory must also be credited to British air superiority, which might not have been achieved without Sarah's intelligence about advanced Turk airplanes.[6]

By November 7, 1917, General Allenby's forces had captured Gaza and begun moving into Palestine. Several days later, Mayor Meir Dizengoff of Tel Aviv sought an audience with Djemal Pasha and pleaded for an end to the Turk's retaliatory measures, which included arrests, beatings, and exile, against the *yishuv* for Nili's activities. Dizengoff, fearing for his life, insisted that only a few Jews had spied for the British. "You found a few spies—and you blame all of us for that? Aren't there spies among the Turks, too? Why is it that your fury falls on the Jews? Why are you torturing us like this? . . . We have not betrayed you and haven't done a thing against [the Empire]!"

Fortunately for Dizengoff, Djemal Pasha's rage was directed at Aaron Aaronsohn. "All my friends warned me, don't trust the Jews, and I treated them well. . . . See how Aaronsohn showed me his honesty and his trustworthiness. I allowed him to travel to Berlin for his alleged scientific purpose—and he escaped to the British and organized spying against me."[7]

On December 11 General Allenby entered Jerusalem, which was the British prime minister's Christmas present to the British people, who celebrated by ringing church bells across England. Less than a year later, on October 30, 1918, the Ottoman Empire signed an armistice with Britain that was "in fact a surrender." Shortly afterward Enver, Talaat, and Djemal fled Constantinople with their German allies. All three former rulers of the Ottoman Empire died violent deaths: Armenian assassins tracked down and killed Talaat in 1921 and Djemal in 1922 (Djemal had little involvement with the Armenian massacres but the assassins weren't making distinctions); and Enver was killed in a battle in 1922 while leading a Muslim militia against the Bolsheviks in the Tajik-Uzbek border region. In 1923 at a multinational peace conference in Lausanne, Switzerland, the boundaries of the modern state of Turkey were carved out of the Ottoman Empire, which passed into history.[8]

On November 11, 1918, less than two weeks after the Ottoman armistice, Germany, on the verge of defeat, signed an armistice (also a surrender) that ended the fighting on the western front. One day before, a pastor brought news to wounded German soldiers in a military hospital near Berlin that the kaiser had abdicated and fled the country, which had been declared a republic, and that the war had been lost. The pastor began sobbing. A twenty-nine-year-old soldier in the hospital, who had been temporarily blinded in a British gas attack a month earlier, also broke down and cried. The weeping soldier asked himself, "So it had all been in vain . . . in vain the death of two millions. Had they died for this? . . . Did all this happen only so that a gang of wretched criminals could lay hands on the Fatherland?"

The pastor's visit proved pivotal for the soldier, Adolf Hitler, who later recounted the following "terrible days and even worse nights. . . . Hatred grew in me, hatred for those responsible for this deed. Miserable and degenerate criminals! . . . My own fate became known to me. I, for my part, decided to go into politics."[9]

The news of Sarah's death in October 1917 slowly spread.

After Liova Schneersohn and Alexander Aaronsohn returned from their October 12 visit to an empty research station in Atlit, they volunteered for the British army. Alexander was made a captain, and Liova was given officer's rank. Alexander went to the Gaza–Beersheba front, but Liova fell ill and could not accompany him. On November 22 Liova, now recovered, was preparing to leave for the front lines when he learned that a Jewish prisoner of war had told British interrogators what had happened to Sarah and the Nili spies in Zichron in early October. The prisoner's account was inaccurate in describing Ephraim's death but not in recounting Sarah's fate.

That night Liova was unable to sleep in his bunk in the military camp. "I was haunted by visions and nightmares: Sarah! Here she is, laughing, here she is—weeping, here she comes towards me, her pale, dainty hands stretched out in greeting. Here she is—among the rocks at Atlit, in a carriage in Cairo, at a concert, she is laughing again, and then again sad. Ah, Sarah, Sarah!"[10]

A day and a half later, Liova reached Alexander's unit on the Mediterranean coast of Palestine. A British soldier took Liova to Alexander's tent, where Alexander sat reading. Alexander rose in excitement at seeing Liova but soon became quiet.

"Go on, man, tell me."

Liova was unable to answer him at first.

"I can see it in your eyes," Alexander told Liova. "Tell me who it is. Don't hold it back."

In a low voice, almost a whisper, because that was all he could manage, Liova said, "Sarah."

Alexander did not move or speak; no tears formed. He just stood there, motionless, frozen. The silence that followed was so unbearable that Liova never forgot it.

Alexander finally asked him how Sarah had died. Liova told him everything but—thanks to a faulty memory or to some merciful instinct on his—left out the report of Ephraim's death, which later proved to be wrong.

Alexander sighed deeply. "First Avshalom. And now Sarah."

Alexander pulled himself together. The two went for a walk by the Mediterranean. "The blue waves of 'our' sea," Liova later wrote, "are coming onto the sand, telling us that once they used to carry our holy girl but now she has gone."

That evening, they listened to Arab workers singing a sad song, over and over. The two men talked for most of the night.[11]

The news reached Aaron's friend Peretz Pascal in Egypt. He wrote a letter to Aaron on December 4. "All our friends share your sorrow and the misfortune which befell you has brought consternation to all of us. Sarah was a heroine and nobody can be blamed for what happened to her. She could have joined [Miriam] and come with her, but as a commander of the ship in danger, she felt it her duty to remain on the bridge until the last."[12]

By then Aaron had left England and was in the United States to publicize the recent Balfour Declaration by Great Britain, the culmination of Zionist ambitions. The declaration stated that "His Majesty's Government view with favour the establishment in Palestine of a national home for the Jewish people, and will use their best endeavours to facilitate achievement of this object." The Balfour Declaration added that "it being clearly understood that nothing shall be done which may prejudice the civil and religious rights of existing non-Jewish communities in Palestine or the rights and political status enjoyed by Jews in any other country." The Balfour Declaration became the diplomatic stepping-stone to an independent Jewish state and is a source of controversy to this day.[13]

After disembarking in New York City in early December 1917, Aaron had lunch with his close friend Judge Mack at the Harvard Club and then went to the office of the Zionist Federation. There he was handed a telegram with information relayed by his brother Samuel, who had left the United States and was then in Egypt. "After torture Sarah died bravely by her own hand." The telegram also mistakenly reported that Ephraim had been killed.

Aaron wrote in his diary that night as though the news of Sarah's death was not unexpected. "The sacrifice is accomplished. I knew that we still had to face the greatest misfortune. But it is one thing to fear it and another to know that all hope is lost. Poor father, poor Sarati. . . . Her loss is the most cruel."[14]

By early 1918 David Ben-Gurion, the future first prime minister of Israel who had been expelled from Palestine at the outset of the war, had changed his position on which side to support. After his expulsion in 1915, Ben-Gurion had gone to the United States to raise a Jewish army that would fight for the Ottoman Empire. Now he supported the British side.[15]

In various ways British officials expressed their deep gratitude to the Aaronsohn family and the Nili spy ring for their services during the war. In early 1918 Rivka Aaronsohn in the United States decided to return to Palestine, but to do so she needed a British passport. Her passport request, perhaps with assistance from her brother Aaron, reached Sir William Ormsby-Gore, a high-ranking intelligence officer in Cairo during the war and now a member of the British Parliament. In a letter supporting Rivka's passport application, Ormsby-Gore wrote, "In my opinion nothing we can do for the Aaronsohn family will repay the work they have done for us and what they have suffered." Rivka returned to Palestine, evidently on a British passport.[16]

After the war, now field marshal Allenby described Nili as "my Field Intelligence Organization behind the Turkish lines." Raymond Savage, a top aide to General Allenby, explained that Allenby's victory in Palestine "was very largely the daring work of young spies, most of them natives of Palestine, which enabled the Field Marshal to accomplish his undertaking so effectively. The leader of the spy ring was a young Jewess, Miss Sarah Aaronsohn." Gen. Gilbert Clayton claimed that "we owe the lives of 30,000 soldiers to the Nili."[17]

Yigal Sheffy in his *British Military Intelligence in the Palestine Campaign*, as already seen, offers a more nuanced view of Nili's accomplishments. What does not appear in dispute is the personal admiration that many British officers had for Sarah and her agents. Captain Weldon of the *Managem* learned after his voyage on October 12, 1917, what had happened to Sarah Aaronsohn. He wrote in his memoir, "Such a suicide finds honor in the Valhalla of brave women. . . . Englishmen often talk about 'playing the game,' but even during the war few Britishers played it to a finer finish than this Jewish girl."[18]

In 1918 after a two-year absence, Aaron returned to Palestine. Upon observing the crops and the still relatively primitive state of Arab agriculture, he wrote in his diary, "There does not seem any change in the country. Still . . . we travel by train—and are with the English! Absa! Absa, where are you? Sarati!" The following year Aaron Aaronsohn was in England to confer with Chaim Weizmann and other Zionist leaders. On May 15, 1919, he boarded an airplane at an airfield in Surrey. His destination was Paris and the Peace Conference, where the final decisions were going to be made concerning the borders of Palestine. Fog and heavy headwinds were the conditions when Aaron's plane took off. His plane never landed in Paris or at any French airfield. A search was mounted in the English Channel, where a captain of a small fishing boat reported hearing an aircraft fly low over his vessel and hit the water fifty yards away. Aaron's body was never recovered.[19]

In the early 1920s Dr. Judah Magnes, the station's trustee to whom Aaron had given "The Confession," his admission to being a spy for the British, visited the Atlit research station. Now head of the Hebrew University in Jerusalem, Magnes found that the Washingtonia palms still lined the road to the station (and stand to this day), but the road itself was overgrown with poppies, thistles, daisies, and weeds. Camels and donkeys grazed in what had been lush fields. A few Arab women lived in the station's building, but the farm equipment and machinery rusted away in the shed. Magnes gathered lavender and roses from bushes, recalling Aaron and his visit to the station many years before, "when we had been happy and full of plans over some cups of tea."[20]

Sarah's journey, however, was not over. For years after her death, Sarah and the Nili spies were regarded as reckless and irresponsible by much of the Jewish community of Palestine, which was now administered by Great Britain under a mandate from the League of Nations. Alexander and Liova may have been the loneliest persons in Palestine. Walking on a street they heard whispers that they were spies. There were demands to expel the surviving Nili spies, and even their relatives were treated like pariahs.

Gradually the bitterness faded, and a new narrative developed around Sarah. A 1932 memorial pamphlet called her "a national heroine unrivaled in the annals of the Hebrew revival," and in 1933 a play appeared about an underground leader, a thinly disguised Sarah, who eschewed the traditional woman's role of marriage and family for an active political life. Starting in the early 1930s, right-wing movements and youth organizations adopted a model of femininity based on Sarah's biography but with a heavy emphasis on her skill with weapons, such as a sword, and at riding horses; her stoic unemotionality; and her desire for action. The comparisons of Sarah Aaronsohn to Joan of Arc were inevitable.[21]

In October 1932, fifteen years after her death, the first pilgrimage to Sarah's grave was held in Zichron. The second pilgrimage in 1933 attracted two thousand people, and the pilgrimages continued for decades. The pilgrims retraced Sarah's ordeal from her father's home to the Rivniker house, where she had been tortured, and then to her brother's home, where she had shot herself. Starting in 1941, a representative of the British army attended the observance. But, ironically enough, during World War II, Sarah and Nili became the "ideological and operative model for the anti-British Lehi," also known as the Stern Gang.[22]

Myths took hold that still survive. One was that T. E. Lawrence had fallen in love with Sarah. The basis for the myth was the dedication in Lawrence's postwar memoir, *Seven Pillars of Wisdom*, to an "S.A."

To S.A.

I loved you, so I drew these tides of men into my hands
 and wrote my will across the sky in stars
To earn you Freedom, the seven pillared worthy house,
 that your eyes might be shining for me
  When we came . . .

In fact, there is no evidence that Sarah and Lawrence ever met. Neither wrote about meeting, and they were never in the same place at any point in the war (when Sarah went to Cairo, Lawrence was not even in Egypt). Ronald Florence carefully analyzed the issue in *Lawrence and Aaronsohn* and concluded that "although her initials fit, Sarah Aaronsohn almost certainly was not the S.A. of Lawrence's dedication." Scott Anderson, in *Lawrence in Arabia*, explained that S.A. stood for Salim Ali, a young Arab companion of Lawrence's. Citing the noted stanzas, Anderson wrote that the poem reflects Lawrence's reaction at learning of Salim Ali's death from typhus.[23]

Another myth was that survivors of Nili had murdered the women identified in Sarah's suicide note out of revenge. Israeli writer Hillel Halkin devoted years of research and a book, *A Strange Death*, to confirming the revenge story, but he could cite no persuasive evidence that, in fact, this happened.

Even after the establishment in 1948 of Israel, the first independent Jewish state in two thousand years, Sarah and the Nili spies did not receive official recognition. That changed in late 1967, the fiftieth anniversary of Sarah's death, with a startling discovery.

For decades after returning to Zichron, Sarah's sister, Rivka, had devoted herself to preserving the Aaronsohn family's homes, the Aaronsohns' letters, the letters of the Nili spies, and related documents and materials. One morning in late 1967, Rivka Aaronsohn's young secretary opened a newspaper and immediately went to see Rivka.

In his spare time, Israeli police officer Shlomo Ben-Elkanah was a student of the Bedouin tribes in the Negev and Sinai Deserts. Reading a history of the Nili spy ring, Ben-Elkanah's attention was riveted by the mention of a Bedouin from the El-Ramyelet tribe who claimed to know the location of Avshalom Feinberg's grave. According to the Bedouins, the gravesite was on the southern side of the railroad station in Rafah in the Sinai Desert; it could be approached on a trail leading from the east. The exact site was under a wild date palm tree.

Ben-Elkanah was confident that with the assistance of local Bedouins, he could find Avshalom Feinberg's grave, but in 1966 the Sinai Desert was part of Egypt, an enemy of Israel's. In August the head of the Israeli police force told Ben-Elkanah that "as long as you are a member of the

Israeli police force, you are not allowed to investigate matters that the Israeli police did not order you to deal with."

In June of the following year, the Israelis captured, among other territories, the Sinai Desert in the Six-Day War. By then Ben-Elkanah was serving with the Israel Defense Forces (IDF). His commanding officer gave him permission to look for Avshalom's grave. Ben-Elkanah asked his friend Sheikh Frayah Farhan el Masdar of the respected Nasayrat tribe to learn what he could about the location of Avshalom's remains.

In October 1967 the sheikh told Ben-Elkanah the story he had learned from Bedouin eyewitnesses. Around the time that the British took Rafah in early 1917, a Bedouin had come running to the tent of the leader of the El-Ramyelet tribe and shouting, "Juassis, juassis" (Spies, spies). Two strangers, disguised as Bedouins, had been spotted in the area, riding camels in the direction of the British lines (the account did not mention the guide). Turks and Bedouins rode out to intercept them, and shooting started. One of the suspected spies was wounded and fell; the other managed to escape.

The wounded spy continued to fight and shot one of the Turks, but "the Turks finished him" by shooting the spy in the head. Discovering that the spy was likely a Jew, the Turks ordered the Bedouins to bury him. A year later, a wild palm tree grew out of the burial site. The Bedouins decided that the buried Jew "was a righteous man." They called the place "Mother of Palm Trees" or "The Jew's Grave."

On October 25, 1967, Ben-Elkanah; several Bedouins, including Sheikh Frayah Farhan el Masdar; and the mayor of Rafah went to the site. The digging began that afternoon under the palm tree. The excavators found a piece of fabric and a button; then, digging deeper, they exposed part of a right shoulder bone, a spinal cord, a skull, and chest bones.

In 1912 Avshalom Feinberg had written to Rivka Aaronsohn about his fantasy that some day he, Rivka, and Sarah would live on an island, where they would not need to die; but if that day came, "the boys will turn into green crowned date palms and next to them their girls will petrify into statues of white marble." Avshalom's remains had become so entwined with the roots of the date palm tree that it took some effort by Ben-Elkanah and the others to extract them. Once removed, the remains were taken to a forensic institute in Tel Aviv. With the assistance of Tzila Feinberg, who recalled that her brother had a cracked upper tooth, the remains were officially confirmed as those of Avshalom Feinberg. The Israeli press widely reported the discovery of the daring young man from the pre-state past who had literally risen from the desert in the wake of the young country's heady military victory.

The presence of a wild date palm tree was explained by Shlomo Ben-Elkanah in his account of finding Avshalom's grave. Based on the position of the roots, he concluded that the Bedouins had searched Avshalom's pockets, found the dates, eaten them, and then spit the seeds into the hole that they had dug for the body. The Nili lore is that Sarah had given Avshalom the dates before he set off into the Sinai Desert.[24]

On November 29, 1967, Avshalom Feinberg was given a state funeral with full military honors and buried in the national cemetery on Mount Herzl, roughly Israel's equivalent of Arlington National Cemetery. His coffin was wrapped in an Israeli flag, decorated with a wreath from the IDF, and surrounded by lit torches. An IDF honor guard stood over the coffin as thousands filed by to pay their respects. The speaker of the Israeli Knesset delivered the eulogy and, on behalf of the Israeli government, asked forgiveness from Avshalom and his comrades for "the tragic misunderstanding, and the failure to recognize their great achievement."

Present at the funeral was an elderly Rivka Aaronsohn, who had never married. In her 1917 letter to Sarah mourning Avshalom's death, Rivka had written, "And now, what meaning, what sense, what purpose is there to my life? The only purpose of my life is to commemorate him. I dream to plant a garden in his memory but for that many things are needed." Some years later, a shoot from the "Mother of Palm Trees" was planted at the head of Avshalom's grave. A large palm tree grows there today.[25]

Surviving Nili members have been decorated with the state "Nili Medal," and some Nili spies have appeared on Israeli postage stamps. In 1978 after a campaign by Rivka Lishansky and then, after her death, by Ivria and Tuvia, Yosef Lishansky was buried next to Avshalom Feinberg after a military funeral. Ivria spoke at her father's funeral.

According to Israeli historian Billie Melman, the discovery of Avshalom's remains coincided with Sarah's "appropriation into the mainstream ethos and consensus and her consolidation as a popular figure." In 1967 the Israel government held its first official ceremony at Sarah's grave in the Zichron cemetery.[26]

Sarah's grave is next to her mother's. The two graves are surrounded by a low iron fence. Jewish custom is to bury someone who committed suicide either outside the cemetery or in an enclosure separate from other graves. Today thirty thousand Israeli schoolchildren annually visit the Aaronsohn homes, which are now a museum; the number would be equivalent in the United States to more than a million such visitors a year. Outside of Israel, including in the United States, Sarah is unknown even though, at the dawn of modern espionage, she proved that women can manage spy networks as effectively as men. By contrast, Mata Hari (whose real name was Margaretha Geertruida Zelle), the Dutch nude dancer and courtesan, is by far the best-known woman spy to emerge from World War I but not because of her espionage achievements. At her sensational spy trial, Mata Hari was accused of using her seductive powers to obtain French military secrets for the Germans, information that allegedly cost the lives of thousands of French soldiers. Despite the lack of evidence, Mata Hari was found guilty. Her execution (days after Sarah's death) made her a legend—half a dozen movies have been made about her—and Mata Hari came to culturally define women in espionage.

In the Aaronsohn homes, the Israeli children are taken on a guided tour to examine the hidden compartment where Sarah kept a pistol; to stare at Aaron's bathroom, kept just as it was on the day that Sarah shot herself; to climb down into the basement and peer at the escape tunnel; and to look at the pictures of the Nili spies on a wall and read their biographies.

The homes are so well preserved that it's easy for a visitor to imagine a scene in 1911 before Malka died, before Sarah married and left for Constantinople, before the war, before the agony and the sorrow. Sitting in the living room of the Aaronsohn family home are Ephraim and Malka, Aaron, Avshalom, Sarah, and Rivka. Alexander is in the

United States, but Zvi and Samuel are present as well. An American friend of Aaron's, on a visit to Palestine, has arrived. For the benefit of his parents, Aaron translates the American guest's words into Yiddish. Avshalom has just returned from Damascus and talks of the little streams that run in the streets, clear and clean like frozen crystal, and of the springs in the mountains, both big and small. The talk is lively, flavored with agronomy, politics, and literature. Rivka holds a book that she glances at from time to time. Sarah sews a stylish dress and interjects herself into the multiple conversations going on in the room, often with an amused smile.

NOTES

The vast majority of archival documents, including Sarah Aaronsohn's letters, are from the Beit Aaronsohn Nili Museum Archive in Zichron Ya'akov, Israel. Therefore, I only provide the name of the archive source if the document came from an archive other than the Beit Aaronsohn Nili Museum Archive.

Introduction

1. Jones, "Women of the CIA" ("Hollywood has convinced us that all women in the CIA belong to a sorority of badass bitches who stab by day and seduce by night"); and Proctor, *Female Intelligence*, 1–2, 133 ("'mata-haridans' continue to appear in various guises in fiction, film, and journalistic accounts today").
2. Pascal, "I Am also a Spy."
3. Foreign Office 371/4167: William Ormsby-Gore to Foreign Office, March 22, 1918, National Archives, Kew, England.
4. Avshalom Feinberg to Sarah Aaronsohn, June 17, 1914.

1. I Will Be Really Happy

1. Engle, *Nili Spies*, 17; Florence, *Lawrence and Aaronsohn*, 30–33; and Remnick, "Blood and Sand," 72.
2. Shukry [Khoury], *Syria and the French Mandate*, 536. In the second half of the nineteenth century, Palestine was part of the *vilayet*, or first-level administrative division or province, of Syria. In the 1880s, Jerusalem was granted more autonomy and attached to the new *vilayet* of Beirut, itself carved out of Syria. But "in terms of administrative unity Palestine, as such, did not exist before World War I."
3. Schama, *Two Rothschilds*, 61. According to Schama, the Jews were "locked up in the town jail" because the Romanian sponsors of the families "had simply dispensed with the essential formalities of securing authorization, greasing appropriate palms, and taking due precautions against the enforce-

ment of immigration regulations." See Florence, *Lawrence and Aaronsohn*, 32–33. By another account, three ships left Romania carrying fifty-four families. The ships were the *Tetis* (i.e., the *Thetis*), the *Denya*, and the *Iris*. The *Tetis* and *Denya* reached Jaffa, but the third ship, the *Iris*, was unable to land in Palestine and sailed to Alexandria, Egypt. Eventually, with the help of baksheesh, the *Iris* families made their way to Haifa. Dagan and Dagan, *On the First Road*, 77–78.

4. Yazbak, *Haifa in the Late Ottoman Period*, 192–98; "Haifa: History and Overview," Jewish Virtual Library, http://www.jewishvirtuallibrary.org /jsource/Society_&_Culture/haifa.html; and Dagan and Dagan, *On the First Road*, 78.

5. Katz, *Aaronsohn Saga*, 27.

6. Aaronsohn, *Rothschild and Early Jewish Colonization*, 73, 177 (describing how prefabricated wooden cabins were shipped from Romania and reassembled on the main street); Florence, *Lawrence and Aaronsohn*, 33–34; Kennedy, "Geology of Mount Carmel"; and Dagan and Dagan, *On the First Road*, 80–81.

7. Bernstein, *Pioneers and Homemakers*, 34–37.

8. Florence, *Lawrence and Aaronsohn*, 34–35; and Schama, *Two Rothschilds*, 67.

9. Florence, *Lawrence and Aaronsohn*, 37–38; and Halkin, *Strange Death*, 23–25.

10. Florence, *Lawrence and Aaronsohn*, 42 (the Zichron wines struggled to compete in overseas markets); Aaronsohn, "With the Turks," 2–4; Halkin, *Strange Death*, 30; and Dash, *Summoned to Jerusalem*, 85.

11. Aaronsohn, *Sarah: Shalhavet Nili*, 29; and Megged, *Mandrakes from the Holy Land*, 113–14.

12. Engle, *Nili Spies*, 20, 34; Florence, *Lawrence and Aaronsohn*, 39–40; and Bernstein, *Pioneers and Homemakers*, 37–38. The franc, as will be seen, remained in use even during World War I.

13. Sarah and Rivka Aaronsohn to Eliezer Ben-Yehuda, as published in *Hashkafa*, December 3, 1906.

14. Bernstein, *Pioneers and Homemakers*, 66–67, 71; and Dash, *Summoned to Jerusalem*, 85.

15. Engle, *Nili Spies*, 34; Florence, *Lawrence and Aaronsohn*, 154–55; Ben-Zvi, *Coming Home*, 286–87 (uses the word "spurs," which must mean stirrups); and Raz, "Fashion in Eretz Israel," 8.

16. Halkin, *Strange Death*, 269–70, from a conversation with Rivka Aaronsohn.

17. Engle, *Nili Spies*, 22; and Florence, *Lawrence and Aaronsohn*, 42–48.

18. Florence, *Lawrence and Aaronsohn*, 51–52. According to the website of the International Wild Wheat Genome Sequencing Consortium ("About," http://wewseq.wixsite.com/consortium, last visited June 7, 2017), "Since the discovery of the wild wheat ancestor in 1906 by Aaron Aaronsohn in Rosh-Pina Israel, there was a continuous effort to introduce beneficial traits from wild emmer to modern wheat. Yet, the lack of a full genome map of wheat has slowed down this process dramatically."

19. Fairchild, *World Was My Garden*, 366; Barnard, *Forging of an American Jew*, 108–10; and Florence, *Lawrence and Aaronsohn*, 91, 419.

20. Florence, *Lawrence and Aaronsohn*, 83–84.

21. Florence, *Lawrence and Aaronsohn*, 90–91.

22. Florence, *Lawrence and Aaronsohn*, 91–92.

23. According to Felix Frankfurter's unfinished biography of Aaron Aaronsohn, Malka died the "death of kissing." Goldstone, *Aaronsohn's Maps*, 95. The term "death of kissing," which describes a painless death, has a distinct progeny in Deuteronomy 34:5, which states, "And Moses, servant of God, died there, in the land of Moab, by the mouth of God." The Midrash Rabba (a compilation of rabbinic homiletic literature whose date is unknown but probably around 900 CE), chapter 11, after recounting the discussion between Moses and God's refusal to permit Moses to enter Israel, states, "At that time [point] the Holy One, Blessed Be He, kissed [Moses] and took his soul from him via a kiss of the mouth." Goldstone wrote that Malka's father had been tortured to death in a Romanian pogrom. His death may have left Malka with a sense of foreboding, if not dread, in her new land, but Goldstone acknowledges that "the family record is silent as to whether [Malka's] despair drove her to suicide."

24. Sarah Aaronsohn to Aaron Aaronsohn, October 19, 1912. Zalig and Sonia Suskin were acquaintances of Aaron's in Hamburg. According to Ronald Florence, many years earlier Aaron had fallen in love with Sonia, but she was reluctant to "allow the relationship to go too far." Florence, *Lawrence and Aaronsohn*, 51.

25. Sarah Aaronsohn to Aaron Aaronsohn, November 10, 1912.

26. Ben-Zvi, *Coming Home*, 286; and Engle, *Nili Spies*, 33.

2. Two Cannot Take Three Places

1. Dagan and Dagan, *On the First Road*, 47–48, 221–23, 231–32, 330.

2. Engle, *Nili Spies*, 30–31; Florence, *Lawrence and Aaronsohn*, 87–88; and Katz, *Aaronsohn Saga*, 63, 77.

3. Engle, *Nili Spies*, 32–34.

4. Ben-Zvi, *Coming Home*, 286.

5. Avshalom Feinberg to Sarah Aaronsohn, March 21, 1912; and Avshalom Feinberg to Rivka Aaronsohn, March 1, 1911.

6. Avshalom Feinberg to Rivka Aaronsohn, March 1, 1911.

7. Gorny, *Zionism and the Arabs*, 56.

8. Baruch Ben-Azar testimony, September 1, 1954 (transcribed by Haya Ironi), Haganah Archives, Tel Aviv (courtesy Israel Defense Forces Archives), 1; and Engle, *Nili Spies*, 31–32.

9. Avshalom Feinberg to Sarah Aaronsohn, February 27, 1911.

10. Avshalom Feinberg to Sarah Aaronsohn, June 7, 1911.

11. Avshalom Feinberg to Sarah Aaronsohn, March 14, 1912.

12. Avshalom Feinberg to Sarah Aaronsohn, October 3, 1913.

13. Avshalom Feinberg to Sarah Aaronsohn, June 9, 1912; and Engle, *Nili Spies*, 35.

14. Halkin, *Strange Death*, 270 (conversation with Rivka Aaronsohn); Engle, *Nili Spies*, 39 ("Sarah was the woman he loved"); Katz, *Aaronsohn Saga*, 86 ("it seems likely that Sarah was herself in love with Avshalom"); and Rivka Aaronsohn to Avshalom Feinberg, undated.

15. Avshalom Feinberg to Rivka Aaronsohn, March 1, 1911; and December 3, 12, and 14, 1911.

16. Avshalom Feinberg to Rivka Aaronsohn, March 1, 1911.

17. Avshalom Feinberg to Rivka Aaronsohn, March 14, 1912.

18. Avshalom Feinberg to Rivka Aaronsohn, December 14, 1911. In this letter, Avshalom quotes from Rivka's reproachful letter. See also Halkin, *Strange Death*, 268. In a conversation with Hillel Halkin, a much older Rivka recalled that "women were different in those days. They had . . . *l'honneur de leur chasteté*. They knew the meaning of restraint."

19. Engle, *Nili Spies*, 38–39; Katz, *Aaronsohn Saga*, 85–86; and Daniel Abraham, "Haim Abraham," http://www.danielabraham.net/tree/abraham/haim/. Daniel Abraham is the great-nephew of Sarah's husband. He set up the website to provide information about his great-uncle because "there is more to his story" than the "many . . . unflattering descriptions" that have appeared "in various books about Nili."

20. Avshalom Feinberg to Sarah Aaronsohn, April 29, 1913.

21. Sarah Aaronsohn to Aaron Aaronsohn, June 6, 1913; and Katz, *Aaronsohn Saga*, 25.

22. Engle, *Nili Spies*, 38.

23. Dwight, "Life in Constantinople," 523, 531–32, 534, 539; and Emmerson, *1913*, 358–59.

24. Emmerson, *1913*, 368–69; Dwight, "Life in Constantinople," 538–39; and "City Government," 228.

25. Florence, *Lawrence and Aaronsohn*, 157.

26. Boyar and Fleet, *Social History*, 302–4, 306–7.

27. Avshalom Feinberg to Sarah Aaronsohn, June 17, 1914.

3. Don't You Feel?

1. Kissinger, *Diplomacy*, 209–17; Tuchman, *Guns of August*, 91, 149–51, 154–55; Herwig, *The Marne*, 14; Dews, "The Family Relationship that Couldn't Stop World I"; and Otte, *July Crisis*, 277.

2. Advertisement, *Daily Telegraph*, August 5, 1914, 1, http://www.telegraph.co.uk/news/ww1-archive/11004294/Daily-Telegraph-August-5-1914.html.

3. Davis, *Short History*, 258–60; Rogan, *Fall of the Ottomans*, 27; and Gibb, "Turkey," 426–27. Bell quoted in Fromkin, *Peace to End All Peace*, 34–35, 43–44.

4. Davis, *Short History*, 367; Fromkin, *Peace to End All Peace*, 43–47; and Dwight, *Life in Constantinople*, 521.

5. Rogan, *Fall of the Ottomans*, 3–4; and Ulrichsen, *First World War*, 17–18.

6. Rogan, *Fall of the Ottomans*, 75; Gibb, "Turkey," 426; and McMeekin, *Ottoman Endgame*, 11.

7. Rogan, *Fall of the Ottomans*, 46–51. The lira was the main unit of currency in the Ottoman Empire, but gold and silver were legal tender. Gibb, "Turkey," 441.

8. Rogan, *Fall of the Ottomans*, 41–42, 55–57.

9. Postcard from Sarah Aaronsohn to Rivka Aaronsohn, August 24, 1914; and Sarah Aaronsohn to Rivka Aaronsohn, August 25, 1914. Two dates appear on the postcard—the nineteenth and the twenty-fourth. It is possible that Sarah wrote the postcard on the nineteenth but that it wasn't postmarked until the twenty-fourth.

10. Ben-Bassat, "Enciphered Ottoman Telegrams," 282–85, 289, 296, and appendix B; and Fromkin, *Peace to End All Peace*, 211.

11. Florence, *Lawrence and Aaronsohn*, 131.

12. Schneersohn, *Miyomano shel ish Nili*, 9–10; Engle, *Nili Spies*, 48–50; and Florence, *Lawrence and Aaronsohn*, 132–33. Engle's account is based verbatim on Liova Schneersohn's undated and unpublished manuscript "Tale

of the Thirteen," in the National Library of Israel in Jerusalem. In this instance, I relied on the English translation of "Tale of the Thirteen" in Engle, *Nili Spies*. According to "Tale of the Thirteen," the Hadera men were held, not in a jail, but in a hotel.

13. McGilvary, *Dawn of a New Era*, 145–47.

14. Engle, *Nili Spies*, 49–50. In another version, Nissan Rotman, a Hadera resident, galloped to Zichron to warn both Avshalom and Aaron about the arrests. Avshalom and Aaron went to Haifa, where they talked to Ottoman authorities, and then Avshalom returned to Hadera to join the arrested men. Livneh, Nedava, and Efrati, *Nili*, 64.

15. Aaronsohn, *Sarah*, 3; Engle, *Nili Spies*, 40.

16. Sarah Aaronsohn to Tzila Feinberg, August 8, 1915.

17. Auron, *Banality of Indifference*, 176–77; and Katz, *Aaronsohn Saga*, 88–89.

18. Raz, "Fashion in Eretz Israel," 3–4.

4. What Sights Her Eyes Have Seen

1. Aaronsohn, "With the Turks," 3–4; and Halkin, *Strange Death*, 265.

2. Florence, *Lawrence and Aaronsohn*, 70–71, 76; Katz, *Aaronsohn Saga*, 67, quoting N. Vatik, "From Zichron Ya'akov," *Ha'ahdut* (The unity), May 15, 1914, 17–18; and Finn, *Byeways in Palestine*, 348, for a mid-nineteenth-century traveler's description of runnels of water used to supply fruit plantations in Lebanon.

3. Aaronsohn, "With the Turks," 6–8. This account was written after Aaron, Alexander, and Avshalom formed the espionage ring and makes no mention of any espionage activities.

4. Aaronsohn, "With the Turks," 11–12, 15–17, 23–27, 29–31.

5. Aaronsohn, "With the Turks," 33–34.

6. Rogan, *Fall of the Ottomans*, 52; and Morgenthau, *Ambassador Morgenthau's Story*, 161–62.

7. Rogan, *Fall of the Ottomans*, 106.

8. Rogan, *Fall of the Ottomans*, 106–14; and Fromkin, *Peace to End All Peace*, 120–22.

9. Rogan, *Fall of the Ottomans*, 116.

10. McMeekin, *Ottoman Endgame*, 158–59; and Bruce, *Last Crusade*, 22–23.

11. Rogan, *Fall of the Ottomans*, 119–22.

12. Rogan, *Fall of the Ottomans*, 67–70; and Fromkin, *Peace to End All Peace*, 121.

13. Aaronsohn, "With the Turks," 44.

14. McMeekin, *Ottoman Endgame*, 161; and Anderson, *Lawrence in Arabia*, 103–5.

15. Martin Sugarman, "The Zion Muleteers of Gallipoli: March 1915–May 1916," Jewish Virtual Library, https://www.jewishvirtuallibrary.org/jsource /History/gallipoli.html.

16. Fromkin, *Peace to End All Peace*, 134–36; and Danforth, "Forget Sykes-Picot."

17. Rogan, *Fall of the Ottomans*, 135–38; McMeekin, *Ottoman Endgame*, 191–96; and Fromkin, *Peace to End All Peace*, 152.

18. Morgenthau, *Ambassador Morgenthau's Story*, 210–22. Morgenthau, who was Jewish, observed that the Turks were quite willing to have the assistance, if not the leadership, of the Christian Germans.

19. Dane, *British Campaigns*, 1:56–59; Anderson, *Lawrence in Arabia*, 106; Fromkin, *Peace to End All Peace*, 134–36, 152–54; Reynolds, Churchill, and Miller, *Story of the Great War*, 3:432–33; and Verrier, *Agents of Empire*, 120.

20. Meyer, *World Undone*, 311.

21. Rogan, *Fall of the Ottomans*, 214, 230.

22. Rogan, *Fall of the Ottomans*, 86–87.

23. Balakian, *Armenian Golgotha*, 34, 47, 77–79.

24. Morgenthau, *Ambassador Morgenthau's Story*, 236, 290, 307–12, 321–23, 385; "Forgotten Holocaust"; and Manne, "Turkish Tale" (discussing the impact of the Gallipoli landings on the Armenian genocide).

25. De Waal, *Great Catastrophe*, 34–41; "Forgotten Holocaust"; Balakian, *Armenian Golgotha*, 79–80, 94–95, 119–20; Fromkin, *Peace to End All Peace*, 212–13; and Tharoor, "Is This Genocide?"

26. Auron, *Banality of Indifference*, 176–77; and Florence, *Lawrence and Aaronsohn*, 178–79. While en route, Sarah had sent Aaron a telegram from Aleppo that she would be arriving in Palestine in a few days. Auron, *Banality of Indifference*, 176.

5. They Must Attack Immediately

1. Engle, *Nili Spies*, 63; and Ben-Zvi, *Coming Home*, 217–19, 223, 271–78, 285–89.

2. Engle, *Nili Spies*, 52–53; and Florence, *Lawrence and Aaronsohn*, 165–67.

3. Rivka Aaronsohn to her family, June 25, 1915; Aaronsohn, "With the Turks," 64–69, 78–80; and Florence, *Lawrence and Aaronsohn*, 167–68.

4. Aaronsohn, "With the Turks," 80–85; and "The Syrian Protestant College in the Great War" (Online Exhibit), University Libraries, American University of Beirut, http://www.aub.edu.lb/ulibraries/asc/online-exhibits/exhibits /show/wwi/1915, last visited June 6, 2017.

5. Sarah Aaronsohn to Tzila Feinberg, August 8, 1915.

6. Florence, *Lawrence and Aaronsohn*, 168–69.

7. Wilson, *Lawrence of Arabia*, 167–68; and Webber, *In the Shadow of the Crescent.*

8. Florence, *Lawrence and Aaronsohn*, 104; Wilson, *Lawrence of Arabia*, 174; and Dunn, "The British Military Intelligence Section in Cairo 1914, Part III."

9. Dunn, "'Such a Band of Wild Men'"; Herbert, *Mons, Anzac and Kut*, 49; "Lawrence of Arabia: Stamp Designer"; Anderson, *Lawrence in Arabia*, 86–87; and Wilson, *Lawrence of Arabia*, 174.

10. Wilson, *Lawrence of Arabia*, 168–69, 173–75 (characterizing Lloyd's outlook based on comments of one of his friends); and Anderson, *Lawrence in Arabia*, 87.

11. Wilson, *Lawrence of Arabia*, 173.

12. Florence, *Lawrence and Aaronsohn*, 169–70.

13. Florence, *Lawrence and Aaronsohn*, 126–27; Rogan, *Fall of the Ottomans*, 290; and Aaronsohn, "With the Turks," 51.

14. Pasha, *Memories of a Turkish Statesman*, 12, 24; and Morgenthau, *Ambassador Morgenthau's Story*, 171–73.

15. Rogan, *Fall of the Ottomans*, 288–89.

16. Florence, *Lawrence and Aaronsohn*, 128–130; Katz, *Aaronsohn Saga*, 81–82; Anderson, *Lawrence in Arabia*, 108–10; and Engle, *Nili Spies*, 45.

17. Tamari, *Year of the Locust*, 102–3, describes the imposition of fines on persons between the ages of fifteen and sixty for failing to collect twenty kilograms of eggs; and M'Lachlan and Pocock, "Locust," 857–58, describes locust cannibalism.

18. Florence, *Lawrence and Aaronsohn*, 130. While the author apparently refers to the collection of locusts, it appears more likely that the citizenry had been ordered to gather the eggs. See Tamari, *Year of the Locust*, 102–3.

19. Engle, *Nili Spies*, 56; and Florence, *Lawrence and Aaronsohn*, 171–72.

20. Woolley, *As I Seem to Remember*, 88–92; and Wilson, *Lawrence of Arabia*, 167.

21. Sheffy, *British Military Intelligence*, 116–22.

22. Weldon, *"Hard Lying,"* 163–64; and Sheffy, *British Military Intelligence*, 79–80, details the use of motor launches from the mother ship that then release the surfboat. The term "hard lying" refers to the extra pay received by the crew on small craft, such as destroyers, torpedo boats, and trawlers. Weldon, *"Hard Lying,"* vi.

23. Sheffy, *British Military Intelligence*, 80–81.

24. Weldon, *"Hard Lying,"* 11, 104–5; Engle, *Nili Spies*, 57; and Florence, *Lawrence and Aaronsohn*, 172.

25. Engle, *Nili Spies*, 59; and Livneh, Nedava, and Efrati, *Nili*, 391.

26. Avshalom Feinberg to Rivka Aaronsohn, September 26, 1915.

27. Avshalom Feinberg to Rivka Aaronsohn, October 22, 1917.

28. Verrier, *Agents of Empire*, 133; Florence, *Lawrence and Aaronsohn*, 173–74; Engle, *Nili Spies*, 59; and Weldon, *"Hard Lying,"* 110.

29. Verrier, *Agents of Empire*, 135–38; and Florence, *Lawrence and Aaronsohn*, 176.

30. Engle, *Nili Spies*, 59.

31. Florence, *Lawrence and Aaronsohn*, 176; and Farrin, *Abundance from the Desert*, 211.

6. The Wait

1. Aaronsohn Diary, February 19, 1917, in Verrier, *Agents of Empire*, 242 (Cairo–Port Said–*Managem*; recounting a later conversation that Aaron had with a British officer who had been on the ship); and Engle, *Nili Spies*, 61.

2. Schneersohn, *Miyomano shel ish Nili*, 13.

3. Engle, *Nili Spies*, 62.

4. Schneersohn, *Miyomano shel ish Nili*, 13.

5. Woodfin, *Camp and Combat*, 16–17.

6. Florence, *Lawrence and Aaronsohn*, 205; and Anderson, *Lawrence in Arabia*, 181.

7. Livneh, Nedava, and Efrati, *Nili*, 392; and "History of Rishon LeZion," http://www.rishonlezion.muni.il/eng/pages/historyofrishonlezion.aspx.

8. Engle, *Nili Spies*, 63–64.

9. Engle, *Nili Spies*, 64; and Florence, *Lawrence and Aaronsohn*, 206.

10. Schneersohn, *Miyomano shel ish Nili*, 13–14.

11. Florence, *Lawrence and Aaronsohn*, 206.

12. Schneersohn, *Miyomano shel ish Nili*, 14.

13. Avshalom Feinberg to Sarah Aaronsohn, January 29, 1916.

14. Sarah Aaronsohn to Haim Abraham, January 23, 1916.

15. Engle, *Nili Spies*, 64.

16. Sarah Aaronsohn to Haim Abraham, February 12, 1916.

17. Sarah Aaronsohn to Haim Abraham, March 7, 1916.

18. Sarah Aaronsohn to Haim Abraham, March 20, 1916.

19. Katz, *Aaronsohn Saga*, 98.

20. Florence, *Lawrence and Aaronsohn*, 208.

21. Baruch Ben-Azar testimony (Israel Defense Forces Archives), 3. Ben-Azar worked in the locust campaign and spent time at Atlit.

22. Ben-Zvi, *Coming Home*, 288–92. See also Florence, *Lawrence and Aaronsohn*, 208; and Engle, *Nili Spies*, 66. Years later Rahel became the wife of Israel's second president.

23. Verrier, *Agents of Empire*, 193; Florence, *Lawrence and Aaronsohn*, 209; and Anderson, *Lawrence in Arabia*, 181.

24. Engle, *Nili Spies*, 76–77.

25. Livneh, Nedava, and Efrati, *Nili*, 392–96; and Engle, *Nili Spies*, 58–59.

26. Sheffy, *British Military Intelligence*, 160, describing reporting structure; and Engle, *Nili Spies*, 77.

27. Sarah Aaronsohn to Avshalom Feinberg, August 7, 1916.

28. Sarah Aaronsohn to Avshalom Feinberg, undated. The letters in which Sarah describes her health appear to be from 1916.

29. Avshalom Feinberg to Sarah Aaronsohn, May 9, 1916.

30. Florence, *Lawrence and Aaronsohn*, 179–80.

31. Engle, *Nili Spies*, 77; and Katz, *Aaronsohn Saga*, 143.

32. Avshalom Feinberg to Sarah Aaronsohn, December 16, 1916.

7. Aaron Aaronsohn's Journey

1. Katz, *Aaronsohn Saga*, 97–98.

2. Florence, *Lawrence and Aaronsohn*, 210–11.

3. Florence, *Lawrence and Aaronsohn*, 213.

4. Schneersohn, *Miyomano shel ish Nili*, 22–24.

5. Florence, *Lawrence and Aaronsohn*, 213–15; Katz, *Aaronsohn Saga*, 103–4; and Evelyn, *English Wife in Berlin*, 158.

6. Katz, *Aaronsohn Saga*, 107–8. In the end, Alexander Dushkin, a companion of Magnes, may have taken the letter to the United States. Florence, *Lawrence and Aaronsohn*, 219.

7. Morton, *Spies of the First World War*, 169–80; Davies, "During World War I."

8. Katz, *Aaronsohn Saga*, 109, 125–26; and Rivka Aaronsohn to Sarah Aaronsohn, July 7, 1917.

9. Thomson, *Queer People*, 201–2.

10. Verrier, *Agents of Empire*, 181, 189; and Ministry of Defence, "The Old War Office Building."

11. Anderson, *Lawrence in Arabia*, 229; Katz, *Aaronsohn Saga*, 117–19; and Florence, *Lawrence and Aaronsohn*, 224.

12. Verrier, *Agents of Empire*, 196.

13. Prior and Wilson, *The Somme*, 38; and Gilbert, *First World War*, 258–60, 299.

14. Monger, *Patriotism and Propaganda*, 19–20; and Loconte, *A Hobbit, a Wardrobe*, 61–62.

15. Verrier, *Agents of Empire*, 199; and Katz, *Aaronsohn Saga*, 121–23.

16. Aaronson Diary, December 12–13, 1916 (Port Said), and December 14, 1916 (Alexandria), in Verrier, *Agents of Empire*, 224–25.

17. Aaronsohn Diary, December 14–16, 1916 (Alexandria), in Verrier, *Agents of Empire*, 225–26; and Florence, *Lawrence and Aaronsohn*, 228.

18. Woolley, *As I Seem to Remember*, 110–13.

19. Aaronsohn Diary, December 16, 1916 (Alexandria), and December 19, 1916 (Alexandria), in Verrier, *Agents of Empire*, 226.

20. Aaronsohn Diary, December 24, 1916 (Port Said), in Verrier, *Agents of Empire*, 227; and Florence, *Lawrence and Aaronsohn*, 230–31.

21. Aaronsohn Diary, December 24, 1916 (Port Said), December 25, 1916 (in sight of Jaffa), and December 26, 1916 (near Sour), in Verrier, *Agents of Empire*, 227–29. According to Ronald Florence, *Lawrence and Aaronsohn*, 231, the surfboat put at least one swimmer in the water, but the rough waves prevented the surfboat from retrieving him. If so, the swimmer evidently did not reach the research station to deliver the news that Aaron was in Egypt. According to Katz, *Aaronsohn Saga*, 138, the swimmers aboard the surfboat decided not to risk the waves and returned to the *Goeland*.

22. Aaronsohn Diary, January 2, 1917 (Alexandria), in Verrier, *Agents of Empire*, 229–30; Fromkin, *Peace to End All Peace*, 169–71; and Anderson, *Lawrence in Arabia*, 225.

23. Aaronsohn Diary, January 5, 1917 (Cairo), and January 11, 1917 (Port Said), in Verrier, *Agents of Empire*, 230–31.

24. Aaronsohn Diary, January 17, 1917 (Cairo), January 20, 1917 (Port Said), and January 22, 1917 (Cairo), in Verrier, *Agents of Empire*, 232–35; and Florence, *Lawrence and Aaronsohn*, 234–35.

25. Aaronsohn Diary, January 20, 1917 (Port Said), and January 24, 1917 (Cairo), in Verrier, *Agents of Empire*, 234–36; Presland, *Deedes Bey*, 12–13, 18–19, 120; Fromkin, *Peace to End All Peace*, 38; Wilson, *Lawrence of Arabia*, 250; and Anderson, *Lawrence in Arabia*, 254.

26. Tucker and Roberts, *Encyclopedia of the Arab-Israeli Conflict*, 1:292; and "Sir Wyndham Deedes."

27. Rogan, *Fall of the Ottomans*, 312–13 (the proposal for an active defense was made in February 1916); Woodward, *Hell in the Holy Land*, 29–30, 33–34; and Murray, *Sir Archibald Murray's Despatches*, 49–50.

28. Rogan, *Fall of the Ottomans*, 313–17; and Murray, *Sir Archibald Murray's Despatches*, 52–54.

29. McMeekin, *Ottoman Endgame*, 348; and Bruce, *Last Crusade*, 105.

30. Rogan, *Fall of the Ottomans*, 316–18; and Bruce, *Last Crusade*, 106–8.

31. "Bedouin," *Encyclopedia Britannica*, 3:622–24.

32. Abu-Rabia, *Bedouin Century*, 14; Gullett, *Australian Imperial Force*, 82, 87, 93, 94–99, 185; and Massey, *Desert Campaigns*, 109.

8. One of Your Men

1. Engle, *Nili Spies*, 78–79.

2. Baruch Ben-Azar testimony (Israel Defense Forces Archives), 4.

3. Avshalom Feinberg to Sarah Aaronsohn, January 7, 1917. Avshalom misremembered Sarah's birthday, which had been the day before. According to some sources (see Melman, "Sarah Aaronsohn, 1890–1917"), Sarah's birthday was January 5, 1890. The Hebrew inscription on her grave, however, gives a date of January 6, 1890.

4. Nedava, *Yosef Lishansky Papers*, 94 (recollection of Rivka Lishansky Lifshitz), 102 (recollection of Ivria Lishansky Rom).

5. Simon, *Date Palm*, 48–49; and Pollack, "Lone Palm Tree."

6. Aaronsohn Diary, January 25, 1917 (Cairo–Port Said), in Verrier, *Agents of Empire*, 236; Engle, *Nili Spies*, 86–87 (suggesting that the guide had betrayed Avshalom and Yosef); and Katz, *Aaronsohn Saga*, 145.

7. Aaronsohn Diary, January 25–26, 1917 (Cairo–Port Said), and January 26, 1917 (Port Said–Cairo), in Verrier, *Agents of Empire*, 236–38.

8. Presland, *Deedes Bey*, 238–40.

9. Aaronsohn Diary, January 28, 1917 (*L'Arbalète*), in Verrier, *Agents of Empire*, 236–38; and Engle, *Nili Spies*, 86–88.

9. What about Avshalom?

1. Schneersohn, *Miyomano shel ish Nili*, 33; Florence, *Lawrence and Aaronsohn*, 132; Engle, *Nili Spies*, 48; Katz, *Aaronsohn Saga*, 96; and Terry, *Reader's Guide to Judaism*, 223.

2. Schneersohn, *Miyomano shel ish Nili*, 23, 33; Engle, *Nili Spies*, 70; and Katz, *Aaronsohn Saga*, 148–49.

3. Schneersohn, *Miyomano shel ish Nili*, 41–42; and Engle, *Nili Spies*, 80–81.

4. Schneersohn, *Miyomano shel ish Nili*, 41–45; Engle, *Nili Spies*, 93–97; and Florence, *Lawrence and Aaronsohn*, 288–89.

5. Aaronsohn Diary, January 30, 1917 (Cairo), in Verrier, *Agents of Empire*, 239.

6. Weldon, *"Hard Lying,"* 160–62.

7. Dagan and Dagan, *On the First Road*, 247.

8. Nedava, *Yosef Lishansky Papers*, 75 (recollection of Atara Ben-Dov, Miriam's daughter). See Dagan and Dagan, *On the First Road*, 249. In the early years of Metula, each farmer was given a decent-size plot of land, a house, a stable, a shed, a horse, and plowing tools.

9. Florence, *Lawrence and Aaronsohn*, 285; and Halkin, *Strange Death*, 158.

10. Assi, "History and Politics of Nomadism," 241, describing how Ha-Shomer adopted "local dress, horseback riding skills, and other fighting customs borrowed from the Bedouin and their European counterparts, the Cossacks."

11. Adler, "The Second Aliyah and Ottoman Governmental Policy."

12. Nedava, *Yosef Lishansky Papers*, 101–3 (recollection of Ivria Lishansky Rom).

13. Gorny, *Zionism and the Arabs*, 17–18; and Dagan and Dagan, *On the Road*, 305–13.

14. Nedava, *Yosef Lishansky Papers*, 94 (recollection of Rivka Lishansky Lifshitz), 101–3 (recollection of Ivria Lishansky Rom). According to a report in 1938 by the Jewish Telegraphic Agency ("Abandoned Colony in Southern Palestine Burned Down by Terrorists"), Arab terrorists burned down Ruchema that year.

15. Aaronsohn Diary, February 19, 1917 (Cairo–Port Said–*Managem*), in Verrier, *Agents of Empire*, 242–43; Schneersohn, *Miyomano shel ish Nili*, 45–51; Engle, *Nili Spies*, 98–99; and Florence, *Lawrence and Aaronsohn*, 266. In *Nili Spies*, Anita Engle suggests that Yosef Lishansky was dropped on the Atlit beach in January, the night after Liebl Bernstein landed. Liova's diary states that this occurred on February 28, but Aaron's diary, which was meticulously maintained, is clear that Lishansky landed on February 19.

16. Aaronsohn Diary, February 21, 1917 (aboard the *Managem*), and March 3, 1917 (Cairo), in Verrier, *Agents of Empire*, 243–45; and Sheffy, *British Military Intelligence*, 83. The *Managem* sailed from Atlit to Beirut before returning to Cairo, and that may explain why the intelligence report was not reviewed in Cairo until March 3.

17. Sarah Aaronsohn to Aaron Aaronsohn, March 6, 1917.

18. Report of Yosef Lishansky, March 4–16, 1917; and Nedava, *Yosef Lishansky Papers*, 95 (recollection of Rivka Lishansky Lifshitz).

19. Sarah Aaronsohn to Aaron Aaronsohn, undated; and Katz, *Aaronsohn Saga*, 228. The "ship is here" evidently refers to the *Managem*, which visited Atlit on or about March 27, 1917. Aaronsohn Diary, March 27, 1917 (Cairo), in

Verrier, *Agents of Empire*, 250. Yosef had not told Sarah of Avshalom's death when Sarah wrote her March 6 letter to Aaron, in which she stated that she was anxious about Avshalom. But Yosef evidently did tell her before the *Managem's* next visit on or about March 27, when the spy ship picked up both the March 6 letter and Sarah's undated letter that began, "It's hard for me to even mention our great disaster in this letter."

20. Sarah Aaronsohn to Alexander Aaronsohn and Rivka Aaronsohn, undated; and Katz, *Aaronsohn Saga*, 228–29. Sarah's letter may have been written and sent while she was in Cairo.

21. Avshalom Feinberg to Sarah Aaronsohn, June 17, 1914.

22. Rivka Aaronsohn to Aaron Aaronsohn, undated but almost certainly written in 1917; and Rivka Aaronsohn to Sarah Aaronsohn, July 10, 1917.

23. Avshalom Feinberg to Sarah Aaronsohn, September 21, 1914.

10. Black Nights

1. Engle, *Nili Spies*, 109–12.

2. Sheffy, *British Military Intelligence*, 165.

3. Aaron Aaronsohn to Sarah Aaronsohn, August 3, 1917; and Sheffy, *British Military Intelligence*, 163.

4. Engle, *Nili Spies*, 112–13 (translated by Nelson Berkoff).

5. Florence, *Lawrence and Aaronsohn*, 205–6; and Katz, *Aaronsohn Saga*, 229.

6. Sarah Aaronsohn to Aaron Aaronsohn, March 6, 1917.

7. Foreign Office 382/1259: Report No. 697, received in Cairo, April 3, 1917, National Archives, Kew, England. Sarah's observations appear in a British report on "economic conditions" in Palestine from an unidentified agent "who travelled NAZARETH–NABLUS–JERUSALEM–RAMLEH between March 6 and March 15, 1917." The report notes that "in general, winter crop prospects are poor. . . . A 3% tax in kind has been exacted from the JERUSALEM olive growers in addition to the tithe." The agent clearly was Sarah. Copies of the report were distributed not just within the British government but also to the Italian, Russian, and French governments. Engle, *Nili Spies*, 103–5.

8. McKenna, *I Was a Spy!*, 50–61, describing how intelligence on train movements from a Belgian woman spy for the British led to a devastating aerial attack on a German munitions train.

9. Dr. Moshe Neumann, "Report of Dr. Neumann" (no date), 1–2 (unpublished English translation); Katz, *Aaronsohn Saga*, 174; and Engle, *Nili Spies*, 105–6. Dr. Neumann's report, an account of his activities as a Nili spy, was

apparently written to British officials at or near the end of the war while seeking compensation for his services and employment.

10. Neumann, "Report of Dr. Neumann," 2–6; and Katz, *Aaronsohn Saga*, 174–75.

11. Katz, *Aaronsohn Saga*, 176–77.

12. Engle, *Nili Spies*, 106; and Katz, *Aaronsohn Saga*, 175.

13. Katz, *Aaronsohn Saga*, 176.

14. Engle, *Nili Spies*, 106–7 (translated by Nelson Berkoff). Sarah's report didn't identify Nahum Wilbushevitz by name, but he was the only Nili spy who was an engineer in the Turkish army. Sarah may also have been able to speak some German. Engle, *Nili Spies*, 35.

15. Engle, *Nili Spies*, 107; Katz, *Aaronsohn Saga*, 233; and Livneh, Nedava, and Efrati, *Nili*, 395–96. According to the biography in *Nili*, Fein's father, a rabbi, was a pioneer of the citron industry in Palestine. Per the biography, Fein's father committed suicide when rabbinical representatives, for unknown reasons, boycotted his citrons.

16. Aaronsohn Diary, March 28, 1917 (Cairo), in Verrier, *Agents of Empire*, 250–51; and Sheffy, *British Military Intelligence*, 81–82.

17. War Office 157/713: EEF [Egyptian Expeditionary Force] Intelligence Diary, March 30, 1917, National Archives, Kew, England.

18. War Office 33/935: General Officer Commanding in Chief, Egypt to War Office, No. A.M. 1745, March 31, 1917, National Archives, Kew, England; War Office 157/713: EEF Intelligence Diary, March 30, 1917, National Archives, Kew, England; Sheffy, *British Military Intelligence*, 165; and Rogan, *Fall of the Ottomans*, 312 ("In April 1916, the Germans assigned a flight of aircraft to Ottoman headquarters in Beersheba. The state-of-the-art planes—powerful Rumplers and Fokker monoplanes that had proved the scourge of the western front—gave the Turks air superiority over the Sinai").

19. Sarah Aaronsohn to Aaron Aaronsohn, June 25, 1917; Florence, *Lawrence and Aaronsohn*, 297–98; Katz, *Aaronsohn Saga*, 232–33; and Engle, *Nili Spies*, 114–15.

20. Engle, *Nili Spies*, 115–16 (translated by Nelson Berkoff); and Sarah Aaronsohn to Aaron Aaronsohn, undated.

11. What I Have Done

1. Engle, *Nili Spies*, 119–21 (translated by Nelson Berkoff); and Sarah Aaronsohn to Aaron Aaronsohn, undated.

2. Sheffy, *British Military Intelligence*, 81–82, describing the British base on Cyprus.

3. Aaronsohn Diary, April 18, 1917 (Cairo), and April 19, 1917 (Port Said), in Verrier, *Agents of Empire*, 255.

4. Gilbert, *First World War*, 313–15, 373–74, 401–2. These dates are based on the calendar in use outside Russia.

5. Gilbert, *First World War*, 306, 318; and Fromkin, *Peace to End All Peace*, 255.

6. Meyer, *World Undone*, 517–21; and Fromkin, *Peace to End All Peace*, 254–55. The abdication of Czar Nicholas II also made it easier for the United States to enter the war since it would not be allied with the repressive Romanov regime. Anderson, *Lawrence in Arabia*, 287.

7. Rogan, *Fall of the Ottomans*, 327.

8. Fromkin, *Peace to End All Peace*, 305–8; Rogan, *Fall of the Ottomans*, 317, 325–27; and Woodfin, *Camp and Combat*, 50–51.

9. Rogan, *Fall of the Ottomans*, 328–29; Aaronsohn Diary, March 29, 1917 (Cairo), in Verrier, *Agents of Empire*, 251; and Woodward, *Hell in the Holy Land*, 56.

10. Murray, *Sir Archibald Murray's Despatches*, 133–34.

11. Gilbert, *First World War*, 344–45; Rogan, *Fall of the Ottomans*, 330–33; and Fromkin, *Peace to End All Peace*, 308.

12. Schneersohn, *Miyomano shel ish Nili*, 62; and Katz, *Aaronsohn Saga*, 239. Liova's diary records that he, Sarah, and Yosef met Aaron in Cairo, while Aaron's diary describes meeting them in Port Said. Aaronsohn Diary, April 19, 1917 (Port Said–Cairo), in Verrier, *Agents of Empire*, 255. In the case of these kinds of direct conflicts, absent other evidence, I have relied on Aaron's diary.

13. Aaronsohn Diary, April 20, 1917 (Cairo), in Verrier, *Agents of Empire*, 255–56; and Schneersohn, *Miyomano shel ish Nili*, 62.

14. "Lawrence of Arabia"; Katz, *Aaronsohn Saga*, 174, 281; and Engle, *Nili Spies*, 86, 218.

15. Aaronsohn Diary, April 20, 1917 (Cairo), and April 23, 1917 (Cairo), in Verrier, *Agents of Empire*, 255–58.

16. Pascal, "I Am also a Spy"; and Engle, *Nili Spies*, 129. The Pascal article does not provide a date for the conversation with Captain Edmonds; therefore, I assume it took place before Sarah's anticipated departure from Egypt in April. Pascal mentions in the article that he and Aaron had decided not to let her return to Palestine. The day after Sarah's arrival, as pointed out, Aaron had tried to persuade her not to return. Aaron Aaronsohn Diary, April 20, 1917 (Cairo), in Verrier, *Agents of Empire*, 255–56.

17. Aaronsohn Diary, April 21, 1917 (Cairo), in Verrier, *Agents of Empire*, 256.

18. Wilson, *Lawrence of Arabia*, 388–89.

19. Aaronsohn Diary, April 21, 1917 (Cairo), in Verrier, *Agents of Empire*, 256.

20. Aaronsohn Diary, Sunday, April 22, 1917 (Cairo–Port Said–Cairo), in Verrier, *Agents of Empire*, 256–57. In his diary, Aaron wrote, "We promised to see each other again in three weeks." Sarah may have appeased Aaron by offering to return in three weeks, but there is no indication that her visit would be anything other than a short stay.

21. Liova Schneersohn, "To Sarah" (unpublished manuscript, 1917), 1.

12. To Sarah

1. Weldon, *"Hard Lying,"* 162.
2. Aaronsohn Diary, April 28, 1917 (Cairo), in Verrier, *Agents of Empire*, 261–62.
3. Aaronsohn Diary, April 19, 1917 (Port Said–Cairo), in Verrier, *Agents of Empire*, 255.
4. Leslie, *Mark Sykes*, 8, 16–17; Fromkin, *Peace to End All Peace*, 146; and Rockwell quoted in Burton, *Historical Dictionary*, 256.
5. Leslie, *Mark Sykes*, 18, 20; and Anderson, *Lawrence in Arabia*, 153–54.
6. Anderson, *Lawrence in Arabia*, 162–63; and Kramer, "Sykes-Picot and the Zionists."
7. Wilson, *Lawrence of Arabia*, 236–37. Sean McMeekin points out that the most "notorious post-Ottoman boundaries," such as those separating Palestine from (Trans)Jordan or Syria from Iraq, were not drawn up by Sykes and Picot. McMeekin, *Ottoman Endgame*, introduction, xix–xx.
8. Kramer, "Sykes-Picot and the Zionists"; and Aaronsohn Diary, January 15, 1917 (Cairo), in Verrier, *Agents of Empire*, 231–32.
9. Leslie, *Mark Sykes*, 62; and Anderson, *Lawrence in Arabia*, 396–97.
10. Aaronsohn Diary, April 27, 1917 (Cairo), in Verrier, *Agents of Empire*, 260–61 (emphasis in original).
11. Anderson, *Lawrence in Arabia*, 301–2; Ben-Bassat, "Enciphered Ottoman Telegrams," 286–87; and Green, "This Day in Jewish History."
12. Anderson, *Lawrence in Arabia*, 302.
13. Anderson, *Lawrence in Arabia*, 302–4. The participants fully understood what they were doing. On May 9 a pro-Zionist member of Parliament William Ormsby-Gore, who had come to know and admire Aaron while assigned to the Arab Bureau, cabled Mark Sykes that "we ought to use the pogroms in Palestine as propaganda. Any spicy tales of atrocity would be eagerly welcomed here." Anderson, *Lawrence in Arabia*, 302–3.
14. Engle, *Nili Spies*, 117–18; and Florence, *Lawrence and Aaronsohn*, 273.

15. Aaronsohn Diary, April 19, 1917 (Port Said–Cairo), in Verrier, *Agents of Empire*, 255; and Anderson, *Lawrence in Arabia*, 304–5.

16. Sarah Aaronsohn to Aaron Aaronsohn, April 30, 1917.

17. Schneersohn, *Miyomano shel ish Nili*, 73–74.

18. Sarah Aaronsohn to Aaron Aaronsohn, undated (the letter was written on the stationery of the "George Nungovich Egyptian hotels"); and Katz, *Aaronsohn Saga*, 239.

19. Schneersohn, *Miyomano shel ish Nili*, 64.

20. Schneersohn, *Miyomano shel ish Nili*, 63–65; and Aaronsohn Diary, May 8, 1917 (Cairo), in Verrier, *Agents of Empire*, 263.

21. Aaronsohn Diary, May 14, 1917 (Cairo), in Verrier, *Agents of Empire*, 266; and Engle, *Nili Spies*, 130–31.

22. Livneh, Nedava, and Efrati, *Nili*, 145, quoting Yosef Alhadeff to Dr. Yaacov Harozen, April 10, 1943.

23. Aaronsohn Diary, May 14, 1917 (Cairo), in Verrier, *Agents of Empire*, 266; and Engle, *Nili Spies*, 131.

24. Engle, *Nili Spies*, 131; and Aaronsohn Diary, May 15, 1917 (Cairo–Port Said) in Verrier, *Agents of Empire*, 266.

25. Schneersohn, *Miyomano shel ish Nili*, 70–72; and Engle, *Nili Spies*, 131–32.

26. Schneersohn, "To Sarah," 19–30, 32.

27. Sarah Aaronsohn to Liova Schneersohn, April 17–18, 1917. These dates appear in Sarah's letter; she was then on her way from Atlit to Egypt. Schneersohn's "To Sarah," however, begins on April 25 "in the Mediterranean" and thereafter contains specific references to dates on which Liova made entries. It may be that Liova wrote an earlier version of "To Sarah" on the *Managem* after they left Atlit, gave it to Sarah, and then reworked it over the succeeding weeks.

28. Engle, *Nili Spies*, 133 (translated by Nelson Berkoff).

29. Aaronsohn Diary, May 31, 1917 (Cairo), in Verrier, *Agents of Empire*, 269–70.

30. Aaronsohn Diary, June 11, 1917 (Cairo), in Verrier, *Agents of Empire*, 273–74.

31. Schneersohn, *Miyomano shel ish Nili*, 79–80.

32. Engle, *Nili Spies*, 137.

13. We Are Watched by a Thousand Eyes

1. Sarah Aaronsohn to Aaron Aaronsohn, June 25, 1917.

2. Sarah Aaronsohn to Liova Schneersohn, June 25, 1917.

3. Sarah Aaronsohn to Liova Schneersohn, June 25, 1917; and Sarah Aaronsohn to Aaron Aaronsohn for the following dates: June 25, 1917; July 14, 1917; and July 24, 1917.

4. Florence, *Lawrence and Aaronsohn*, 254–55.

5. Sarah Aaronsohn to Aaron Aaronsohn, June 25, 1917; and Engle, *Nili Spies*, 138.

6. Sarah Aaronsohn to Aaron Aaronsohn, June 25, 1917; and Katz, *Aaronsohn Saga*, 248–49.

7. Sarah Aaronsohn to Aaron Aaronsohn, July 14, 1917; Engle, *Nili Spies*, 32.

8. Sarah Aaronsohn to Aaron Aaronsohn, July 14, 1917; and Engle, *Nili Spies*, 140–43.

9. Aaron Aaronsohn to Sarah Aaronsohn, August 3, 1917.

10. Aaron Aaronsohn Diary, July 26, 1917 (Cairo), in Verrier, *Agents of Empire*, 285.

11. War Office 157/717, July 25, 1917, National Archives, Kew, England. A summary of Sarah's report evidently was wired to Cairo by the Eastern Mediterranean Special Intelligence Bureau, likely from a base on Cyprus. See Extract from Report CX 176, July 24, 1917, communicated by E.M.S.I.B., National Archives, Kew, England; and Katz, *Aaronsohn Saga*, 241–42.

12. Sarah Aaronsohn to Aaron Aaronsohn, June 25, 1917. In this letter, Sarah describes how she had planned to leave Zichron on the morning of June 22, get to Dr. Neumann (which would have required a full day's carriage ride), and return on the twenty-third. She had trouble finding a carriage, so she "was late to catch the Managem." She apparently wrote the June 25 letter in the hopes that the *Managem* might return shortly. Aaron's diary records that when on June 26 the *Managem* came to Atlit, "no one was waiting for them," and the landing party was fired on, evidently by a local patrol. Aaronsohn Diary, June 28, 1917 (Cairo), in Verrier, *Agents of Empire*, 276–77. That the airplane report did not reach the British in Egypt until about July 25 suggests that the *Managem* didn't pick up Sarah's June 25 letter and Dr. Neumann's airplane report until a visit around July 25, and then the crew wired the report to Cairo from Cyprus. The date in the British war diary of "about June 23" is roughly consistent with Sarah's chronology of her visit to Ramle. Sheffy, *British Military Intelligence*, 164–65.

13. Aaronsohn Diary, June 28, 1917 (Cairo), in Verrier, *Agents of Empire*, 276–77; and Sheffy, *British Military Intelligence*, 169.

14. Copping, "Honoured"; and Brown, "Remembered at Last."

15. Aaronsohn Diary, July 7, 1917 (Cairo), in Verrier, *Agents of Empire*, 281 ("[Capt. Philip] Graves was surprised that even one out of six arrived"); Woodward, *Hell in the Holy Land*, 16–18; and Engle, *Nili Spies*, 148.

16. Sheffy, *British Military Intelligence*, 164–66, quoting War Office 157/718: EEF Intelligence Diary, August 8, 1917, National Archives, Kew, England. Several of Sheffy's examples of Nili's dated intelligence concerned the movements of Turk divisions. In each instance, the movement had been reported by a deserter, or was known because of a wireless intercept, before the Nili report on the divisions' movements reached the British. Another example concerns a deserter whom Nili first hid and then put on board the *Managem*. According to Sheffy, by the time the deserter reached Egypt, "his operational and tactical information became dated (although he contributed a great deal of basic information later on)." By contrast, Sheffy notes, "field intelligence" interrogated at least fifty-eight additional defectors from the deserter's division who had "fresh, albeit more limited, information." As to the airplanes, as a result of Nili's intelligence, improved British planes "were rushed in in time to restore British air superiority before the third battle of Gaza." Sheffy, *British Military Intelligence*, 165.

14. Everywhere I Turn I Feel His Absence

1. Aaron Aaronsohn to Sarah Aaronsohn, August 3, 1917; and Katz, *Aaronsohn Saga*, 180–82.
2. Sarah Aaronsohn to Aaron Aaronsohn, August 23, 1917; and Livneh, Nedava, and Efrati, *Nili*, 393. The idea apparently was that Halperin, who had been working in Atlit, would go back and forth from Zichron on long errands. His absence while serving as a swimmer-courier on the *Managem* would therefore not be noticed.
3. Sarah Aaronsohn to Aaron Aaronsohn, July 21, 1917.
4. Sarah Aaronsohn to Aaron Aaronsohn, August 23, 1917.
5. Sarah Aaronsohn to Aaron Aaronsohn, August 23, 1917; and Katz, *Aaronsohn Saga*, 255.
6. Sarah Aaronsohn to Aaron Aaronsohn, August 23, 1917.
7. Sarah Aaronsohn to Aaron Aaronsohn, August 23, 1917; and Katz, *Aaronsohn Saga*, 254–55.
8. Sarah Aaronsohn to Aaron Aaronsohn, July 24, 1917; and Aaron Aaronsohn to Sarah Aaronsohn, August 3, 1917.
9. Sarah Aaronsohn to Aaron Aaronsohn, June 25, 1917; and Florence, *Lawrence and Aaronsohn*, 302–3.
10. Sarah Aaronsohn to Aaron Aaronsohn, June 25, 1917; Sarah Aaronsohn to Aaron Aaronsohn, July 14, 1917; Sarah Aaronsohn to Aaron Aaronsohn, August 23, 1917; Sarah Aaronsohn to Liova Schneersohn, September 12, 1917; and Sarah Aaronsohn to Aaron Aaronsohn, September 10, 1917.

11. Livneh, Nedava, and Efrati, *Nili*, 398; and Sarah Aaronsohn to Aaron Aaronsohn, August 23, 1917.

12. Sarah Aaronsohn to Aaron Aaronsohn, August 23, 1917; and Engle, *Nili Spies*, 159.

13. Sarah Aaronsohn to Rivka Aaronsohn, undated but likely in January 1917; Sarah Aaronsohn to Liova Schneersohn, June 25, 1917; Sarah Aaronsohn to Aaron Aaronsohn, August 8, 1917; Katz, *Aaronsohn Saga*, 180, 243; and Livneh, Nedava, and Efrati, *Nili*, 396–97.

14. Sheffy, *British Military Intelligence*, 165; and Katz, *Aaronsohn Saga*, 252, 259–60.

15. Sarah Aaronsohn to Aaron Aaronsohn, August 23, 1917.

16. Sarah Aaronsohn to Aaron Aaronsohn, July 14, 1917; and Sarah Aaronsohn to Aaron Aaronsohn, July 21, 1917.

17. Sarah Aaronsohn to Aaron Aaronsohn, July 24, 1917.

18. Sarah Aaronsohn to Aaron Aaronsohn, undated. The letter was apparently written in early September because in it Sarah passed on to Aaron an acquaintance's Yom Kippur greetings. That year Yom Kippur was in September. See "Calendar for Year 1917 (Israel)," Time and Date.com, http://www.timeanddate.com/calendar/?year=1917&country=34. See also Engle, *Nili Spies*, 166. The Fontaine fable that Sarah refers to is apparently *The Wolf and the Dog*, about a stray dog whose collar has been removed but he remains loyal to his master.

19. Sarah Aaronsohn to Aaron Aaronsohn, June 25, 1917.

20. Sarah Aaronsohn to Aaron Aaronsohn, July 14, 1917; Sarah Aaronsohn to Aaron Aaronsohn, July 24, 1917; and Aaron Aaronsohn to Sarah Aaronsohn, August 3, 1917. By ending the relationship with Zvi, Sarah presumably meant any working relationship, for example, in farming or business.

21. Yosef Lishansky to Aaron Aaronsohn, July 7, 1917.

22. Aaron Aaronsohn to Sarah Aaronsohn, August 3, 1917.

23. Sarah Aaronsohn to Aaron Aaronsohn, August 23, 1917; and Engle, *Nili Spies*, 139.

24. Sarah Aaronsohn to Aaron Aaronsohn, August 23, 1917.

25. Katz, *Aaronsohn Saga*, 177–78.

26. Sarah Aaronsohn to Aaron Aaronsohn, September 21, 1917; and Katz, *Aaronsohn Saga*, 263–64.

27. Aaronsohn Diary, July 17, 1917 (Cairo), in Verrier, *Agents of Empire*, 283–84.

28. Rogan, *Fall of the Ottomans*, 289, 292–98; McMeekin, *Ottoman Endgame*, 305–7; and Anderson, *Lawrence in Arabia*, 121–23, 179–81, 183–84.

29. Lawrence, *Seven Pillars of Wisdom*, 222, 226, 246–47, 253–56; Anderson, *Lawrence in Arabia*, 258, 270, 288, 310–14; Florence, *Lawrence and Aaronsohn*, 257–62; and Wilson, *Lawrence of Arabia*, 422.

30. Wilson, *Lawrence of Arabia*, 443. Lawrence first sent the letter to Gen. Gilbert Clayton, who decided not to send it to Sykes. Wilson, *Lawrence of Arabia*, 445.

31. Aaronsohn Diary, August 12, 1917 (Cairo), in Verrier, *Agents of Empire*, 289.

32. Leslie, *Mark Sykes*, 271–72; and Anderson, *Lawrence in Arabia*, 294.

33. Anderson, *Lawrence in Arabia*, 357–58, quoting Aaron Aaronsohn, "The Jewish Colonies," *Arab Bulletin*, no. 64 (September 27, 1917); and Florence, *Lawrence and Aaronsohn*, 198.

34. Aaronsohn Dairy, August 24, 1917 (Cairo), in Verrier, *Agents of Empire*, 291.

35. Anderson, *Lawrence in Arabia*, 359, quoting Reginald Wingate to Arthur Balfour, August 20, 1917.

36. Aaronsohn Diary, August 27, 1917 (Cairo), in Verrier, *Agents of Empire*, 292.

37. Aaronsohn Diary, August 16, 1917 (Cairo), in Verrier, *Agents of Empire*, 290 (describing a landing on August 14).

38. Aaronsohn Diary, August 26, 1917 (Cairo), in Verrier, *Agents of Empire*, 291–92; and Engle, *Nili Spies*, 174–75. According to Anita Engle, one reason that the *Managem* did not come was that the swimmer-courier, Liebl Bernstein, had gone on strike. His wife had apparently told him that while spying for the British was a fine thing, given the risks, Liebl wasn't being paid enough. He demanded more money, the British refused to pay it, and Liebl refused to swim. It seems likely that the British could have found another swimmer—for example, Yitzhak Halperin might have been available by then—and when the sea was calm, a swimmer wasn't needed, since the surfboat could get to the beach or at least close to it. The principal reason for the *Managem*'s delay appeared to be the bad weather.

39. Sarah Aaronsohn to Liova Schneersohn, September 12, 1917; and Engle, *Nili Spies*, 170–72.

40. Sarah Aaronsohn to Aaron Aaronsohn, September 10, 1917; and Sarah Aaronsohn to Aaron Aaronsohn, August 23, 1917.

41. Nedava, *Yosef Lishansky*, 96 (recollection of Rivka Lishansky Lifshitz), 106 (recollection of Ivria Lishansky Rom).

42. Anderson, *Lawrence in Arabia*, 360.

15. The Situation Is Getting Worse

1. Sarah Aaronsohn to Aaron Aaronsohn, September 10, 1917; Anderson, *Lawrence in Arabia*, 376; and Katz, *Aaronsohn Saga*, 258.

2. Sarah Aaronsohn and Yosef Lishansky to Aaron Aaronsohn, September 25, 1917. The source of this information is unclear, and the account is short on details.

3. Tauber, "Capture of the NILI Spies," 701–10. The account comes from Aziz Bek, who was the head of the intelligence service of the Ottoman Fourth Army. Bek's credibility is suspect because his first account of the Nili ring, written in 1932, made no mention of the capture of the Arab spies. In a later, supposedly better researched book, Bek claimed that Sarah met with Djemal Pasha in late 1914 in Palestine and learned about his preparations for the attack on the Suez Canal. In fact, Sarah was then in Constantinople. Captain Weldon of the *Managem*, furthermore, insisted in his own memoir that the British were careful to bring only coins into Palestine dated no later than 1914. Weldon, *"Hard Lying,"* 188.

4. Sarah Aaronsohn to Aaron Aaronsohn, September 21, 1917.

5. Engle, *Nili Spies*, 180–82; and Katz, *Aaronsohn Saga*, 264–65.

6. Nedava, *Yosef Lishansky*, 340–41 (recollection of Eitan Belkind); and Livneh, Nedava, and Efrati, *Nili*, 252.

7. Halkin, *Strange Death*, 173–76 (account of Yanko Epstein as told to Hillel Halkin). Epstein recalled that Avshalom Fein accompanied him, along with Sonia Belkind, but Eitan Belkind recalls Fein as being at the meeting in Gedera. It is more likely that Fein returned with Lishansky's carriage. The purpose of Sonia's trip to Beersheba and what she expected to accomplish there are unclear.

8. Sarah Aaronsohn to Aaron Aaronsohn, September 21, 1917; and Engle, *Nili Spies*, 180–81.

9. Raz, "Fashion in Eretz Israel," 8–9.

10. Sarah Aaronsohn to Aaron Aaronsohn, September 21, 1917; Florence, *Lawrence and Aaronsohn*, 303; and Engle, *Nili Spies*, 178–79.

11. Sarah Aaronsohn to Aaron Aaronsohn, September 21, 1917.

12. Engle, *Nili Spies*, 187–88; and Katz, *Aaronsohn Saga*, 199–200. Shmuel Katz suggests that Fein's report had a decisive impact on the British strategy for breaking through the Gaza–Beersheba line, but he cites no evidence to support this. In all likelihood, Fein's report may have been important intelligence but was only part of a mosaic of information from a variety of sources, including air reconnaissance and wireless intercepts.

13. Schneersohn, *Miyomano shel ish Nili*, 95–100; Katz, *Aaronsohn Saga*, 266; and Florence, *Lawrence and Aaronsohn*, 303. While Liebl Bernstein appar-

ently was on board, no mention is made in the various accounts that a swimmer was needed. The night of September 21 was apparently calm enough for the surfboat to get all the way to the beach.

14. Schneersohn, *Miyomano shel ish Nili*, 100–106. Yosef told Liova another version of Naaman Belkind's capture. In this account, Bedouins from a tribe allied with the Turks stopped Naaman and his Bedouin guide in the desert. They kept Belkind's gun and money and handed him over to the Turks. Belkind was able to bury his papers in the sand, however, before the Bedouins subdued him. Parenthetically Liova may have been involved in the Tyre evacuations. Engle, *Nili Spies*, 184 (describing the evacuation of the agent and his family at Tyre).

15. Schneersohn, *Miyomano shel ish Nili*, 100–106; Engle, *Nili Spies*, 184–85; and Katz, *Aaronsohn Saga*, 266.

16. Schneersohn, *Miyomano shel ish Nili*, 106–7; and Weldon, *"Hard Lying,"* 193.

17. Katz, *Aaronsohn Saga*, 267; and Engle, *Nili Spies*, 182–83.

18. Engle, *Nili Spies*, 185.

19. Sarah Aaronsohn to Liova Schneersohn, September 25, 1917; Schneersohn, *Miyomano shel ish Nili*, 108–9; Katz, *Aaronsohn Saga*, 266–67; and Weldon, *"Hard Lying,"* 193–94.

20. Schneersohn, *Miyomano shel ish Nili*, 108–9.

21. Engle, *Nili Spies*, 186–87 (translated by Nelson Berkoff). Sarah's note acknowledged that "the moon won't allow you more than a short visit but [we] will be ready and waiting for you."

22. Weldon, *"Hard Lying,"* 194.

23. Engle, *Nili Spies*, 189.

24. Engle, *Nili Spies*, 186–87, 204.

25. Sarah Aaronsohn to Aaron Aaronsohn, September 12, 1917; Sarah Aaronsohn to Aaron Aaronsohn, July 14, 1917; and Sarah Aaronsohn to Aaron Aaronsohn, July 24, 1917. Sarah's July 14 letter to Aaron had only described a Turkish defeat in the "south." Her July 24 letter to Aaron evidently assumed that he understood that Sarah had been describing Beersheba when she used the word "south."

26. Hughes, *Allenby and British Strategy*, 46.

27. Cutlack, *Australian Flying Corps*, 8:69–72, 80–81; and Sheffy, *British Military Intelligence*, 165.

28. Bruce, *Last Crusade*, 144–45. "The chances of the British deception succeeding were greatly enhanced by the changing balance of power in the skies. German dominance of the airspace above the battlefield was brought to an

end by the autumn of 1917 with the arrival of new British aircraft, including the Bristol fighter, which outperformed the opposition."

29. Jeffery, *MI6*, 132.

30. Schneersohn, *Miyomano shel ish Nili*, 112–15. Liova writes of two landings—one on October 12, the other on October 14. The first landing was relatively brief. No Nili spy was at the shore, so the *Managem* left and returned two days later. Engle, *Nili Spies*, 189–91 (describing one landing). In his own account, Captain Weldon describes two landings. On the second landing, he "sent three agents ashore. They went right up to the colony [meaning, presumably, the research station], but returned after about two hours and reported that as far as they could see the place was deserted." Weldon, *"Hard Lying,"* 198–99.

16. She Is Worth a Hundred Men

1. Halkin, *Strange Death*, 176–77; and Livneh, Nedava, and Efrati, *Nili*, 270–71.

2. Nedava, *Yosef Lishansky*, 96 (recollection of Rivka Lishansky Lifshitz); and Livneh, Nedava, and Efrati, *Nili*, 271.

3. Miller, Papelka, and Griffin, "Confirming Torture."

4. Nemat, *Prisoner of Tehran*, 18.

5. The source of Sarah's words is a document in the Beit Aaronsohn Nili Museum Archive. The document does not identify the author, but Sarah's urgings to her father likely were reported by Zvi Aaronsohn, who was present during Ephraim's torture. Email from Beit Aaronsohn Nili Museum Archive to Gregory J. Wallance, June 30, 2016.

6. Livneh, Nedava, and Efrati, *Nili*, 272; and Florence, *Lawrence and Aaronsohn*, 324. Her father's rebuke appears in Engle, *Nili Spies*, 193.

7. Yaffe, *"Dor ma'apilim" zikhronot*, 387.

8. Nedava, *Yosef Lishansky*, 107 (recollection of Ivria Lishansky Rom).

9. Nedava, *Yosef Lishansky*, 107–8 (recollection of Ivria Lishansky Rom), 111 (recollection of Tuvia Lishansky).

10. Nedava, *Yosef Lishansky*, 107 (recollection of Ivria Lishansky Rom); and Engle, *Nili Spies*, 198–99.

11. Sarah's statements to the Turks during her own torture may have come from Zvi Aaronsohn's wife, based on what Zvi told her. Email from Beit Aaronsohn Nili Museum Archive to Gregory J. Wallance, June 30, 2016; and Engle, *Nili Spies*, 199.

12. Nedava, *Yosef Lishansky*, 107–8 (recollection of Ivria Lishansky Rom); and Engle, *Nili Spies*, 199.

13. Katz, *Aaronsohn Saga*, 273.

14. Livneh, Nedava, and Efrati, *Nili*, 272.

15. Nedava, *Yosef Lishansky*, 96 (recollection of Rivka Lishansky Lifshitz).

16. Undated note from Sarah Aaronsohn; Livneh, Nedava, and Efrati, *Nili*, 275–76; and Katz, *Aaronsohn Saga*, 333–34. My translator's translation of the note was close to but differed from the Katz translation in *Aaronsohn Saga*. In particular, Sarah did not write that her people were "mean"; instead, they were "despicable."

17. Nedava, *Yosef Lishansky*, 108 (recollection of Ivria Lishansky Rom); and Engle, *Nili Spies*, 200–202.

18. Yaffe, *"Dor ma'apilim" zikhronot*, 388–90; Engle, *Nili Spies*, 220; and Katz, *Aaronsohn Saga*, 277–78. Some accounts suggest that Sarah wrote her suicide note in Aaron's bathroom (Engle, *Nili Spies*, 200–21), but that seems unlikely, given the length of the note and the statement in it, "I shall try to get hold of some small firearm or poison." She already had a pistol when she went into Aaron's bathroom.

19. Engle, *Nili Spies*, 203; and Katz, *Aaronsohn Saga*, 275–76.

17. The Boys Will Turn

1. Katz, *Aaronsohn Saga*, 278; Neumann, "Report of Dr. Neumann," 7; and Engle, *Nili Spies*, 197, 204–8.

2. Nedava, *Yosef Lishansky*, 93–100 (recollection of Rivka Lishansky Lifshitz), 296–98 (recollection of Yitzhak Halperin); Engle, *Nili Spies*, 205–6; and Livneh, Nedava, and Efrati, *Nili*, 395, 397–98.

3. Livneh, Nedava, and Efrati, *Nili*, 291–96; Katz, *Aaronsohn Saga*, 279–287; Nedava, *Yosef Lishansky*, 296–98 (recollection of Yitzhak Halperin); and Engle, *Nili Spies*, 209–10, 220.

4. Katz, *Aaronsohn Saga*, 292–93. Eitan Belkind was told he would be sentenced to death, but the execution of his sentence was postponed due to his age (he was seventeen). He managed to escape from prison.

5. Katz, *Aaronsohn Saga*, 288–92.

6. Bruce, *Last Crusade*, 154–59; and Van-Dyk, "The Charge of the 4th Light Horse Brigade at Beersheba."

7. Dizingoff, *Im Tel Aviv Bagola*, 388–90.

8. Fromkin, *Peace to End All Peace*, 372; Rogan, *Fall of the Ottomans*, 347, 389–90; and McMeekin, *Ottoman Endgame*, 487.

9. Shirer, *Rise and Fall*, 29–32.

10. Katz, *Aaronsohn Saga*, 295; and Schneersohn, *Miyomano shel ish Nili*, 118.

11. Schneersohn, *Miyomano shel ish Nili*, 120–21.

12. Peretz Pascal to Aaron Aaronsohn, December 4, 1917.

13. Schneer, *Balfour Declaration*, 341–42.

14. Florence, *Lawrence and Aaronsohn*, 341–42.

15. Fromkin, *Peace to End All Peace*, 211.

16. Foreign Office 371/4167: William Ormsby-Gore to Foreign Office, March 22, 1918, National Archives, Kew, England.

17. Engle, *Nili Spies*, 101; Verrier, *Agents of Empire*, 206–7, 320n13 (claim of thirty thousand lives saved based on "private information"); and Florence, *Lawrence and Aaronsohn*, 419.

18. Weldon, *"Hard Lying,"* 199–200. In the same passage, Weldon complimented Yosef Lishansky but based on the mistaken belief that Lishansky, to spare the *yishuv* more suffering, had voluntarily surrendered to the Turks.

19. Florence, *Lawrence and Aaronsohn*, 361–62, 416–18.

20. Engle, *Nili Spies*, 224–25, quoting a letter from Judah Magnes to the Rosenwelds, friends in the United States who had severed their connection to the research station upon learning that Aaron was engaged in espionage.

21. Melman, "Legend of Sarah," 290–92, 301–7; and Florence, *Lawrence and Aaronsohn*, 362.

22. Melman, "Legend of Sarah," 295–96.

23. Anderson, *Lawrence in Arabia*, 462; and Florence, *Lawrence and Aaronsohn*, 459–62.

24. Shlomo Ben-Elkanah, "My Actions to Find the Remains of Avshalom Feinberg," in Nedava, *Yosef Lishansky*, 351–54; and Katz, *Aaronsohn Saga*, 297–301.

25. Rivka Aaronsohn to Sarah Aaronsohn, undated but likely written in 1917; Bar, *Landscape and Ideology*, 168; and Katz, *Aaronsohn Sage*, 299–300.

26. Melman, "Legend of Sarah," 310–11.

BIBLIOGRAPHY

Aaronsohn, Alexander. *Sarah: Shalhevet Nili* [Sarah: The flame of Nili]. Translated by I. M. Lask. (English manuscript, 1965.) Jerusalem: 1943.

———. *With the Turks in Palestine.* Boston: Houghton Mifflin, 1916.

Aaronsohn, Ran. *Rothschild and Early Jewish Colonization in Palestine.* Jerusalem: Hebrew University Magnes Press, 2000.

"Abandoned Colony in Southern Palestine Burned Down by Terrorists." Jewish Telegraphic Agency, September 9, 1938. http://www.jta.org/?s=Ruchema &orderby=date&order=desc.

Abu-Rabia, Aref. *A Bedouin Century: Education and Development among the Negev Tribes in the 20th Century.* New York: Berghahn Books, 2001.

Adler, Gerald M. "The Second Aliyah and Ottoman Governmental Policy, 1904–1914." In *The Israeli-Palestinian Conflict, 1860–2006: Legal Aspects in a Historical and Political Context*, August 2008. http://www.arab-israel-legal -issues.com/chapter8.htm.

Anderson, Scott. *Lawrence in Arabia: War, Deceit, Imperial Folly and the Making of the Modern Middle East.* New York: Doubleday, 2013.

Assi, Seraje. "History and Politics of Nomadism in Modern Palestine (1882– 1948)." PhD diss., Georgetown University, May 30, 2016. https://repository .library.georgetown.edu/bitstream/handle/10822/1041811/Assi_georgetown _0076D_13431.pdf?sequence=1.

Auron, Yair. *The Banality of Indifference: Zionism and the Armenian Genocide.* New Brunswick NJ: Transaction Publishers, 2000.

Balakian, Grigoris. *Armenian Golgotha: A Memoir of the Armenian Genocide, 1915–1918.* Translated by Peter Balakian and Aris Sevag. New York: First Vintage Books, 2010.

Bar, Doron. *Landscape and Ideology: Reinterment of Renowned Jews in the Land of Israel (1904–1967).* Berlin: Walter de Gruyter, 2016.

Barnard, Harry. *The Forging of an American Jew: The Life and Times of Judge Julian W. Mack.* New York: Herzl Press, 1974.

"Bedouin." *Encyclopedia Britannica.* Vol. 3. 13th ed. Cambridge: University of Cambridge Press, 1910, 1926.

Ben-Bassat, Yuval. "Enciphered Ottoman Telegrams from the First World War Concerning the *Yishuv* in Palestine." *Turcica* 46 (2015): 279–99. DOI: 10.2143/TURC.46.0.3087638.

Ben-Zvi, Rahel Yanait. *Coming Home.* New York: Herzl Press, 1964.

Bernstein, Deborah S., ed. *Pioneers and Homemakers: Jewish Women in Pre-State Israel.* Albany: State University of New York Press, 1992.

Boyar, Ebru, and Kate Fleet. *A Social History of Ottoman Istanbul.* Cambridge: Cambridge University Press, 2010.

Brown, Jonathan. "Remembered at Last: Animals Who Served in Wartime." *Independent,* November 24, 2004. http://www.independent.co.uk/news/uk /this-britain/remembered-at-last-animals-who-served-during-wartime -5350916.html.

Bruce, Anthony. *The Last Crusade: The Palestine Campaign in the First World War.* London: Thistle Publishing, 2013.

Burton, Alan. *Historical Dictionary of British Spy Fiction.* London: Rowman & Littlefield, 2016.

"City Government: Public Safety: Fire." *Municipal Journal and Engineer* 9 (July–December 1900). http://bit.ly/2pTHiwi.

Copping, Jason. "Honoured: The WW1 Pigeons Who Earned Their Wings." *Telegraph,* January 12, 2014. http://www.telegraph.co.uk/history/world-war -one/10566025/Honoured-the-WW1-pigeons-who-earned-their-wings.html.

Cutlack, F. M. *The Australian Flying Corps in the Western and Eastern Theatres of War, 1914–1918.* Vol. 8. of *Official History of Australia in the War of 1914–1918.* 11th ed. East Sussex: Naval and Military Press, 1941. https://www.awm.gov.au /collection/AWMOHWW1/?conflict=1.

Dagan, Shaul, and Ruth Dagan. *On the First Road to Zion: Stories of the First Aliyah Colonies.* Haifa: Arison Foundation, 1998.

Dane, Edmund. *British Campaigns in the Nearer East, 1914–1918: From the Outbreak of War with Turkey to the Armistice.* Vol. 1, *The Days of Adversity.* London: Hodder and Stoughton, 1919.

Danforth, Nick. "Forget Sykes-Picot. It's the Treaty of Sèvres That Explains the Modern Middle East." *Foreign Policy,* 2015. http://foreignpolicy.com/2015/08 /10/sykes-picot-treaty-of-sevres-modern-turkey-middle-east-borders-turkey/.

Dash, Joan. *Summoned to Jerusalem: The Life of Henrietta Szold.* New York: Harper & Row, 1979.

Davies, David. "During World War I, Germany Unleashed 'Terrorist Cell in America.'" Interview with Howard Blum. *Fresh Air.* NPR, January 25, 2014.

http://www.npr.org/2014/02/25/282439233/during-world-war-i-germany
-unleashed-terrorist-cell-in-america.

Davis, William Stearns. *A Short History of the Near East: From the Founding of
Constantinople (330 A.D. to 1922)*. New York: Macmillan, 1922.

De Waal, Thomas. *Great Catastrophe: Armenians and Turks in the Shadow of
Genocide*. Oxford: Oxford University Press, 2015.

Dews, Fred. "The Family Relationship that Couldn't Stop World I."
Brookings Now (blog), December 20, 1913. https://www.brookings.edu
/blog/brookings-now/2013/12/20/the-family-relationships-that-couldnt
-stop-world-war-i/.

Dizengoff, Meir. *Im Tel Aviv Bagola* [With Tel Aviv in exile]. Tel Aviv: Beit Ha-
Tanakh, 2000.

Dunn, Michael Collins. "The British Military Intelligence Section in Cairo
1914, Part III: The Five New Men." Editor's Blog. *Middle East Journal*, January 5, 2015. http://mideasti.blogspot.com/2015/01/the-military-intellignce
-section-in.html.

———. "'Such a Band of Wild Men': The British Military Intelligence Section
in Cairo, December 1914, Part I." Editor's Blog. *Middle East Journal*, December 30, 2015. http://mideasti.blogspot.com/2014/12/such-band-of-wild-men
-british-military.html.

Dwight, H. G. "Life in Constantinople." *National Geographic* 26, no. 6
(December 1914).

Emmerson, Charles. *1913: In Search of the World before the Great War*. New York:
PublicAffairs, 2013.

Engle, Anita. *The Nili Spies*. London: Hogarth Press, 1959.

Evelyn, Princess Blücher. *An English Wife in Berlin: A Private Memoir of Events,
Politics and Daily Life in Germany throughout the War and the Social Revolution of 1918*. New York: E. P. Dutton, 1920.

Fairchild, David. *The World Was My Garden: Travels of a Plant Explorer*. New
York: Charles Scribner's Sons, 1938.

Farrin, Raymond. *Abundance from the Desert: Classical Arab Poetry*. Syracuse:
Syracuse University Press, 2011.

Finn, James. *Byeways in Palestine*. New York: Dossier Press, 1872.

Florence, Ronald. *Lawrence and Aaronsohn: T. E. Lawrence, Aaron Aaronsohn,
and the Seeds of the Arab-Israeli Conflict*. New York: Viking, 2007.

"The Forgotten Holocaust: The Armenian Massacre that Inspired Hitler." *Daily
Mail*, October 11, 2007. http://www.dailymail.co.uk/news/article-479143
/The-forgotten-Holocaust-The-Armenian-massacre-inspired-Hitler.html.

Fromkin, David. *A Peace to End All Peace: The Fall of the Ottoman Empire and the Creation of the Modern Middle East*. New York: Henry Holt, 1989.

Gibb, Elias John Wilkinson. "Turkey." *Encyclopedia Britannica*. Vols. 27–28. 13th ed. New York: Encyclopedia Britannica, 1911, 1926.

Gilbert, Martin. *The First World War: A Complete History*. New York: Henry Holt, 1994.

Goldstone, Patricia. *Aaronsohn's Maps: The Untold Story of the Man Who Might Have Created Peace in the Middle East*. Orlando: Harcourt, 2007.

Gorny, Yosef. *Zionism and the Arabs, 1882–1948: A Study of Ideology*. New York: Oxford University Press, 1987.

Green, David B. Green. "This Day in Jewish History, 1917: Ottoman Authority Orders Jews to Evacuate Tel Aviv." *Haaretz*, April 6, 2014. www.haaretz.com /jewish/this-day-in-jewish-history/1.583953.

Gullett, H. S. *The Australian Imperial Force in Sinai and Palestine*. Vol 7 of *Official History of Australia in the War of 1914–1918*. Sydney: Angus & Robertson, 1922. https://archive.org/stream/australianimperi07gulluoft/australianimperi 07gulluoft_djvu.txt.

Halkin, Hillel. *A Strange Death: Espionage, Betrayal and Vengeance in a Village in Old Palestine*. London: Weidenfeld & Nicolson, 2006.

Herbert, Aubrey. *Mons, Anzac and Kut*. London: Hutchinson,1919.

Herwig, Holger H. *The Marne, 1914: The Opening of World War I and the Battle That Changed the World*. New York: Random House, 2009.

Hughes, Matthew. *Allenby and British Strategy in the Middle East, 1917–1919*. London: Frank Cass , 1999.

Jeffery, Keith. *MI6: The History of the Secret Intelligence Service, 1909–1949*. London: Bloomsbury, 2010.

Jones, Abigail. "Women of the CIA: The Hidden Story of American Spycraft." *Newsweek*, September 21, 2016. http://www.newsweek.com/2016/09/30 /cia-women-national-security-500312.html.

Katz, Shmuel. *The Aaronsohn Saga*. Jerusalem: Gefen, 2007.

Kennedy, Elaine. "The Geology of Mount Carmel, Israel." *Geoscience Reports* 33 (Spring 2002): 1–8. http://grisda.net/publications/georeports/33.pdf.

Kissinger, Henry. *Diplomacy*. New York: Simon & Schuster, 1994.

Kramer, Martin. "Sykes-Picot and the Zionists." *The American Interest*, May 19, 2016. http://www.the-american-interest.com/byline/martin-kramer/.

Lawrence, T. E. *Seven Pillars of Wisdom: A Triumph*. New York: Anchor Books, 1991.

"Lawrence of Arabia: Stamp Designer." Egypt in the Golden Age of Travel, October 14, 2012. http://grandhotelsegypt.com/?p=724.

Leslie, Shane. *Mark Sykes: His Life and Letters.* New York: Charles Scribner's Sons, 1923.

Livneh, Eliezer, Yosef Nedava, Yosef, Yoram Efrati. *Nili: Toldoteha shel he'azah medinit* [Nili: A story of political daring]. Tel Aviv: Schocken, 1961.

Loconte, Joseph. *A Hobbit, a Wardrobe, and a Great War: How J.R.R. Tolkien and C.S. Lewis Rediscovered Faith, Friendship, and Heroism in the Cataclysm of 1914–1918.* Nashville: Nelson Books, 2015.

Manne, Robert. "A Turkish Tale: Gallipoli and the Armenian Genocide." *The Monthly*, February 2007. https://www.themonthly.com.au/monthly-essays -robert-manne-turkish-tale-gallipoli-and-armenian-genocide-459.

Massey, William T. *The Desert Campaigns.* New York: G. P. Putnam's Sons, 1918.

McGilvary, Margaret. *The Dawn of a New Era in Syria.* New York: Fleming H. Revell, 1920.

McKenna, Marthe. *I Was a Spy!* New York: Robert M. McBride, 1933.

McMeekin, Sean. *The Ottoman Endgame: War, Revolution, and the Making of the Modern Middle East, 1908–1923.* New York: Penguin Books, 2015.

Megged, Aharon. *Mandrakes from the Holy Land.* Translated by Sondra Silverston. New Milford CT: Toby Press, 2005.

Melman, Billie. "The Legend of Sarah: Gender, Memory, and National Identities (*Eretz Yisrael*/Israel, 1917–1990)." In *Jewish Women in Pre-State Israel: Life, History, Politics and Culture*, edited by Ruth Kark, Margalit Shilo, and Galit Hasan-Rokem, 285–320. Waltham MA: Brandeis University Press, 2008. Kindle edition.

———. "Sarah Aaronsohn, 1890–1917." *Jewish Women: A Comprehensive Historical Encyclopedia.* Jewish Women's Archive, March 1, 2009. https://jwa.org /encyclopedia/article/aaronsohn-sarah.

Meyer, G. J. *A World Undone: The Story of the Great War, 1914–1918.* New York: Bantam Dell, 2006.

Miller, Christine, Jessica Popelka, and Nicole Griffin. "Confirming Torture: The Use of Imaging in Victims of Falanga." *Forensic Magazine*, August 2014. http://www.forensicmag.com/article/2014/08/ confirming-torture-use-imaging-victims-falanga.

Ministry of Defence. "The Old War Office Building: A History." Whitehall: UK Ministry of Defence, 2001. https://www.gov.uk/government/uploads /system/uploads/attachment_data/file/49055/old_war_office_build.pdf.

M'Lachlan, Robert, and Reginald Innes Pocock. "Locust." *Encyclopedia Britannica.* Vol. 16. 13th ed. New York: Encyclopedia Britannica, 1926.

Monger, David. *Patriotism and Propaganda in First World War Britain: The National Civilian War Aims Committee and Civilian Morale*. Liverpool: Liverpool University Press, 2012.

Morgenthau, Henry. *Ambassador Morgenthau's Story*. Garden City NY: Double Day, Page, 1919.

Morton, James. *Spies of the First World War: Under Cover for King and Kaiser*. Surrey: National Archives, 2010.

Murray, Sir Archibald. *Sir Archibald Murray's Despatches: June 1916–June 1917*. London: J. M. Dent & Sons, 1920. https://archive.org/details /sirarchibaldmurr00murrrich.

Nedava, Yosef, ed. *Yosef Lishansky Papers and Letters: Ish Nili: Ketavim, mikhtavim divre zikhronot* [A man of Nili: Writings, letters and memorials]. Jerusalem: Hadar Publishing, 1977.

Nemat, Marina. *Prisoner of Tehran: A Memoir*. New York: Free Press, 2007.

Otte, T. G. *July Crisis: The World's Descent into War, Summer 1914*. Cambridge: Cambridge University Press, 2014.

Pascal, Peretz. "I Am also a Spy." *Doar Hayom* (Jerusalem), October 27, 1920.

Pasha, Djemal. *Memories of a Turkish Statesman, 1913–1919*. New York: George H. Doran, 1922.

Pollack, Shalom. "The Lone Palm Tree." *Jerusalem Post*, October 2, 2010. http:// m.jpost.com/Christian-In-Israel/Features/The-lone-palm-tree#article =0RDM3MDY0NUZGQ0Q2MzU0M0VCMzM5NjM4RTUyQ0I1MTU=.

Presland, John. *Deedes Bey: A Study of Sir Wyndham Deedes, 1883–1923*. London: Macmillan, 1942.

Prior, Robin, and Trevor Wilson. *The Somme*. New Haven: Yale University Press, 2005.

Proctor, Tammy M. *Female Intelligence: Women and Espionage in the First World War*. New York: New York University Press, 2003.

Raz, Ayala. "Fashion in Eretz Israel: What We Were Wearing in the Early Days of This Century." Israel Ministry of Foreign Affairs, January 7, 1999. mfa.gov.il /MFA/MFA . . . /Ayala%20raz%20-%20fashion%20in%20eretz-Israel.aspx.

Remnick, David. "Blood and Sand." *New Yorker*, May 5, 2008. http://www .newyorker.com/magazine/2008/05/05/blood-and-sand-books-david-remnick.

Reynolds, Francis J., Allen L. Churchill, and Francis T. Miller, eds. *The Story of the Great War: History of the European War from Official Sources*. Vol. 3. New York: P. F Collier, 1916. Google Play Books.

Rogan, Eugene. *The Fall of the Ottomans: The Great War in the Middle East*. New York: Basic Books, 2015.

Schama, Simon. *Two Rothschilds and the Land of Israel*. New York: Alfred A. Knopf, 1978.

Schneer, Jonathan. *The Balfour Declaration: The Origins of the Arab-Israeli Conflict*. New York: Random House, 2010.

Schneersohn, Liova. *Miyomano shel ish Nili* [Diary of a man of Nili]. Haifa: Renaissance, 1967.

Sheffy, Yigal. *British Military Intelligence in the Palestine Campaign, 1914–1918*. London: Frank Cass, 1998.

Shirer, William L. *The Rise and Fall of the Third Reich: A History of Nazi Germany*. New York: Simon & Schuster, 1960.

Shukry [Khoury], Phillip S. *Syria and the French Mandate: The Politics of Arab Nationalism, 1920–1945*. Princeton: Princeton University Press, 1987.

Simon, Hilda. *The Date Palm: Bread of the Desert*. New York: Dodd, Mead, 1978.

"Sir Wyndham Deedes, Distinguished Visitor, Is Feted by Zionists." Jewish Telegraphic Agency, March 21, 1927. http://www.jta.org/1927/03/21/archive/sir-wyndham-deedes-distinguished-visitor-is-feted-by-zionists.

Tamari, Salim. *Year of the Locust: A Soldier's Diary and the Erasure of Palestine's Ottoman Past*. Berkeley: University of California Press, 2011.

Tauber, Eliezer. "The Capture of the NILI Spies: The Turkish Version, Intelligence and National Security." *Intelligence and National Security* 6, no. 4 (1991): 701–10. http://www.tandfonline.com/doi/abs/10.1080/02684529108432128?journalCode=fint20.

Terry, Michael, ed. *Reader's Guide to Judaism*. Chicago: Fitzroy Dearborn, 2000.

Tharoor, Ishan. "Is This Genocide? What Four Americans Saw Happening to Armenians 100 Years Ago." *Washington Post*, April 22, 2015. https://www.washingtonpost.com/news/worldviews/wp/2015/04/22/what-these-four-americans-saw-happening-to-armenians-100-years-ago-sounds-like-genocide.

Thomson, Basil. *Queer People*. London: Hodder and Stoughton, 1922.

Tuchman, Barbara. *The Guns of August*. New York: Dell, 1962.

Tucker, Spencer, and Priscilla Mary Roberts, eds. *The Encyclopedia of the Arab-Israeli Conflict: A Political, Social and Military History*. Santa Barbara: ABC-CLIO, 2008.

Ulrichsen, Kristian Coates. *The First World War in the Middle East*. London: C. Hurst, 2014.

Van-Dyk, Robyn. "The Charge of the 4th Light Horse Brigade at Beersheba." Australian War Memorial, October 30, 2007. https://www.awm.gov.au/articles/blog/the-charge-of-the-4th-light-horse-brigade-at-beersheba.

Verrier, Anthony, ed. *Agents of Empire: Anglo-Zionist Intelligence Operations, 1915–1919: Brigadier Walter Gribbon, Aaron Aaronsohn, and the NILI Ring, 1915–1919*. London: Brassey's (UK), 1995.

Webber, Kerry. *In the Shadow of the Crescent: The Life and Times of Colonel Stewart Frances Newcombe* (blog). http://shadowofthecrescent.blogspot.com/p /sf-newcombe-short-biography.html.

Weldon, L. B. *"Hard Lying": Eastern Mediterranean, 1914–19*. London: Herbert Jenkins, 1925.

Wilson, Jeremy. *Lawrence of Arabia: The Authorized Biography of T. E. Lawrence*. New York: Atheneum, 1990.

Woodfin, Edward C. *Camp and Combat on the Sinai and Palestine Front: The Experience of the British Empire Soldier, 1916–18*. London: Palgrave Macmillan, 2012.

Woodward, David R. *Hell in the Holy Land: World War I in the Middle East*. Lexington: University Press of Kentucky, 2006.

Woolley, Sir Leonard. *As I Seem to Remember*. London: Facsimile, 1962.

Yaffe, Hillel. *"'Dor ma'apilim' zikhronot, mikhtavim ve yoman"* [Generation of pioneers: Memoirs, letters and diary]. Jerusalem: Jewish Agency Publishing House, 1971.

Yazbak, Mahmoud. *Haifa in the Late Ottoman Period, 1864–1914: A Muslim Town in Transition*. Leiden: E. J. Brill, 1998.

INDEX

Note: In the interest of brevity, Sarah Aaronsohn and her sister and brothers (Aaron, Alexander, Rivka, Samuel, and Zvi) are noted by their first names in subentries.

Aaronsohn, Alexander: arrest, imprisonment, and torture of, by Turks, 48–49, 223; and Avshalom Feinberg's death, 129–30, 239; in British army, 238; and British intelligence, 64, 66–67, 213; and evacuation of Nili spies, 217, 220–21; and final message from Sarah, 229; and Gideonites, 46–47, 87; and Nili funds from United States, 185; in Ottoman army, 36, 44, 46–48; in Palestine after World War I, 241; and plans to spy for British, 60–64; and Sarah's death, 238–39; in United States, 27, 44, 46, 71, 188, 198, 213; Zvi's resentment of, 174

Aaronsohn, Avner, 225, 229–30

Aaronsohn, Ephraim, 5, 11, 174, 186, 223–25, 232, 238–39, 246, 251n23, 273n5

Aaronsohn, Malka, 5, 11, 14, 18, 132, 232, 246, 251n23

Aaronsohn, Miriam, 185–86, 215–17, 239

Aaronsohn, Rivka: and Aaronsohn homes, preservation of, 243; appearance and character of, 23–24; and Avshalom Feinberg's death, 129–32; and Avshalom Feinberg's grave discovery, 243–45; and Avshalom Feinberg's island fantasy, 244; at Avshalom Feinberg's state funeral, 245; and Beirut, 48; birth of, 9; and British intelligence, 62–64; education of, 9–10; engagement of, to Avshalom Feinberg, 18, 26, 252n18; friendship of, with Avshalom Feinberg, 19–26; and letters from Avshalom Feinberg, 73–75; and return to Palestine

from United States, 240; at Syrian Protestant College, 48, 63; in United States, 44, 71, 96–97

Aaronsohn, Samuel, 9, 87, 185, 215, 239

Aaronsohn, Sarah: appearance and character of, 10–11; and appeasement of Jewish community, 175; and Armenian genocide, 57–58, 80–81; arrest and torture of, 222–30, 273n5, 273n11; and Atlit, 114–20, 149–50, 170–71, 182–201, 217, 264n16; and Avshalom Feinberg's capture, 79; and Avshalom Feinberg's death, 128–32, 135, 139, 169, 189–93; and Avshalom Feinberg's island fantasy, 244; and beach rendezvous with *Managem*, 133–35; birth and background of, 1–3, 9; British officers' admiration for, 240–41; burial of, 232, 246; in Cairo, 143–45, 149–55, 161–71, 264n12, 264n16, 265n20; and carrier pigeons, 180–81, 202–3; in Constantinople, 28–31, 36–38, 42–44; and criticism of British intelligence, 185; on Dardanelles campaign, 54; death of, 230–32, 238–39, 240–41; and death of Avshalom Feinberg's mother, 21–22; and death of mother, 14, 18, 22; and *dibs* (grape syrup), 89–90, 110; and Djemal Pasha, 271n3; education of, 9–10; engagement and marriage of, to Haim Abraham, 26–28; English lessons of, 161; in Europe, 14–16; final request of, 232; friendship of, with Avshalom Feinberg, 19–26; and gender role expectations, 10–11; grave of, 246; health of, 90, 149,

164, 170, 177, 200; homesickness of, 28–31, 36–38, 42–44; and joining Nili, 2; as leader of Nili, 110; letters to and from, 81–83, 91–92, 109–10, 127–32, 186–87, 199, 228–30; and Liova Schneersohn, 80–81, 116, 143, 153–54, 162, 165–71; memorial celebrations of, 242; as model for World War II anti-British Lehi (Stern Gang), 242; and money misunderstandings, 186; myths about, 242–43; on Nili finances, 186–87, 250n12; Nili learns of, 79; and opposition of Jewish community to Nili work, 141–42, 160–61, 172–78, 208–10; personal relationship of, with Avshalom Feinberg, 130–31; pilgrimages to gravesite of, 242; and Rahel Yanait, 59–60, 84–86; and reasons for working with Nili, 188–89, 269n18; and recruiting spies and managing Atlit research station, 86–92; and relief funds from British for Jews in Palestine, 160; and return to Palestine from Constantinople, 44–45, 57–58, 255n26; spying talent and value of, 97, 140, 160; suicide threats of, 151–52, 172, 217; and T. E. Lawrence, 242–43; and torture of father, 224, 273n5; on wartime conditions in Constantinople, 36–38; and Yosef Lishansky, 135–40, 144, 162–64, 201, 262n7; and Zichron community council, 208–10; and Zvi, 189–90, 200, 269n20

Aaronsohn, Yardena, 231

Aaronsohn, Yedidia, 185–86, 215–17

Aaronsohn, Zvi: and Alexander, 174; arrest and torture of, 223–24, 234; and Avshalom Feinberg's death, 189–90; birth of, 9; career of, prewar, 87; and escape from Romania to Palestine, 5; helpfulness of, 135; and opposition of Jewish community to Nili work, 173–74, 176; and Sarah, 189–90, 200, 269n20; on Sarah's health, 90; and torture of father, 273n5; and torture of Sarah, 273n11

Aaronsohn homes museum, 246–47

Abdullah (swimmer), 118

Aboulafia, Raphael, 73, 87, 134, 180

Abraham, Daniel, 252n19

Abraham, Haim: engagement and marriage of, to Sarah, 26–28; and letters from Sarah, 81–83; and money for refugee relief, 186–87, 250n12; Sarah's affection for, 83; website about, 252n19

Aenne Rickmers, 73, 75, 121

aerial warfare, 140–41, 263n18

AFC (Australian Flying Corps), 219

al-Din, Baha, 187, 214

Alhadeff, Yosef, 163

Allenby, Edmund, 149, 193, 196, 218–20, 236–37, 240

Allenby and British Strategy in the Middle East (Hughes), 219

Alter, Albert, 224–25

Anderson, Scott, 66, 243; *Lawrence in Arabia*, 243

anti-Semitism, British, 98

Arab Revolt, 103, 152, 193–97

Armenian genocide, 2, 39, 45, 55–59, 80–81, 98–99, 227, 237

Asquith, Herbert, 52

Atatürk (Mustafa Kemal), 54

Australian Flying Corps (AFC), 219